This book provides an authoritative account of Hegel's social philosophy at a level that presupposes no specialized knowledge of the subject. Hegel's social theory was designed to reconcile the individual with the modern social world. Michael O. Hardimon explores the concept of reconciliation in detail and discusses Hegel's views on the relationship between individuality and social membership, and on the family, civil society, and the state.

The book is an important addition to the group of major studies of Hegel published by Cambridge University Press. It will interest a broad swathe of readers in philosophy (both students and specialists), and it can be used in courses on political and social theory.

D0076401

HEGEL'S SOCIAL PHILOSOPHY:
THE PROJECT OF RECONCILIATION

MODERN EUROPEAN PHILOSOPHY

Executive editor
ROBERT PIPPIN, UNIVERSITY OF CHICAGO

Editorial board
HIDE ISHIGURO, KEIO UNIVERSITY, JAPAN
ALAN MONTEFIORE, BALLIOL COLLEGE, OXFORD
MARY TILES, UNIVERSITY OF HAWAII

David Bakhurst, *Consciousness and Revolution in Soviet Philosophy*
R. M. Chisholm, *Brentano and Intrinsic Value*
Maudemarie Clark, *Nietzsche on Truth and Philosophy*
Raymond Geuss, *The Idea of a Critical Theory:
Habermas and the Frankfurt School*
Gary Gutting, *Michel Foucault's Archaeology of Scientific Reason*
David Holdcroft, *Saussure: Signs, System, and Arbitrariness*
Karel Lambert, *Meinong and the Principle of Independence*
Frederick Neuhouser, *Fichte's Theory of Subjectivity*
Charles Taylor, *Hegel and Modern Society*
Mary Tiles, *Bachelard: Science and Objectivity*
Robert S. Tragesser, *Husserl and Realism in Logic and Mathematics*
Stephen K. White, *Political Theory and Postmodernism*
Peter Winch, *Simone Weil: The Just Balance*

HEGEL'S SOCIAL PHILOSOPHY
THE PROJECT OF RECONCILIATION

MICHAEL O. HARDIMON

Massachusetts Institute of Technology

CAMBRIDGE
UNIVERSITY PRESS

Published by the Press Syndicate of the University of Cambridge
The Pitt Building, Trumpington Street, Cambridge CB2 IRP
40 West 20th Street, New York, NY 10011-4211, USA
10 Stamford Road, Oakleigh, Melbourne 3166, Australia

© Cambridge University Press 1994

First published 1994

Printed in the United States of America

Library of Congress Cataloging-in-Publication Data
Hardimon, Michael O.
Hegel's social philosophy: the project of reconciliation /
Michael O. Hardimon.
p.   cm. – (Modern European philosophy)
Includes bibliographical references and index.
ISBN 0-521-41852-6 (hard). – ISBN 0-521-42914-5 (pbk.)
1. p. cm. 2. Hegel, Georg Wilhelm Friedrich, 1770–1831 – Political
and social views. 3. Social policy – History – 19th century.
4. Political science – Philosophy – History – 19th century.
5. Reconciliation.   I. Title.   II. Series.
B2949.S6H35   1994
193 – dc 20   93-21079
                                              CIP
A catalog record for this book is available from the British Library.

ISBN 0-521-41852-6 hardback
ISBN 0-521-42914-5 paperback

TO MARY

CONTENTS

vii

ACKNOWLEDGMENTS

One of the nicest things about completing a book is that you finally get to thank the people who helped you write it. First thanks go to Raymond Geuss and John Rawls, my two mentors. Their criticisms and comments have helped shape this book. Many of the ideas in it derive from Raymond, who taught me how to read and think about Hegel. Josh Cohen, Fred Neuhouser, and Ken Westphal probably read more drafts of more versions of the book than they care to remember. For their extensive and detailed comments I am extremely grateful. I also thank David Brink, Steve Engstrom, Hans Friedrich Fulda, Paul Hoffman, Tim Scanlon, and Gisela Striker for comments on various parts of the manuscript. I am indebted to Bill deVries and Terry Nichols, who read and criticized the complete manuscript of the first version of the book. To Terry I owe additional thanks for the labor of checking the textual references and assisting in the preparation of the final manuscript. Shelly Kagan and Judy Thomson provided a special kind of hard-nosed criticism I found tremendously useful. To George Boolos, John Carriero, Gary Ebbs, Steve Erickson, Victor Gourevitch, Jim Higgenbotham, Tom Kuhn, Marcus Otto, Robert Pippin, Georges Rey, Amélie Rorty, Michael Sandel, and Rob Stainton I express my gratitude for comments and conversations. To Craig Hardimon, my brother, I owe thanks for technical assistance. Without the daily encouragement, constant conversation, and nearly endless editing of my colleague and spouse, Mary Devereaux, I would not have completed this book. I thank her in particular for her support during the hard summer of 1991. To all of these colleagues, and the many other friends who saw me through the writing and rewriting of this book, I say thank you. Finally, special thanks to Winston Hughes. In the preparation of the manuscript for publication, it was a pleasure to work with Pamela J. Bruton and with Terence Moore and Martin Dinitz of the Cambridge University Press editorial staff.

The first version of this book was completed with a fellowship from the Ford Foundation's Postdoctoral Fellowship for Minorities Program. I am grateful for its financial and moral support. I also thank the Department of Linguistics and Philosophy at MIT, which has been extremely generous about granting, and helping to fund, the release from teaching and other responsibilities that made it possible for me to write the book.

ABBREVIATIONS

Standard English translations will be cited along with the original, with English pagination following German pagination, separated by a slash (/). In works cited by section (§), remarks are indicated by an "R" and additions by "Z" (*Zusatz*). Thus, PR, §261R, means the remark to §261. PR, §261Z, means the addition to §261. A comma used before "R" or "Z" means "and." Thus, PR, §261, R means §261 and the remark to §261; PR, §261, Z means §261 and the addition to §261; and PR, §261, R, Z means §261 and the remark and addition to §261.

Werke   *Hegel: Werke Theorie Werkausgabe.* Frankfurt: Suhrkamp Verlag, 1970. Cited by volume number.

D   *Differenz des Fichteschen und Schellingschen Systems der Philosophie* (1801). *Werke* 2. Cited by page number.

       The Difference between Fichte's and Schelling's System of Philosophy. Translated by H. S. Harris and Walter Cerf. Albany: SUNY Press, 1977. Cited by page number.

EG   *Enzyklopädie der philosophischen Wissenschaften*, vol. 3 (1817, rev. 1827, 1830). *Werke* 9. Cited by section (§) number.

Hegel's Philosophy of Mind. Translated by William A. Wallace and A. V. Miller. Oxford: Oxford University Press, 1971. Cited by section (§) number.

EL   *Enzyklopädie der philosophischen Wissenschaften,* vol. 1 (1817, rev. 1827, 1830). *Werke* 8. Cited by section (§) number.

Hegel's Logic. Translated by William Wallace. Oxford: Oxford University Press, 1975. Cited by section (§) number.

ER   "Ueber die englische Reformbill" (1831). In *Werke* 11. Cited by page number.

"The English Reform Bill." In *Hegel's Political Writings.* Translated by T. M. Knox. Oxford: Oxford University Press, 1964. Cited by page number.

PCR   *Die Positivität der christlichen Religion.* In *Werke* 1. Cited by page number.

The Positivity of the Christian Religion. In *Early Theological Writings.* Translated by T. M. Knox. Philadelphia: University of Pennsylvania Press, 1971. Cited by page number.

PhG   *Phänomenologie des Geistes* (1807). *Werke* 3. Cited by page number.

Hegel's Phenomenology of Spirit. Translated by A. V. Miller. Oxford: Oxford University Press, 1977. Cited by page number.

PR   *Grundlinien der Philosophie des Rechts oder Naturrecht und Staatswissenschaft im Grundrisse* (1821). *Werke* 7. Cited by section (§) number. Preface cited by paragraph (¶) number.

Hegel: Elements of the Philosophy of Right. Translated by H. B. Nisbet, edited by Allen W. Wood. Cambridge: Cambridge University Press, 1991. Cited by section (§) number. Preface cited by paragraph (¶) number.

Hegel's Philosophy of Right. Translated with notes by T. M. Knox. New York: Oxford University Press, 1967. Cited by section (§) number. Preface cited by paragraph (¶) number. Citations from this translation are listed as "Knox."

VA   *Vorlesungen über die Äesthetik*. 3 vols. *Werke* 13–15. Cited by volume and page number.

      Aesthetics: Lectures on Fine Arts. 2 vols. Translated by T. M. Knox. Oxford: Oxford University Press, 1988. Cited by volume and page number.

VD   "Die Verfassung Deutschlands" (1801–2). In *Werke* 1. Cited by page number.

      "The German Constitution." In *Hegel's Political Writings*. Translated by T. M. Knox. Oxford: Oxford University Press, 1964. Cited by page number.

VG   *Die Vernunft in der Geschichte*. Edited by J. Hoffmeister. Hamburg: Felix Meiner Verlag, 1955. Cited by page number.

      Lectures on the Philosophy of World History. "Introduction." Translated by H. B. Nisbet. Cambridge: Cambridge University Press, 1975. Cited by page number.

VGP   *Vorlesungen über die Geschichte der Philosophie*. 3 vols. *Werke* 18–20. Cited by volume and page number.

      Hegel's Lectures on the History of Philosophy. 3 vols. Translated by Elizabeth Haldane. New York: Humanities Press, 1968. Cited by volume and page number.

VPG   *Vorlesungen über die Philosophie der Geschichte*. *Werke* 12. Cited by page number.

      The Philosophy of History. Translated by J. Sibree. New York: Dover, 1956. Cited by page number.

VPRG   *Vorlesungen über Rechtsphilosophie*, vol. 4. Edited by K.-H. Ilting. Transcription of the 1824–5 lectures by K. G. von Griesheim. Stuttgart: Fromman Verlag, 1974. Cited by page number.

VPRHN *Philosophie des Rechts: Die Vorlesung von 1819/20.* Edited by Dieter Henrich. Frankfurt: Suhrkamp Verlag, 1983. Cited by page number.

VPRHO *Vorlesungen über Rechtsphilosophie,* vol. 3. Edited by K.-H. Ilting. Transcription of the 1822–3 lectures by H. G. Hotho. Stuttgart: Fromman Verlag, 1974. Cited by page number.

VPRJ *Vorlesungen über die Philosophie der Religion. Ausgewählte Nachschriften und Manuscripte.* 5 vols. Edited by Walter Jaeschke. Hamburg: Felix Meiner Verlag, 1983. Cited by volume and page number.

Lectures on the Philosophy of Religion. 4 vols. Edited by Peter C. Hodgson, translated by R. F. Brown, P. C. Hodgson, J. M. Stewart, with the assistance of J. P. Fitzer and H. S. Harris. Berkeley and Los Angeles: University of California Press, 1984. Cited by volume and page number.

VPRW *Die Philosophie des Rechts: Die Mitschriften Wannenmann (Heidelberg 1817/18) und Homeyer (Berlin 1818/19).* Edited by K.-H. Ilting. Transcriptions of the 1817–18 lectures by P. Wannenmann and of the 1818–19 lectures by C. G. Homeyer. Stuttgart: Klett-Cotta Verlag, 1983. Cited by page number.

W "Verhandlungen in der Versammlung in der Landstände des Königsreichs Württemberg im Jahre 1815 und 1816" (1817). *Werke* 4. Cited by page number.

"Proceedings of the Estates Assembly in the Kingdom of Wurtemberg, 1815–1816." In *Hegel's Political Writings.* Translated by T. M. Knox. Oxford: Oxford University Press, 1964. Cited by page number.

WL *Wissenschaft der Logik* (1812–16). *Werke* 5–6. Cited by volume and page number.

Hegel's Science of Logic. Translated by A. V. Miller. London: George Allen & Unwin, 1969. Cited by page number.

INTRODUCTION

The central aim of Hegel's social philosophy was to reconcile his contemporaries to the modern social world. Hegel sought to enable the people of the nineteenth century to overcome their alienation from the central social institutions – the family, civil society, and the state – and to come to 'be at home' within them. 'The project of reconciliation' is the name I have given to this enterprise. My aim in this book is to explain what the project of reconciliation is.

I

Hegel's project merits close examination for at least three sorts of reasons. The first has to do with our own cultural concerns – concerns that might equally well be classified as 'political' or 'personal.' Our social world – the present-day social world of Europe and North America – is a world of alienation *(Entfremdung)*. It characteristically gives rise to the felt experience of alienation. Many people feel 'split' from its institutions, regarding them as foreign, bifurcating, and hostile or indifferent to their needs. Many people also feel split within themselves, divided by the conflicting aims of realizing their individuality and being members of the community.[1] Not everybody

---

1 Hegel does not, it is true, use the word *Entfremdung* to describe this form of division. Moreover, the structure of this form of division differs from the structure of the form of consciousness he discusses in the section of the PhG entitled "Self-

feels this way, of course, but many do. A felt sense of division and conflict is a pervasive feature of our world.[2] Alienation is a problem for all of us in the sense that it is a problem of *our* culture. Not the least reason for looking at the project of reconciliation, then, is that it addresses a problem that is – or ought to be – of concern to us.

A closely related reason for looking at Hegel's project is that it articulates an ideal that is of interest to us: the ideal of reconciliation. We may not initially think of ourselves as caring about reconciliation, but an interest in reconciliation flows naturally out of concern with alienation. 'Reconciliation' (*Versöhnung*), as Hegel uses it, is a technical term referring to the process of overcoming alienation.[3] It is the process of overcoming the splits that divide the self from the social world and the attendant splits that divide the self from the self. Reconciliation is also the state in which the process of overcoming alienation results – the state that Hegel characterizes as being at home in the social world. In Hegel's view, the experience of alienation is directed toward the ideal of reconciliation, and the ideal of reconciliation is contained within the experience of alienation. Looking at Hegel's project can help us understand what reconciliation is. His project seeks to show that reconciliation represents a coherent and attractive aspiration – an important social ideal. Hegel's project can help us articulate an aspiration we may implicitly hold, allowing us to add reconciliation to our vocabulary of social ideals.

alienated Spirit" ("Der sich entfremdete Geist"; PhG, 359-441/294-363). Nonetheless, it is clear – and uncontroversial – that Hegel's social philosophy is meant, among other things, as a response to the problem that is now standardly called alienation. For Hegel's general view that modern social life is characterized by splits and divisions, see the early D (20–2/89–91) and the much later VA (1:81/ 1:55), constructed by H. C. Hotho from his notes on Hegel's lectures. For a useful discussion of the philology of the word 'alienation', see Schacht 1971.

2   I emphasize the felt experience of alienation because it provides a natural starting place for thinking about Hegel's project. But it is important to note that although Hegel thinks that alienation can be manifested in people's feelings, he does not regard it as a mere feeling. What is centrally at issue for Hegel in determining whether people are alienated or at home in the social world is their *structural relation* to the central social institutions. This topic is taken up in Chapter 3.

3   It should be noted here at the outset that the negative connotations of the English word 'reconciliation' (e.g., the suggestion of resignation) are not shared by *Versöhnung,* the German word Hegel uses, which is far more positive than the English and essentially involves an element of affirmation. The differences between 'reconciliation' and *Versöhnung* are discussed briefly in Chapter 1 and at greater length in Chapter 3.

Hegel's project does not, however, speak directly to us. The people Hegel seeks to reconcile are his contemporaries, the people of the nineteenth century.[4] And the social world he seeks to reconcile them to – the social world of the nineteenth century – is presumably rather different from our own. The state, as he represents it, is a (constitutional) monarchy; the rural nobility and the peasantry constitute important social groups; and women are excluded from civil society and the state. We cannot assume that the alienation experienced by people in Hegel's world is identical to the alienation experienced by people in ours. Nor can we assume that the answers Hegel offers to the problem of alienation in his social world will answer the problem of alienation in ours. Nonetheless, the general problem that pushes Hegel's project, *alienation*, and the general ideal that pulls it, *reconciliation*, are matters of concern to us, and this gives us a reason to examine Hegel's project. Moreover, even if the social world Hegel seeks to reconcile his contemporaries to is not identical to our own, it is not radically different from it either. It is a world that includes the nuclear bourgeois family, the modern market, and the modern political state. Not the least important thing we can get from reading Hegel is insight into the structure of our social world.

The second category of reasons for looking at Hegel's project is scholarly. Reconciliation is the main goal and central organizing category of Hegel's social philosophy (PR, ¶14, §360). It is also the main goal and central organizing category of Hegel's philosophy as a whole (VA, 1:81/1:55; VG, 78/67; VGP, 3:69/3:165).[5] If we want to understand Hegel's social philosophy, we must understand the role that reconciliation plays within it. In considering Hegel's social philosophy *as* a project of reconciliation, we attempt to understand it through its aim – an approach that provides an especially illuminating way of thinking about his philosophy's shape and structure. Focusing on reconciliation can also help us understand what makes Hegel's social philosophy distinctive – for the emphasis his social philosophy places on reconciliation is clearly one of its most distinctive features.

---

4 A more precise specification of Hegel's audience is provided in Chapter 4, section I.

5 The project of reconciling people to the social world is one part of the larger project of reconciling them to the world as a whole, which is, in turn, a part of the still larger project of reconciling *Geist* (spirit, mind) to the world as a whole and thereby to itself.

Interpreting Hegel's social philosophy as a project of reconciliation has the further advantage of making it possible to avoid placing Hegel in one or the other of two established drawers: progressive or conservative, liberal or communitarian. At the same time,
this approach helps us understand the compulsion to pigeonhole
him in this way. A focus on reconciliation brings the opposing tendencies of his social thought – progressive *and* conservative, liberal
and communitarian – into clearer view. This tack similarly enables
us to avoid the temptation of reading Hegel as either a left or a right
Hegelian (as an advocate of criticism and revolution or an advocate of quietism and accommodation).[6] The project of reconciliation
is, among other things, an attempt to reconcile the conflicting political tendencies (toward criticism and quietism, revolution and
accommodation) that, taken by themselves, lead in the directions
of left and right Hegelianism. To the extent that we view Hegel as
engaged in the project of reconciliation, we can see him, not as a
left or a right Hegelian, but instead as a *Hegelian.*

Obviously, the idea that Hegel's social philosophy is a project of
reconciliation is one among many possible interpretations. One
could, for example, make Hegel's notion of *Geist* (mind, spirit) the
central concept of one's interpretation. Hegel uses *Geist* to refer to
human individuals, to human culture and society, and to God. Or
one could attempt to construe Hegel's social philosophy in terms
of the "categories" *(Denkbestimmungen)* of Hegel's *Science of Logic* –
his account of the determinations of thought he regards as delin-
eating the fundamental structure of the self and the world. Or again,
one might try to make Hegel's concept of freedom the center of
one's exposition. The advantage of starting with reconciliation
rather than *Geist* or the *Science of Logic* is that doing so makes it easier
to see Hegel's social thought as rooted in a set of concerns we share
with him: alienation and the wish to overcome it. The advantage of
starting with reconciliation rather than freedom is that doing so
makes it easier to escape the tightly closed circle of notions within
which Hegel works, and so makes it easier for us to get an initial
purchase on his thought.

That reconciliation is central to Hegel's social philosophy is a
familiar idea in the literature. Scholars have long recognized that
reconciliation is the central aim of Hegel's social philosophy and

---

6 For discussions of left and right Hegelianism, see Crites 1967; Löwith 1941, 1964;
   and Toews 1980.

of his philosophy as a whole.[7] But the point of studying Hegel, like that of studying any other important historical philosopher, is not to come up with radically new and different things to say; rather, it is to deepen our understanding of his view. Thus it is by no means distressing that the claim that reconciliation is central to Hegel's social philosophy is not new. It would rather be cause for worry if no one had appreciated the importance of reconciliation before. But it is one thing to recognize in a general way that reconciliation is the aim of Hegel's social philosophy and another to give this point content. That this idea is familiar does not mean that it has been properly understood. I believe that this idea still stands in need of philosophical clarification. I also believe that there is still a need for a systematic account of Hegel's social philosophy *as* a project of reconciliation.[8] My aim in this book is to address this dual need.

In any case, the very idea that Hegel's social philosophy can be taken seriously as a project of reconciliation has recently become controversial. In his excellent book *Hegel's Ethical Thought,* Allen Wood acknowledges that Hegel's social philosophy aims at reconciliation. He says that "Hegel seeks to overcome alienation by rationally reconciling us to the world, comprehending a divine reason, akin to our own, immanent in it." But then he goes on to say:

> Few of Hegel's readers today find it natural to adopt rational theodicy as their fundamental relation to their cultural predicament. Accordingly, they should be more willing than he was to consider Hegel's conception of the vocation of modern individuals and its fulfillment in the modern state in their practical meaning – as a project in rational ethics. To read Hegel in this way is, admittedly, to read him in some measure against his own self-understanding; it is nevertheless *the only way* in which most of us, if we are honest with ourselves, *can read him seriously at all.*[9] (My emphasis)

It will come as no surprise that I think Wood wrong on this point. But Wood makes it clear that the idea that Hegel's social philosophy can be taken seriously as a project of reconciliation is something that needs to be shown. One of my central aims in this book is precisely to show that – and how – it can.

7 Recent commentators include Pippin (1981, 510), Taylor (1989, 430), and Wood (1990, 6).
8 Plant (1973) emphasizes the idea of reconciliation in Hegel's social thought, but I have tried to provide a treatment of the topic that is more analytical and systematic.
9 Wood 1990, 8.

The third sort of reason for looking at Hegel's project is philosophical. Reconciliation represents an important philosophical topic in its own right. One philosophical reason for looking at Hegel's project is for the light it sheds on this topic. But, of course, reconciliation is not generally recognized as an important philosophical field of inquiry by analytical philosophers. Indeed, within the analytical tradition, reconciliation is not generally recognized as a philosophical concern at all. This suggests a somewhat different reason for looking at Hegel's project: doing so may enable us to see that reconciliation is in fact an important topic for philosophy.

It should be clear why one might want to make reconciliation an object of philosophical reflection. Reconciliation is an important cultural, political, and personal concern, and thinking about such concerns is a traditional aim of philosophy. One of the perennial sources of attraction of Hegel's writing consists in its attempt to address important matters of cultural, political, and personal concern in a philosophical way.

It may also help to note that concern with reconciliation is not as far removed from mainstream analytical work as one might initially think. Thus, for example, John Rawls maintains that one of the various roles that political philosophy has as a part of culture is "reconciliation" – a role that he notes was emphasized by Hegel. "Political philosophy calms our frustration and rage against our social world by showing us the way in which its institutions, when properly understood from a philosophical point of view, are rational."[10] Moreover, reconciliation can be seen as forming an important concern within the tradition of modern political philosophy, which analytical philosophers recognize as their own. Rousseau, Kant, and Marx all offer visions of reconciliation, broadly understood.

But in order to make good on the claim that the topic of reconciliation is genuinely philosophical, it is not enough to name names or point to a tradition: the claim that the topic is genuinely philosophical is something that must be shown. The best way to do that is to put the notion of reconciliation to philosophical work. And the best way to do that is to look at Hegel. Hegel was the first modern thinker explicitly to claim that reconciliation is the proper aim of political philosophy. His is the deepest and most comprehensive philosophical treatment of this problem available. If under-

10 Rawls 1987, 1.

standing Hegel provides a *historical* reason for looking at the project of reconciliation, understanding how reconciliation could be a philosophical topic constitutes a *philosophical* reason for looking at Hegel.

A closely related philosophical reason for examining Hegel's project is that it raises an important philosophical question. Hume asked: What is causation? Wittgenstein asked: What is it to follow a rule? The philosophical question Hegel asks is: Can I be reconciled to the social world?

One difference between Hegel's question and the questions Hume and Wittgenstein posed stands out immediately. Unlike the questions they posed, Hegel's question does not belong to the recognized philosophical canon. But, of course, one of the basic motivations for turning to the history of philosophy is precisely to expand our sense of what the philosophical questions are. Serious work in the history of philosophy begins in the conviction that philosophers of the past can help us in this endeavor. To my mind, the most important philosophical lesson we can draw from Hegel's social philosophy is that Can I be reconciled to the social world? is an important philosophical question. Showing the philosophical interest and importance of this question is another of my aims in this book.

The way in which I propose to show the philosophical interest and importance of this question is by showing that it allows of an interesting philosophical answer: the answer that Hegel gives. In this respect my approach to Hegel's social philosophy reverses the usual order of things: my presentation of Hegel's *answer* is driven by the aim of motivating his *question*. I am far more concerned with showing that his question is philosophically interesting and important than in establishing the correctness or incorrectness of his answer. Indeed, one of my central aims is to show that we can regard this question as philosophically important even if we do not finally accept the answer that Hegel gives. This does not mean, however, that we can simply ignore Hegel's answer. On the face of things the question, Can I be reconciled to the social world? is extremely abstract and general. It is not initially clear what is being asked when these words are uttered. Nor is it immediately clear what would count as a possible answer. Still less is it initially obvious what turns on the question being answered one way or the other. In order to appreciate the philosophical force of Hegel's question, we must work our way through the details of his view.

II

In what follows I present a *philosophical reconstruction* of Hegel's project. If we are to see Hegel's answer to the question as a philosophical response, we must be able to understand it. And before his answer can be understood, it must be reconstructed. Hegel's technical vocabulary is too obscure to be used without clarification and too foreign for those of us trained within the analytical tradition to ever take it over as our own. My guiding principle has been to avoid using Hegel's technical vocabulary, to minimize reliance on his metaphysics, and to present his view in terms that we can understand. One consequence of this decision is that the language and structure of my presentation differ dramatically from Hegel's own. My hope is that the gains in clarity and perspicuity will offset the regrettable loss of connection with his text. My aim of presenting Hegel's view clearly and intelligibly forces me to forgo making exegesis a central part of my discussion. The interpretation provided in this book is rooted in close readings of the text, but extended textual discussion would ensnare us in the very aspects of Hegel's prose the reconstruction is meant to avoid.

In addition to reconstructing the terminology of Hegel's discussion, this book also reconstructs its structure. Although the notion of reconciliation is absolutely central to Hegel's thought, his own exposition obscures the central role it plays. The reconstruction provided in this book brings the centrality of this notion into plain view. It is designed to make the role that reconciliation plays in Hegel's social philosophy transparent. It is meant to make it possible for us to see his social philosophy *as* a project of reconciliation.

One crucial substantive respect in which my account is a reconstruction is that it abstracts the project of reconciling people to the social world from the two larger projects of which it is a part: the project of reconciling people to the world as a whole and the project of reconciling *Geist* to the world as a whole and to itself. My central focus is on the relation of people to the modern social world.

I should note that for the most part I deliberately avoid engagement in scholarly disputes. I do so not out of ingratitude, indifference, or hostility to Hegel scholarship but rather with the aim of presenting as clear and uncluttered a reconstruction of Hegel's view as possible. This book is intended to be a contribution to the scholarly study of Hegel, but the contribution it seeks to make is not itself scholarly. I mean to contribute to the scholarly study of Hegel by presenting an account of his project of reconciliation that is especially clear and illuminating. I hope that by giving shape, clarity, and form to the familiar idea that reconciliation is the main goal and central organizing category of Hegel's social philosophy, my reconstruction will make it possible for scholars to see Hegel's social philosophy in a new and different way.

Throughout the book I seek to observe the principles of intelligibility and fidelity. The principle of intelligibility requires that Hegel's thought be presented in a manner that is clear and understandable. The principle of fidelity requires that one remain faithful to the distinctive character of his thought. My fundamental interpretive task is to manage the tension between these two principles. My goal is to present a Hegel that is both understandable and Hegelian.

Characterizing my enterprise as a 'philosophical reconstruction' could be misleading, since there are at least two ways in which it differs from 'philosophical reconstruction' as standardly practiced. First, I do not attempt to transform Hegel into a contemporary. The Hegel I 'reconstruct' remains someone whose philosophical views and approach to philosophy are strikingly different from our own. The point of my reconstruction is to facilitate – not obviate – contact with the 'otherness' of his thought. Approaching Hegel, like approaching Plato, Aquinas, or Descartes, involves entering a foreign philosophical world; my reconstruction seeks to respect this fact. Second, this book does not attempt to reconstruct Hegel's philosophy as providing answers to the questions that are generally regarded by contemporary philosophers as being philosophical. It seeks instead to learn from Hegel what *he* took the philosophical questions to be and to reconstruct the answers that he gives in a form we can understand.

One other point needs to be made clear at the outset. My aim in this book is to reconstruct *one central aspect* of Hegel's social philosophy: his attempt to reconcile people to the modern social world. This book does not purport to give a complete account of Hegel's thought. Nor does it attempt to discuss Hegel's social and political philosophy in a comprehensive way. It seeks instead to pursue in some depth one single strand of Hegel's thought, in the hope that doing so will illuminate his thought as a whole.[11]

---

11 Taylor (1975) offers what is perhaps the best general discussion of Hegel's philosophy. Plant (1973) offers an excellent general discussion of Hegel's political philosophy. The best general account of Hegel's ethical theory is to be found in Wood 1991.

From a textual standpoint, my discussion restricts itself to Hegel's *Rechtsphilosophie* (philosophy of right), the social philosophy he presented in the *Grundlinien der Philosophie des Rechts oder Naturrecht und Staatswissenschaft im Grundrisse* (1821),[12] in the section "Der objektive Geist" of the *Enzyklopädie der philosophischen Wissenschaften,* vol. 1 (1817, rev. 1827, 1830), and in the lectures given in Heidelberg and Berlin between 1817 and 1831. I have decided to concentrate on this section of Hegel's corpus because it constitutes the most mature and systematic presentation of his social thought and because limiting myself in this manner facilitates my attempt to reconstruct Hegel's social thought in a clear and systematic way. In any case, the *Rechtsphilosophie* is more than rich and interesting enough to sustain one book.[13]

III

This book is divided into two parts. Part I, "An Approach to Hegel's Project," provides the orientation necessary to understand Hegel's project. Chapter 1, "The Problems of Hegel's Project," begins by addressing the initial difficulties encountered in understanding the project, using them to provide an entrée into the project.

Chapter 2, "*Geist* and the *Doppelsatz,*" is intended to convey a sense of Hegel's philosophical point of view by providing an account of two ideas central to that view: *Geist* (spirit, mind) and the *Doppelsatz* (the double dictum), Hegel's famous doctrine that proclaims the 'actuality' of the 'rational' and the 'rationality' of the 'actual.'

Chapter 3, "The Concept of Reconciliation," provides a preliminary account of the basic notion of Hegel's project: reconciliation. It elucidates the ordinary use of the word 'reconciliation' (and of *Versöhnung,* the German term Hegel uses) and provides a reconstruction of Hegel's technical sense of the term. It also draws a contrast between reconciliation, on the one hand, and resignation and consolation, on the other, and discusses the relation between reconciliation and happiness.

Part II, "The Project of Reconciliation," lays out Hegel's project. Chapter 4, "The Anatomy of the Project," draws on the chapters

---

12 For a discussion of the publication of the *Grundlinien der Philosophie des Rechts* and a statement of the view that its publication date was actually 1820, see Peperzack 1987, 1ff.

13 Readers interested in a developmental approach to Hegel's thought can profitably consult Fulda 1981 and Plant 1973.

that precede it to present the basic elements of Hegel's project in a clearly structured way. It specifies the project's aim, who gets reconciled, and what they get reconciled to. It also explains why the project is necessary, how it proceeds, and how it is possible. Its final section shows how the project can be seen as involving a process of self-transformation.

Chapter 5, "Individuality and Social Membership," provides a reconstruction of Hegel's conceptions of individuality and social membership. It shows why, according to Hegel, it is possible to be both a "full-fledged" individual and a "full-fledged" social member, and that modern individuality and social membership are intertwined inextricably. More specifically, it shows how, for Hegel, modern individuality is made possible by modern social membership and how, in his view, modern social membership essentially includes an individualistic dimension.

Chapter 6, "The Family, Civil Society, and the State," presents Hegel's account of the central social institutions of the modern social world – the family, civil society, and the state – and attempts to show why Hegel thought that these institutions were worthy of reconciliation.

The final chapter, "Divorce, War, and Poverty," considers the difficulties these problems pose for Hegel's project and explains why Hegel thinks they do not undermine the modern social world's claim to be a home.

A few words about my strategy. After considering the initial difficulties Hegel's project may pose for us, I am going to step back and present his view in a relatively detached, historical way. The complexity of Hegel's view is such that we need to begin by postponing assessment and focusing more or less exclusively on understanding what the view is. Once we have gotten a basic grip on his view, it will be possible to consider certain criticisms as we go along, but understanding rather than assessment is my central concern in the book. Nonetheless, I do think it important to stand back from Hegel's project at some point and say something about how we are to view it. I take up this task in the Conclusion. I should also note that this book forms a whole. Its discussion proceeds from the abstract to the concrete, the later chapters providing the context for the material presented in the earlier ones. Only when the reader has gone through the whole book will he or she be in a position to understand its component parts.

I

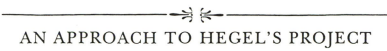

AN APPROACH TO HEGEL'S PROJECT

THE PROBLEMS
OF HEGEL'S PROJECT

As soon as one begins to think about Hegel's project, a family of problems arises. The project might, for example, seem alien, threatening, or misguided. Even before the problems are clearly formulated, they can produce the conviction that the project cannot be taken seriously. The mere sense that the problems exist is an impediment.[1] But perhaps we would be less inclined to dismiss Hegel's project if we were to arrive at a better understanding of what these problems are. There would still, of course, be questions concerning how we are to regard Hegel's project ultimately, but we could, at least, begin by taking the project seriously. What we need to do, then, is to consider whether there may not be an initial way of addressing these difficulties that would make it possible for us to approach Hegel's project in a serious way. Considering these problems should also have the further, desirable effect of drawing us into Hegel's project. I will begin by considering five sorts of difficulties Hegel's project may raise.

I. The problem of foreignness

The first problem is that Hegel's project may seem alien. There are at least three reasons why this may appear to be so.

1 See, e.g., Wood 1990, 8.

1. Hegel's project may seem alien, or foreign, first of all, because the very idea of the 'social world' may seem alien.[2] What are we talking about when we talk about the social world?[3] We can start by saying that the expression refers to society or a society of a certain type. Somewhat more precisely, we can say that it refers to the framework of the central institutions and practices of social and political life of society or a society of a certain type. The idea of the social world is thus very closely related to Rawls's idea of the "basic structure," by which he means the basic structure of society, which structure he takes to consist of the scheme formed by the main social and political institutions of society or the way in which these institutions fit together.[4]

As I am using the expression, 'the social world' does not refer to social subspheres or subcultures – for example, the 'world' of punks, artists, factory workers, or lawyers. It refers instead to society, or a type of society, considered as a whole – without, however, carrying the implication that the institutions and practices of society must form some kind of highly interconnected whole; logically speaking, a social world need not form a 'system' or a 'totality.' This point deserves emphasis since Hegel thinks that the modern social world does form a system or a totality. The use of 'the social world' I am recommending makes it possible to coherently ask whether a given social world forms an interconnected whole and to coherently deny that a particular social world (or, for that matter, that any social world) forms a system or totality. It should be pointed out that 'the social world' also refers to the particular roles that people have within the central social institutions. Thus, for example, Hegel thinks of the modern social world as including the roles of family member, member of civil society (*Bürger*, 'burgher'), and citizen.

The expression 'the social world' is roughly synonymous with 'society'. Why, then, speak of a social *world*? The term is suggestive in a way in which 'society' is not; in particular, it conveys the idea

2 The expression 'the social world' belongs to my reconstruction. To my knowledge, Hegel does not himself use its German equivalent, *die soziale Welt*; he certainly does not use it in any systematic way. The general term Hegel uses to refer to what I am calling the social world is *die sittliche Welt* (the ethical world). My reason for not using this term is that it expresses a philosophical thesis – that the social world is an *ethical* world – about which I would like to remain noncommittal.

3 I shall occasionally use the word 'world' as an abbreviation for 'social world', allowing context to make clear that I am not then changing the subject from the social world to the world in general.

4 Rawls 1971, 7–11.

that society forms a 'world' – the world of social institutions and practices into which human beings are born, within which they live, and in which they die. Hegel thought of the *modern* social world as a specifically modern type of society, realized to a greater or lesser degree by the European states of the early nineteenth century such as England, France, and Prussia. More will be said about Hegel's conception of the modern social world in Chapters 6 and 7, but it should be noted that the idea of the social world can be applied to any particular historical era. Thus, for example, we can speak meaningfully of the ancient and medieval social worlds and not just the modern social world.

It should also be pointed out that speaking of the social world in the recommended sense does not commit one to the Hegelian idea that for any given historical era there will be one dominant structure of social and political institutions (VG, 155–7/129–31). Nor does it commit one to the Hegelian idea that the central social institutions of the modern social world consist of the family, civil society, and the state (PR, §157); the bare idea of the social world (or, for that matter, the bare idea of the *modern* social world) contains no such commitment.

One last remark on 'the social world'. The expression can also be used to refer to the particular social world that a particular group of people inhabit. We can, for example, speak of our social world as 'the' social world. We can also speak of Hegel's social world as 'the' social world. This usage does not involve a conflation of a particular society with 'society' as such. It instead provides a useful way of expressing the point that a particular social world may represent 'the' social world for the people who inhabit it. It is, so to speak, *the* social world *for them*, for it is the social world into which they are born and carry out their lives.

2. A second reason the project of reconciliation may seem alien is that becoming reconciled to the social world is a matter of *taking a particular attitude* toward the social world or of *relating to* the social world in a particular way – and these ideas may seem alien.[5] Thus someone might say: "I have no attitude toward *the* social world. I have an attitude toward my father, toward my boss, toward the president of the United States, but not toward the social world itself." Here it is important to recall that what is at issue when one

---

5 My use of 'relating to' and 'taking an attitude toward' (the social world) corresponds broadly to Hegel's use of the term *Gesinnung* (disposition or outlook).

speaks of relating to 'the' social world is one's relation to one's own social world – the social world in which one lives. One might deny that one has any attitude toward one's social world. To this it could be replied that one need not have an *explicit* attitude toward one's social world as such in order to be correctly said to have *an* attitude toward it. One's attitude toward one's social world may be implicit, expressed by the way in which one *relates* to the central institutions and practices of the society. 'Relating to an institution' is a matter of conducting oneself in a certain way with a certain frame of mind with respect to that institution. Thus, for example, performing jury duty out of a sense of civic duty, performing jury duty with a sense of resentment, and avoiding jury duty altogether, all represent different ways of 'relating' to the judicial system.

It seems plausible to suggest that people do, generally speaking, have an attitude (or range of attitudes) toward their social world. Their attitude (or attitudes) may be implicit, inchoate, or fragmentary. They may even have no explicit conception of the social world. But people will presumably have some attitude toward the central institutions of their society, even if it is only one of indifference. A person for whom marrying, finding a job, and voting raise no particular personal or political issues has one sort of attitude toward the social world; the person for whom any of these activities raises acute personal and political questions, another. Generally speaking, the more problematic one's relation to the social world, the more likely one is to be aware of having an attitude toward the social world. But it is no less true that the person whose basic relation to the social world is unproblematic also has *an* attitude (or range of attitudes) toward the social world. Such a person may, for example, unreflectively think that its institutions are perfectly acceptable. And, obviously, the person who self-consciously endorses the basic institutional arrangements of his or her social world – for example, the person who thinks that the social world is a wonderful place – has an attitude toward that world.

The idea of relating to the social world in an explicit or self-conscious way can be evoked by thinking about what it would be to relate in this manner to a particular sphere of the social world: the political order. Imagine what it would be like to live in Nazi Germany. Political circumstances would force one to take an explicit attitude toward the political order. One would be faced with a range of questions: What does it mean that I am a citizen of a country with this sort of regime? How am I to relate to it? Ought I to resist? To comply? To leave if I can? How can I protect myself from it? How can I avoid complicity in its evil? The problem of what attitude to adopt toward a regime like that of Nazi Germany is one we can all understand.

Once we have a grip on the idea of relating to the political order in a self-conscious way, it is easy to extend the idea to relating to the other central institutions of society. Consider the issues that will arise for the woman who despises the institution of the family. Will she address her parents as 'mother' and 'father'? Will she think of them as standing in these roles? She will, of course, recognize that they occupy these roles. But will she think of these roles as part of their 'identity'? Will she think of these roles (and her role as 'daughter') as structuring their relationship? How will she deal with her mother and father if they attempt to relate to her *as* mother and father? And if for some practical reason she marries, how will she think of herself and her spouse? Will she think of him as her 'husband'? Of herself as a 'wife'? How will she respond when people regard her as a 'wife,' when, for example, they address her as 'Mrs.'? How will she respond to her spouse's inclinations to treat her as his 'wife'? And how will she deal with the objective features of society (e.g., differential wages) that make it difficult to avoid the traditional role of wife?[6] These problems are certainly familiar.

But even if one gets a grip on the idea of relating to the social world in an explicit or self-conscious way, the idea of *being reconciled* to the social world may still seem foreign. Few of us begin employing the category of reconciliation in the context of our relation to the social world. We are far more likely to first use this notion in interpersonal contexts, thinking about the possibility or impossibility of becoming reconciled with co-workers, colleagues, friends, or family members. Or again we may use the notion with reference to collectivities or groups. We might, for example, ask about the possibility of reconciliation between white and black Americans or between Israeli Jews and Palestinians. But the notion of reconciliation – like that of alienation – allows of extension to the social world. Just as one can speak of alienation from the social world so too one can speak of reconciliation with the social world.

3. Still another reason the project of reconciliation may seem alien is that it is a kind of social theodicy (see VG, 48/42) – and this idea may strike us as foreign. 'Social theodicy' is a social and politi-

6 One point this example brings out is that one of the central ways in which people relate to institutions is by relating to the roles contained within them.

cal variant of the traditional theological enterprise.[7] As traditionally conceived, theodicy seeks to justify the ways of God to man. Social theodicy seeks to justify the ways of society to its members. By showing that the world is ultimately good, traditional theodicy seeks to reconcile man to God; by showing that the social world is ultimately good, social theodicy seeks to reconcile people to the social world. We can think of Hegel's social theodicy as responding to two problems: the problem of alienation and the problem of social evil. And, accordingly, we can think of his social theodicy as functioning as a response to each of these two problems.

This point is worth emphasizing because the distinction between these two subtasks is often overlooked. The problem of alienation, as Hegel understands it, was that his contemporaries (or, in any case, many of the intellectuals within his social world) were not 'at home' in their social world.[8] They regarded their central social institutions as foreign, bifurcating, and hostile or indifferent to their needs. Hegel's social philosophy was to function as a social theodicy, first of all, by showing that, contrary to appearances, their social world was in fact a 'home'. It was to establish that the modern social world was the kind of place in which its members could genuinely be at home by showing that society's central institutions were not foreign, bifurcating, hostile or indifferent to their needs. The idea was that once his audience grasped that their social world was a home, they would come to be at home there, and so be reconciled.

The problem of social evil, as Hegel understands it, arises because the social world contains problematic features that intuitively appear to be evil, such as divorce (PR, §176) and war (PR, §324), and one central feature, poverty (PR, §§244–5), that is genuinely evil. Moreover, Hegel recognizes that particular families, forms of civil society, and states will inevitably exhibit defects and imperfections, some of which are quite serious.

The second way in which his social philosophy is to function as a social theodicy, then, is by showing (i) that divorce and war each have a rational element in the light of which they can be affirmed, (ii) that the evil of poverty does not undermine the basic goodness of the social world, and (iii) that the general fact that particular social institutions exhibit defects and imperfections is ultimately accept-

7 The term 'social theodicy' belongs to my reconstruction. Hegel uses the term 'theodicy' (*Theodizee*).
8 The issue of how widespread Hegel takes alienation to be is addressed in Chapter 4.

able because defects and imperfections are the unavoidable price of finitude, the unavoidable price of having social institutions that are realized in the finite sphere of human life and action, which is to say, realized at all. (The problems posed by divorce, poverty, and war are taken up in Chapter 7; the general problem of the imperfection of particular institutions is addressed in Chapter 2.) It is perhaps worth mentioning that the problem of social evil can be subsumed under the problem of alienation if the problem of social evil is regarded as a possible source of alienation. This, then, suggests that the task of responding to alienation, broadly understood, is ultimately the more fundamental of the two subtasks of Hegel's social theodicy.

Now clearly there is something foreign about this enterprise. Social theodicy is not among the tasks we normally think of as belonging to social philosophy. However congenial the idea of extending the traditional idea of theodicy to the social world may have been to Hegel's contemporaries, it is not an idea that seems natural and intuitive to most people today. Nonetheless, the enterprise is not completely and utterly foreign. Social theodicy represents a response to the question, How shall I relate to the social world? that takes the question seriously. And this is a question that we can take seriously; it is a question that many people today face in everyday life. Moreover, social theodicy addresses two problems we can recognize as real: the problem of alienation and the problem of coming to terms with the fact that the social world will inevitably exhibit defects and imperfections. Considered as *a* response to these problems, the enterprise of social theodicy becomes accessible.

We need not suppose that social theodicy can succeed in order to find it interesting. Indeed, the enterprise is no less interesting if it cannot succeed. Were we to find out that the social world does not allow of a successful social theodicy, that would represent an important discovery, for, presumably, the way in which we would relate to a social world that *allows* of a successful social theodicy – if such there be – is rather different from the way in which we would relate to a social world that does *not* allow of one. If a social world allows of a successful social theodicy, acceptance, support, and endorsement may recommend themselves as ways of relating to it. If, on the other hand, the social world does not allow of a successful social theodicy, retreat, resistance, and revolution may recommend themselves as possible responses.

II. The problem of optimism

A second difficulty with Hegel's project of reconciliation is that it may seem wildly optimistic. As we have seen, Hegel maintains that his social world really is 'a home', despite the fact that it appears to be alien, bifurcating, and hostile or indifferent to its members' needs. In his view, what prevents them from coming to be at home is not so much a problem with their social world as it is a problem with their understanding – with their understanding of their social world and their understanding of themselves. The real reason they are alienated is that they fail to understand that the modern social world is a place where they can be at home and that they are the kind of agents who can be at home in the social world they inhabit.

It is clear, then, that there is an important respect in which Hegel's conception of the modern social world is very optimistic. If we do not share this outlook, it would be only natural to regard Hegel's project with scepticism. But the question at hand is not whether we should accept Hegel's conclusions. It is whether the optimism of Hegel's project is such as to prevent us from taking it seriously. I have already sketched the first line of response. We need not assume that Hegel's social theodicy can succeed in order to take his project seriously. Nor need we share Hegel's optimism in order to take his project seriously – at least from a historical point of view. Here it perhaps is worth recalling that doing the history of philosophy, doing it properly, essentially involves a willingness to take seriously views that one does not share.

In any case, Hegel's optimism is far less extreme than might at first appear. Hegel does not think that the modern social world is perfect in each and every respect. He is not the Pangloss of the social world. We have seen that Hegel maintains that some of its fundamental features such as divorce and war are problematic, that he regards poverty as an evil, and that he recognizes that particular families, civil societies, and states will inevitably be defective in various ways. It is clear, then, that Hegel does not think that reconciliation is possible because he believes that everything is perfect. He maintains that reconciliation is possible because the basic features of the central institutions of the modern social world – the family, civil society, and the state – are acceptable and because these structures are realized to a significant degree. (This point is taken up in Chapter 2.)

It is perhaps worth pointing out that Hegel's optimism is actually far less removed from common sense than one might think. There is a familiar, moderate position fairly common today that resembles it in certain respects. Many people think that the social, political, and economic system of the United States, or, more generally, representative democracies with market economies coupled with welfare provisions, are basically acceptable. Although they may regard the existing instantiation of these structures as defective in various respects, they endorse the basic structures and, furthermore, think that these structures are in fact adequately realized. From this standpoint, Hegel's view is not so wildly optimistic. It might be thought of as an interesting radicalization of this commonsense point of view.

But, of course, we may be less sanguine about our own social world. Some will be inclined to doubt that its basic structures are genuinely acceptable, even in principle. (Here I must confess to sharing these doubts.) In that case Hegel becomes interesting for another reason. His optimism represents a clearly articulated, sharply focused, radical alternative to one's own view – a view against which one can clarify one's own position. Indeed, one of the striking features of Hegel's philosophy is the appeal it holds for radical critics of society. Then, again, if one is unclear about one's basic attitude toward one's social world, Hegel is useful in another way. His social philosophy can deepen one's understanding of the different ways in which the social world can be assessed and of the sorts of considerations that go into making such assessments. It can put us in a better position to determine how we are to relate to the social world.

III. The problem of pessimism

A third difficulty Hegel's project raises is, paradoxically, that it may seem pessimistic and demoralizing. One source of this impression is linguistic. 'Reconciliation' is the English word I am using to represent *Versöhnung*, the German word Hegel uses. One of the peculiarities of 'reconciliation' is that it can mean *resignation*. This may suggest that the real aim of Hegel's project is resignation, which can sound pessimistic and demoralizing. The difference between 'resignation' and *Versöhnung* is a main topic of Chapter 3, but it should be noted here that *Versöhnung* cannot mean 'resignation'. The attitude *Versöhnung* conveys is positive. *Versöhnung* essentially involves affirmation. The aim of Hegel's project of reconciliation is not to bring about a transition from a state of alienation to a state of resignation to the social world. The final state at which it aims is one in which people will rationally endorse and affirm the social world.

The impression that Hegel's project is pessimistic does not, however, derive solely from the English translation of *Versöhnung* and is by no means unique to his non-German-speaking readers. Even if one recognizes that Hegel's social philosophy is not *intended* to be a philosophy of resignation, one might still wonder whether his project of reconciliation does not ultimately *collapse* into a project of resignation. The seriousness of the problems that Hegel's social world exhibits might well lead one to think that it does. As we have seen, his world (like ours) includes not only divorce and war but also poverty, and Hegel thinks that becoming reconciled to the modern world involves accepting it as a world that contains these features. One might well then wonder whether this sort of acceptance does not ultimately amount to resignation. This is not, however, a matter we can settle at the outset. Indeed, before we can consider whether the project of reconciliation does or does not collapse into a project of resignation, we will need to consider it as a whole.

IV. The threat of conservatism, ideology, and the suppression of individuality

The fourth problem Hegel's project raises is that it may seem threatening. I will consider several reasons why this may be so.

1. The first reason is that it may appear to be conservative. It may appear to

  (i) Endorse the status quo merely because it is in place
  (ii) Exclude reform
  (iii) Require the abandonment of criticism and opposition

Let me consider these three, closely related, features in turn.

(i) Why Hegel's project may appear to endorse the status quo is easy to see. To begin with, Hegel's *Doppelsatz*, or 'double dictum', one of the most famous passages in the Preface to the *Philosophy of Right*, proclaims:

> What is rational is actual
> and what is actual is rational. (PR, ¶12)

In one very natural reading, this slogan asserts that everything that exists is rational and suggests that it is rational simply because it exists.[9] This reading only seems confirmed by Hegel's further claim that "*what is* is reason" (PR, ¶13). Moreover, the aim of Hegel's social philosophy is not to reconcile people to a reformed or revolutionized future social world but instead to reconcile them to the 'actual' social world – the social world in which they live. It is precisely to make this point that Hegel cites the saying

Ἰδοὺ ῾Ρόδος, ἰδοὺ καὶ τὸ πήδημα.
Hic Rhodus, *hic* saltus.
[*Here* is Rhodes, jump *here.*] (PR, ¶13)

One is not to attain reconciliation in some distant time and place, like Rhodes, the place where the braggart claimed to have made a jump none of the Olympic victors could equal. One is to become reconciled *here and now*, in the city in which one lives. "Here is Rhodes" means *this* social world is the world to which one is to become reconciled. "Jump here" means the task is to become reconciled at *this* time to *this* world. Hegel denies that his social world has to undergo revolutionary transformation or be reformed in order to become worthy of reconciliation; he thinks that it is *already* worthy of reconciliation.

This is why Hegel holds that the saying "here is Rhodes, jump here" could with but "little alteration" be rendered as "*here* is the rose, dance here" (PR, ¶14). To say "*here* is the rose" (a pun on the Latin word *Rhodus*, which means both 'Rhodes' and 'rose') is to say that a form of social life that provides satisfaction is to be found here and now in this social world. To say "dance here" (a pun on the Latin word *salta*, which means both 'jump' and 'dance') is to say that one can find satisfaction by participating in the central arrangements of the modern social world.

One final reason for thinking that Hegel's project may endorse the status quo as such is that endorsement *is* a crucial component of reconciliation. Until and unless one endorses the social world in which one lives, one has not attained reconciliation. Reconciled individuals endorse their social world.

But for all this, Hegel does not endorse the status quo as such. Contrary to appearances, the *Doppelsatz* does not maintain that everything that exists is rational. Nor is it meant to suggest that

9 See Haym 1857, 367–8ff.

things are rational merely because they exist. Indeed, Hegel explicitly denies that everything that exists is rational (EL, §6). As we shall see in Chapter 3, Hegel employs the word 'actual' (*wirklich*) in a technical sense. In his usage, what is 'actual' is to be contrasted with what merely exists (that which exhibits mere *Dasein* or *Existenz*). Hegel understands 'actuality' (*Wirklichkeit*) to be the unity of essence (*Wesen*) and existence (*Existenz*) (EL, §142). Things are 'actual' only to the extent that they realize their 'essence', their underlying rational structure. When Hegel says "*what is* is reason," he is not using the expression 'what is' to refer to everything that exists but instead to refer to that which 'genuinely' is, that which is actual.

Hegel does, of course, endorse the family, civil society, and the state. But he does not endorse them merely because they are in place. He affirms them because he believes they have an underlying rational structure that is realized to a significant degree in the modern social world. (By an 'underlying rational structure' Hegel means a philosophically accessible structure that is rationally intelligible and reasonable or good.) And he maintains, quite generally, that *particular* families, civil societies, and states are worthy of affirmation only to the extent that they realize the underlying rational structure of the family, civil society, and the state.

Although endorsement is a crucial component of reconciliation, it is not necessary to endorse each and every feature of one's social world in order to be reconciled. One need (and should) endorse particular families, civil societies, and states *only* to the extent that they realize their underlying rational structures. Reconciled individuals do endorse their social world, but they do not endorse it qua existing social world. They endorse it qua actual and qua rational. Hegel's aim in the *Philosophy of Right* is inter alia to articulate the rational structure of the modern social world and thereby put his audience in a position to grasp what is genuinely actual in their social world and to affirm it in its rationality.

(ii) We have already touched upon one reason why someone one might hold that Hegel's project excludes reform. Hegel thought that the modern social world was worthy of reconciliation *as it stood*. He did not think it had to be reformed in any way in order to become worthy of reconciliation. Now this may give us pause. But the proposition that the social world does not need to be reformed in order to become worthy of reconciliation does not entail that it does not need to be reformed. Hegel thought that his social world was worthy of reconciliation *and* stood in need of reform. Roughly speaking, he thought that its existing features were sufficiently rational to warrant reconciliation and sufficiently irrational to warrant reform. Thus, for example, he advocated the establishment of a constitutional monarchy (PR, §279, R; VPRHO, 679), a representative bicameral assembly (PR, §§298–320), public criminal trials (PR, §224), and trials by jury (PR, §227R) in Prussia. Now, admittedly, these proposals are not terribly radical by our lights; nor were they all that radical by the standards of Hegel's own time. Nonetheless, Hegel's advocacy of these reforms places him squarely in the camp of the moderate liberal progressives of his age. Indeed, it is now generally recognized that Hegel was not the friend of the Prussian restoration he was once taken to be.[10]

The tension internal to Hegel's view that the modern social world is both worthy of reconciliation and in need of reform is unusual and complex and leads to a natural tendency to push Hegel in one of two directions: *either* toward the extreme view that since the social world is worthy of reconciliation it does not need to be reformed *or* toward the extreme view that since the social world needs to be reformed it is not worthy of reconciliation. The first view represents one of the basic sources of right Hegelianism; the second, one of the basic sources of left Hegelianism.[11] But the crucial fact about Hegel is that he wants to resist both left and right Hegelianism, or, less anachronistically, the sort of views that came to be called by these names. His aim is rather to "maintain the synthesis" according to which the social world, although imperfect, is worthy of reconciliation – a synthesis that would make it possible to unite basic acceptance of the social world with liberalizing reform.

(iii) Finally, one might think that Hegel's project is conservative because it appears to exclude criticism and opposition. One of the main sources of this impression is to be found in his Preface to the *Philosophy of Right*. Speaking of the philosophy of right (*Rechtsphilosophie*) itself, he says there, "As a philosophical composition, it must distance itself as far as possible from the obligation to construct a *state as it ought to be*; such instruction as it may contain cannot be aimed at instructing the state on how it ought to be, but rather at showing how the state, as the ethical universe, should be recognized" (PR, ¶13). Hegel goes on to say that "it is just as foolish to imagine that any

10 For criticisms of this view that Hegel approved of the Prussian restoration, see, e.g., Rosenzweig 1920; Weil 1950; Ritter 1965, 1982; Avineri 1972; and Wood 1990. For the classic statement of this view see Haym 1857.
11 See Introduction, n. 6.

philosophy can transcend its contemporary world as that an individual can overleap his own time or leap over Rhodes" (PR, ¶13).

Now there is no question that the *tone* of these passages is very conservative. Their tone suggests that the proper stance toward the social world does not involve trying to improve it in any way. But if one looks more closely at what Hegel actually says, it becomes clear that his position is rather more circumspect. Instead of addressing the general question of whether it is possible to engage in rational criticism of the state, the longer passage just cited speaks to the much narrower question of whether such criticism belongs to the tasks of philosophy. Hegel's answer to the latter question is no. Philosophy, as he understands it, consists in the activity of grasping 'the actual'. He calls this activity 'speculation' (*Spekulation*) (EL, §82, Z). Thus, he says that "to comprehend *what is* is the task of philosophy, for *what is* is reason" (PR, ¶13).

The social world is a proper object of philosophy precisely to the extent that it is rational. To the extent particular social institutions fail to realize their underlying rational structure, they fall outside the scope of philosophy thus understood. Philosophy must, it is true, account for the general fact that particular social institutions will inevitably fail to realize their underlying rational structure to some degree, but the activity of criticizing particular social institutions is not, in Hegel's view, a philosophical task.

When Hegel says that philosophy cannot "transcend its contemporary world," he does not mean that philosophy is restricted to the activity of providing sheer description of the de facto features of existing social institutions. As we have seen, Hegel maintains that philosophy *can* capture the underlying rational structure of the modern social world. And he holds that his philosophy of right actually does capture this structure.

It should be pointed out that the account the philosophy of right provides can in principle be used as the basis for rational criticism of existing institutions. To the extent that existing social institutions fail to correspond to their underlying rational structures, they are subject to criticism. The very theory that is supposed to make it possible to accept the modern social world – the account of the family, civil society, and state provided in the *Philosophy of Right* – also provides a set of standards on the basis of which defective social institutions can be criticized.[12] Social criticism may not be a *philo-*

12 See Hösle 1986.

sophical activity in Hegel's view, but his social philosophy provides the tools that enable one to engage in *philosophically informed* criticism of the social world.

Within the philosophical framework Hegel provides, it is possible to be reconciled to the social world *and* struggle to overcome its failings. And it is possible to struggle to overcome its failings *and* be reconciled. One might be reconciled in virtue of one's belief that the basic arrangements of the social world – the underlying structures of the family, civil society, and state described in the *Philosophy of Right* – were rational and that these structures were realized to a significant degree. At the same time, one might recognize that the existing arrangements in one's society failed to correspond in various respects to the structures described in the *Philosophy of Right*. And one might attempt to reform those institutions so as to bring them into line with their underlying rational structures. One's struggle would not express opposition to the most basic arrangements of the social world but instead a profound affirmation of these arrangements, for one would be attempting to bring the existing social world into accordance with its own underlying aspirations.

It must, however, be acknowledged that Hegel does not himself emphasize the critical side of his thought. If anything, he downplays it. Indeed, there are places in which he deliberately gives the impression that his social philosophy is quietistic and accommodationist. Hegel's motivation for conveying this impression was partly prudential.[13] He had planned to publish the *Philosophy of Right* in 1819. But in that year the Prussian reform era, which had begun in 1807 under the chancellorship of Karl Freiherr von Stein and continued under the chancellorship of Karl August von Hardenberg, came to an abrupt halt with the assassination of the right-wing playwright August von Kotzebue, who was killed by the student radical Karl Ludwig Sand. A period of political repression followed, marked by the Carlsbad Decrees, which were laws limiting academic freedom and subjecting publications with political content to strict governmental censorship, and the so-called demagogue persecutions, the political persecution of professors associated with student nationalism. And so Hegel, who had been appointed to his chair in Berlin by the progressive minister of education Karl von Altenstein and had generally supported the reforms of Stein and Hardenberg,

---

13 My treatment of Hegel's politics follows Ilting 1973, 25–94, and Wood 1990, 11–14, 257–8.

withdrew his manuscript of the *Philosophy of Right* and revised it to satisfy the censors. Nowhere were these revisions more evident than in the Preface, which Hegel intentionally wrote in such a way as to give the false impression that his social philosophy enjoined the uncritical endorsement of the Prussian state.

But there is also another, less calculated reason why Hegel refused to emphasize the critical side of his thought. Hegel believed that his age was characterized by a tendency to engage in superficial forms of criticism. We can get a sense of this by considering the following passage from his *Lectures on the Philosophy of World History*:

> It is easier to perceive the shortcomings of individuals, states, and the course of world affairs than to understand their true import. For in passing negative judgments, one looks down on the matter in hand with a superior and supercilious air, without having gone into it thoroughly enough to understand its true nature, i.e., its positive significance. The criticism may well be justified, except that it is far easier to detect shortcomings than the true substance (as in works of art, for example). People often think they have done their job, when they have found something which can be justly criticized; they are right, of course, in one respect; but they are also wrong in so far as they fail to recognize the positive factor [*das Affirmative an der Sache*]. To see only the bad side in everything and to overlook all the positive and valuable qualities is a sign of extreme superficiality. Age, in general, takes a milder view, whereas youth is always dissatisfied; this is because age brings with it maturity of judgement, which does not simply tolerate the bad along with the rest out of sheer lack of interest, but has learnt from the seriousness of life to look for the substance and enduring value of things. (VG, 76–7, 66)

Hegel did not think that his (intellectual) contemporaries needed to be encouraged to engage in criticism. They were, in his view, inclined to do that already. Nor did the fact that the social world exhibited shortcomings need emphasis. Its shortcomings were evident enough. What did need to be emphasized was the fact that the shortcomings of the modern social world did not undermine its basic goodness and rationality. The most important thing, according to Hegel, was to grasp and appreciate the basic goodness of the social world. But for this his contemporaries did need guidance. Hence his emphasis on grasping the affirmative. Hegel's aim in his social philosophy was to cultivate an outlook of basic confidence and trust by providing the philosophical apparatus that would make it possible to see the "true substance" of the social world. Thus although Hegel did not advocate the uncritical endorsement of the status quo, he did think that it was far more important to grasp "the positive and valuable qualities" of the modern social world than to detect its shortcomings. The conservative tone of Hegel's writing thus reflects a view that he genuinely held.

2. Hegel's project may also seem threatening because it may appear ideological. To say that a project is 'ideological' is to say that it is or promotes a form of 'false consciousness' (a false account of the social world, its members, or their relation that stabilizes or promotes oppression). Marx offers a very general reason for thinking that Hegel's project is ideological. Hegel maintains that the fact that the modern social world is a home cannot be seen without the aid of theory. Marx, however, argues that a social world is a home only if the fact that it is home is *transparent*, that is, such that it can be understood *without* the aid of theory. In his view, if one needs theory to be at home, the social world one inhabits is not a home. The fact that a social world stands in need of social theodicy is a sure sign that something is deeply wrong with that world. But as we shall see in Chapter 3, Hegel has a conception of what it is for a social world to be a home in which a world can genuinely be a home *and* be in need of theory. He maintains that the historical transformations that made the modern social world a home – transformations that included the emergence of civil society and the modern state – also made the modern social world appear alien and so gave rise to the need for social theory. He also argued, more generally, that the very conditions of modernity – which include the scale and complexity of the modern social world and the fact that modern people demand 'rational insight' into their social arrangements – make social theory indispensable.

If Hegel's understanding of his historical situation is correct – if the modern social world *is* a home – then there is nothing ideological about his enterprise. But if his understanding of his historical situation is wrong – if the modern social world is not a home – then his project will turn out to be ideological. The reason the project will be ideological, however, is that it seeks to reconcile people to a social world that is not a home – not, as Marx was inclined to think, simply because the project is philosophical. We need to say against Marx that the philosophical project of reconciliation is not *inherently* ideological. But we need to say with Marx, or in a Marxist vein, that the risk of ideology is inherent in the enterprise.

A second, more specific reason for thinking that Hegel's project of reconciliation is ideological has to do with his understanding of poverty in the modern social world. Hegel maintains that the modern social world is a home despite the fact that it contains poverty. In his view, poverty is not an accidental or contingent feature of modern society but is instead systematic and structural: the fact that people in modern society tend to fall into poverty and form an underclass is the result of the normal operation of the economy (PR, §241). Even though Hegel is acutely aware of the horrors of poverty, he still maintains that the modern social world is a home. And so it is only natural to wonder whether his project of reconciliation does not turn out to be ideological. How could the attempt to defend a social world that contains poverty and generates an underclass amount to anything else? It is no accident that this question has a Marxist sound: the problems raised by Hegel's account of poverty constitute one obvious source of Marxism.

3. Hegel's project may seem threatening because it may appear to require the suppression or abandonment of individuality. The idea of reconciliation may itself seem to impose this requirement. Reconciliation is a matter of overcoming the splits that divide one from the social world. The idea of reconciliation is an idea of unity with the social world. Being reconciled with the social world involves regarding oneself as a member of the social world in some very strong sense. And so the question naturally arises whether the process of reconciliation does not require the suppression or abandonment of individuality. How could one come to regard oneself as a member of the social world in anything other than a purely external sense without suppressing or abandoning one's individuality?

This worry may be heightened by various passages in which Hegel speaks nostalgically of certain ancient forms of social life in which people were at home in the social world precisely because they lacked individuality.[14] Thus, for example, in the *Positivity of the Christian Religion*, speaking of the Greek polis and the Roman Republic, Hegel writes:

---

14 Hegel's conception of the ancient world is highly idealized and controversial. My concern here is not to defend it but, rather, to account for the role it plays in Hegel's thought. The reconstruction I provide does not in any way depend on its historical accuracy. See Chapter 5, sections I, II, and III, for a more complete discussion of Hegel's attitude toward the ancient Greeks, along with a fuller treatment of what "individuality" means for Hegel and what he thinks it would be to lack it.

As free men the Greeks and Romans obeyed laws laid down by themselves, obeyed men whom they had themselves appointed to office, waged wars on which they had themselves decided, gave their property, exhausted their passions, and sacrificed their lives by thousands for an end which was their own. They neither learned nor taught [a moral system] but evinced by their actions the moral maxims which they could call their very own. In public as in private and domestic life, every individual was a free man, one who lived by his own laws. The idea [*Idee*] of his country or of his state was the invisible and higher reality for which he strove, which impelled him to effort; it was the final end of *his* world or in his eyes the final end of *the* world, an end which he found manifested in the realities of his daily life or which he himself co-operated in manifesting and maintaining. Confronted by this idea, his own individuality vanished; it was only this idea's maintenance, life, and persistence that he asked for, and these were things which he himself could make realities. It could never or hardly ever have struck him to ask or beg for persistence or eternal life for his own individuality. Only in moments of inactivity or lethargy could he feel the growing strength of a purely self-regarding wish. Cato turned to Plato's *Phaedo* only when his world, his republic, hitherto the highest order of things in his eyes, had been destroyed; at that point only did he take flight to a higher order still. (PCR, 204–5/154–5).

Although the basic idea of this passage is clear enough, one point needs clarification. In saying that the individuality of the Greek or Roman "vanished" (*verschwand*) when confronted with the idea of his state or nation, he does not mean that the Greek or Roman somehow ceased to be a separate and distinct human being. What Hegel means is rather that the Greek or Roman ceased to *think* of himself (Hegel is thinking here of men) as an individual – as someone whose separate and particular interests count in their own right – and hence ceased to *be* an individual in the sense of someone who takes his separate and particular interests to count in their own right.

In the *Phenomenology of Spirit*, we find the following, rather more abstract and obscure, but still highly evocative portrait of the ethical life (*Sittlichkeit*) of the ancient world: "This ethical *Substance*, taken in its abstract universality, is only law in the form of *thought;* but it is no less immediately actual *self-consciousness*, or it is *custom*. The single individual consciousness, conversely, is only this existent unit in so far as it is aware of the universal consciousness in its individuality as its *own* being, since what it does and is, is the universal custom" (PhG, 264/212). Here the idea is, roughly, that the individual member of the ethical substance conceives of the shared cultural outlook of his community (the "universal consciousness" of his "ethical substance") as defining his own "being." Indeed, Hegel suggests that the individual member of the ethical substance tacitly believes that he is the person he is ("this existent unit") only insofar as he identifies with the universal consciousness of his ethical substance – only insofar as he takes the shared cultural outlook of his community to define his own being.

Hegel goes on to say:

> Reason is present here as the fluid universal *Substance,* as unchangeable simple thinghood, which yet bursts asunder into many completely independent beings, just as light bursts asunder into stars as countless self-luminous points, which in their absolute being-for-self are dissolved, not merely *implicitly* in the simple independent Substance, but *explicitly for themselves.* They are conscious of being these separate independent beings through the sacrifice of their particularity, and by having this universal Substance as their soul and essence, just as this universal again is their own doing as particular individuals, or is the work that they have produced. (PhG, 265/212–13)

It is precisely by sacrificing their particularity – precisely by abandoning any conception of themselves as individuals apart from their cultural identity and subordinating their separate and particular interests to the shared interests of the community – that the members of the ethical substance come to see themselves as the kind of beings they are: individual instantiations of the shared spirit of their community, the "stars" through which their "ethical substance" shines.

The upshot of these passages is that Hegel holds that the members of ancient *Sittlichkeit* identified wholly and completely with their particular community. They enjoyed the satisfactions of community without the pain of alienation. Hegel characterizes this relation as a "happy state" (*Glück*) (PhG, 266/214) and holds that its "happiness" consists precisely in that absence of separation and division between community members and their community. It is the happiness of "being in the substance" – the happiness of "unity."

Hegel is clearly attracted to this form of social life. He finds in it a dramatic contrast to the division and fragmentation of modern social life. His writing about ancient *Sittlichkeit* reveals a feeling of loss, even a yearning for a return to this simpler and more harmonious way of relating to the social world. Nonetheless, it is equally clear – and generally recognized – that Hegel *rejects* the idea of returning to ancient *Sittlichkeit* or recapturing its immediacy. Hegel thinks such a step would be both impossible and undesirable. It would be impossible because humanity has attained the "principle of particularity" (which recognizes the importance of the separate and particular interests of human beings and their right to develop and pursue them) (PR, §124R) and the "principle of subjective freedom" (which recognizes the importance of private conscience and the right of human beings to act on its basis) (PR, §185R) – a result Hegel takes to be irreversible.[15] Such a step would be undesirable because the attainment of these principles represents one of the fundamental progressive developments of human history. Thus Hegel remarks in the *Philosophy of Right*:

> The right of the subject's *particularity* to find satisfaction, or – to put it differently – the right of *subjective freedom*, is the pivotal and focal point in the difference between *antiquity* and the *modern* age. This right, in its infinity, is expressed in Christianity, and it has become the universal and actual principle of a new form of the world. Its more specific shapes include love, the romantic, the eternal salvation of the individual as an end, etc.; then there are morality and conscience, followed by the other forms, some of which will come into prominence below as the principle of civil society and as moments of the political constitution, while others appear within history at large, particularly in the history of art, the sciences, and philosophy. (PR, §124R)

In Hegel's view, the undivided unity of ancient *Sittlichkeit*, although unalienated and happy, was also primitive. And the reason it was primitive was precisely that it provided no room for particularity, subjectivity, or individuality.

Hegel's aim, then, is not to attempt to reconstitute the harmony of ancient *Sittlichkeit* but rather to find a way of grasping modern social life as combining the fruits of modernity – the principle of particularity and the principle of subjective freedom – with community membership. This is what Hegel has in mind when he speaks

15 Hegel seems to think that these two principles are at root the same. (See PR, §124R.) He also characterizes this principle as the "principle of the self-sufficient and inherently infinite personality of the individual" (which recognizes the existence, value, and rights of the inherently infinite personality of the individual) (PR, §185R) and more succinctly as the "principle of individuality" (VGP, 2:249/ 2:202).

of "preserv[ing] . . . subjective freedom in the realm of the substantial, and at the same time . . . stand[ing] with . . . subjective freedom not in a particular and contingent situation, but in what has being in and for itself" (PR, ¶14).

The upshot is that the idea of reconciliation, as Hegel understands it, does not involve the abandonment or suppression of individuality. For Hegel the crucial fact about *modern* people is precisely that they have attained "the principle of individuality" (VGP, 2:249/2:202). In order for a social world to be a home – a home *for them* – it must be a place in which they can realize themselves as community members without abandoning or suppressing their individuality. That is the point of Hegel's talk of "*preserv[ing]* . . . subjective freedom in the realm of the substantial" (my emphasis). We might say that a process of reconciliation is a process of *reconciliation* only if it preserves the individuality of the people it reconciles. The nightmare of people abandoning their separate and particular interests or private consciences in the hope of attaining unity with their social world *is* indeed a nightmare, but what it dreams of is not reconciliation. The idea of reconciliation does involve the idea of unity with the social world, but the sort of unity that reconciliation involves is quite different from what Hegel took the participants in ancient *Sittlichkeit* to enjoy. It is a form of unity that *preserves* difference. Hegel wants to reconcile the modern individual to the modern social world by showing that individuality and social membership are themselves reconciled within its arrangements.

4. Finally, Hegel's project may seem threatening because it may seem to be accommodationist in the sense of endorsing or affirming evil. And the reason for this is clear. There is a sense (or range of senses) in which the project seeks to convince people to accept divorce, poverty, and war.

The first thing to be pointed out is that there clearly is *a* sense in which Hegel's project is accommodationist. As a social theodicy, his project seeks to accommodate divorce, poverty, and war in the sense of providing a way of making it possible to accept their existence. Accommodating evil in this, neutral, sense is the business of theodicy. It does not, however, follow from this that the project is accommodationist in the invidious sense of endorsing or affirming evil. And indeed one of the constraints on a successful theodicy, at least as Hegel understands it, is that it must make it possible to accept certain things that are intuitively evil, such as divorce, poverty, and war, *without* endorsing or affirming evil as such.

This means that the question whether Hegel's project is accommodationist in the *invidious* sense amounts to the familiar question of whether his social theodicy succeeds. And we have seen that we can take his project seriously without assuming that it will succeed. Although we may well be concerned that Hegel's project will collapse into the invidious form of accommodationism, we should not refuse to consider it on the grounds that this is something at which it aims.

V. The worry about misguidedness

The fifth and final problem that Hegel's project raises is that it may seem fundamentally misguided. I will consider two versions of this concern.

1. The first version of this concern derives from positivism, which takes Hegel's project to be misguided because it attempts to provide (rational, philosophical) orientation with respect to the social world. We can distinguish two reasons the positivists would have for taking his project to be misguided. The first and most obvious reason is that from their standpoint, his attempt to provide orientation with respect to the social world is a special case of the misguided attempt to provide philosophical guidance concerning what is worthwhile, what one should do, and how one should live. The positivists took this enterprise to be misguided because they held that normative and evaluative claims fall outside the realm of rational discussion and evaluation altogether. For them, such claims are 'cognitively meaningless', and lack 'cognitive content'. They are neither analytic (true by virtue of the meaning of their component words) nor potentially true or false. Hence they are not claims, which if true would be knowledge.

Few people today would find this line of reasoning compelling. The conception of meaning that provides its foundation, according to which claims are (cognitively) meaningful only if they are analytical or empirically verifiable, has fallen into disrepute, and the proposition that rational discussion concerning evaluative and normative claims is possible is now widely accepted.

But the second reason the positivists would have for taking Hegel's concern with orientation to be misguided is one that many people would still find compelling. From the positivist point of view, *attitudes* fall outside the realm of rational discussion and evaluation. The positivists regarded attitudes as mere constellations of purely subjective feelings and volitional states. In his attempt to trace the roots of metaphysics to the need to express one's attitude toward life, Carnap makes it clear that he thinks such attitudes lack "theoretical content."[16] He glosses what he calls "a man's attitude in life" (*Lebensgefühl*) as "his emotional and volitional reaction to the environment, society, to the tasks to which he devotes himself, to the misfortunes that befall him."[17] If one shares this conception of attitudes, then the whole idea of providing orientation with respect to attitudes may well seem to be wrongheaded.

But the positivist conception of attitudes is especially ill-suited to describe the sort of attitudes that people hold toward the social world. Such attitudes cannot plausibly be regarded as mere constellations of subjective feelings and volitions, for they also contain beliefs about the social world and may well be informed by reasoned assessments of its institutions. The attitudes people possess about the social world are far richer and more complex than the positivists recognized.

Now if we reject the positivists' view that attitudes are nothing more than constellations of feelings and volitions, the proposition that attitudes toward the social world cannot be rationally discussed or evaluated will no longer seem so attractive. Indeed, the idea that we can discuss our attitudes about the social world in a rational way seems quite plausible. And in fact one of the features that makes Hegel's social philosophy attractive is that he provides a philosophical framework within which it is possible to engage in discussion of this sort.

It is perhaps worth pointing out that the idea that orientation belongs to the tasks of philosophy is by no means idiosyncratic to Hegel. The modern roots of this idea can be traced back to Kant, who regarded reason as the faculty of orientation.[18] Carnap came close to the truth when he said that "metaphysics . . . arises from the need to give expression [*Ausdruck*] to a man's attitude in life."[19] There *is* an important connection between philosophy and the general attitude people have toward life, but Carnap was mistaken about that relation. Rather than being thought of as arising from the need to give *expression* to one's "attitude in life," philosophy is better thought of as arising from, inter alia, the need for orientation with regard to one's attitude in life – that is, the need to *determine* what general attitude is truly appropriate.

16 Carnap 1932, 238; 1959, 78.   17 Carnap 1932, 239; 1959, 79.
18 Kant 1786, 1949.   19 Carnap 1932, 239; 1959, 79.

The tendency to dismiss the need for orientation in general and orientation with respect to attitudes in particular is an unfortunate legacy of positivism. One need not assume, as Hegel does, that philosophy can provide a form of orientation that is systematic, comprehensive, and absolute in order to maintain that orientation represents a legitimate philosophical aim.

2. The second version of the concern that Hegel's project is fundamentally misguided derives from postmodernism.[20] Hegel's philosophy starts from the assumption that division, conflict, and opposition represent 'evils' or 'forms of negativity' to be overcome. Its goal is one of wholeness, harmony, and unity. And in fact the unity at which it aims can be called 'absolute unity'. The project of reconciliation seeks to establish the wholeness of the self by bringing the self into harmonious unity with the social world.

Postmodernists such as Foucault, Lyotard, and Derrida deny that wholeness, unity, and harmony are ideals worth striving for. From their point of view, division, opposition, and conflict are not 'evils' or 'forms of negativity' to be overcome but rather expressions of 'otherness' (that which is other than or different from the self) to be acknowledged, cultivated, and affirmed. They take the Hegelian aim of overcoming division and otherness to be futile, inauthentic, and pernicious. They regard it as *futile* because they believe the divisions that motivate the project can never fully be overcome. We will always be faced with otherness. Our basic circumstance is one of fragmentation and dissonance. We really *are* homeless. They believe Hegel's project is *inauthentic* because they maintain that it is driven by the wish to deny these basic facts. They hold that the project is *pernicious* because they contend that the attempt to establish wholeness, harmony, and unity inevitably results in the disciplining, marginalizing, homogenizing, and devaluation of some other (e.g., a human being or group of human beings of some other race, class, culture, or gender). The real source of misery, the postmodernists maintain, is not division, conflict, and opposition but rather the fantastic idea of overcoming all divisions and forms of otherness. What are we to make of this critique?

We can begin by acknowledging that the postmodernists make it clear that it is an *issue* whether wholeness, harmony, and unity are ideals worth striving for. Contrary to what one might naively think,

---

20 I have been strongly influenced in my treatment of the postmodernists by White (1991).

wholeness, harmony, and unity are far from unquestioned or un-
questionable goods. It is, however, far from clear that the postmodernists have understood Hegel's conception of unity. 'Concrete
unity' as Hegel understands it is not unity *without* difference but
instead unity *in* difference. The Hegelian conception of concrete
unity is quite explicitly defined as one that does not exclude division, conflict, or otherness. Hegel himself rejects the view that division, conflict, and opposition are *simply* evils or forms of negativity
to be overcome. He maintains, on the contrary, that they are essential to the articulation, unfolding, and development of the human
spirit. Indeed, he argues that *any* conception of unity that attempts
to exclude or eliminate conflict and otherness is bound to be inadequate. And he takes criticism of such one-sided and abstract forms
of unity to be a fundamental task of philosophy. In a characteristic
passage, he remarks: "Philosophy affords a reflective insight into
the essence of the opposition only in so far as it shows how truth is
just the dissolving of opposition and, at that, not in the sense, as
may be supposed, that the opposition and its two sides *do not exist
at all*, but that they exist reconciled" (VA, 1:82/1:55). The sort of
unity Hegel calls concrete is meant to be a 'higher unity', one that
preserves and embraces division, conflict, and otherness.

The upshot of this is that Hegel's conception of unity is far more
complicated, subtle, and open to otherness than the postmodernists
seem to recognize. They do not appear to recognize that he shares
their view that the total annulment of conflict, division, and otherness is a bad aim. Nor do they appear to appreciate that he agrees
that there is a sense in which conflict, division, and otherness are
to be preserved. Furthermore, it is far from clear that their critique
of unity applies to the specific sort of unity Hegel takes as his goal.
And so it is far from clear the postmodernists have succeeded in
showing that the ideals of unity, harmony, and wholeness have been
superseded. Doubtless they would argue that Hegel's attempt to
incorporate otherness into a higher unity ultimately represents
nothing more than an insidious and sophisticated way of excluding otherness. But this is something that would have to be shown.
Moreover, the only way in which it could be shown would be by
presenting a criticism of Hegel's conception of unity that was fully
sensitive to its attempt to preserve otherness. In any case, my point
here is not that Hegel's project succeeds, but simply that we should
not think that postmodernism has discredited it, for it has not.

It is worth noting that one can quite consistently maintain that the otherness of other people and cultures are forms of otherness to be embraced while also maintaining that alienation from the basic arrangements of one's social world is a form of otherness to be abhorred. If Hegel needs to be reminded that some forms of otherness are benign, his postmodernist opponents need to be reminded that not all forms are. And so I would like to close this chapter by suggesting that at least as it applies to the social world, Hegel's conception of unity is certainly not one that we should reject out of hand – it may even turn out to be a conception that we will want to embrace.

GEIST AND THE *DOPPELSATZ*

If we are to understand Hegel's project of reconciliation, we must have some acquaintance with the philosophical point of view it presupposes. I have decided to try to convey a sense of this point of view by sketching two ideas central to the view: the concept of *Geist* (spirit, mind) and the *Doppelsatz* (the double dictum).

Geist is the term Hegel employs to refer to human individuals, human culture and society, and God. It constitutes the foundation of Hegel's philosophical anthropology (his philosophical conception of the nature of the human being), which, as we will see, is closely connected with his philosophical sociology and his theory of history and theology. The *Doppelsatz* encapsulates Hegel's basic conception of reason, reality, and the relation between them. It also encapsulates the basic methodological approach and normative outlook of his social philosophy.

I should point out that my purpose in presenting these ideas is not to defend them but rather to make them accessible to readers unacquainted with Hegel's philosophy. And I should stress that my general aim in this reconstruction is to minimize reliance on Hegel's metaphysics. My purpose in this chapter is to provide part of the orientation necessary to approach Hegel's social philosophy.

This chapter has two parts. In the first, I discuss Hegel's concept of *Geist*; in the second, I discuss the *Doppelsatz*.

I. *Geist*

Geist is the basic concept of Hegel's philosophy. *Geist* can be translated as 'mind' or 'spirit'. *Geist*, as Hegel conceives of it, can be thought of as mind because he uses the word to refer to both self-consciousness and the subject of self-consciousness, but for reasons we will consider below, 'spirit' has become the standard translation for Hegel's use of *Geist*.

My discussion of *Geist* divides into three sections. I first provide an initial sketch of the notion of *Geist* by considering the advantages and disadvantages of using 'spirit' as a translation. The next section examines the important but obscure idea that *Geist* is 'self-interpreting'. My discussion of *Geist* concludes with an examination of the respects in which, according to Hegel, human beings are essentially *Geist*. This final section includes a discussion of the relation between absolute *Geist* (Hegel's conception of God) and human beings. I should note that my purpose here is not to provide a comprehensive account of Hegel's notion of *Geist*, but simply to put us in a position to think about how this concept figures in his social philosophy.

1. One basic advantage of 'spirit' as a translation of *Geist* is that Hegel takes social institutions (e.g., the family and the state) and culture (e.g., art, religion, and philosophy) to be paradigmatic expressions of *Geist* – both of which are, perhaps, more idiomatically thought of as forms of spirit than forms of mind. On the other hand, 'spirit' has the disadvantage of suggesting immateriality or incorporeality. As Charles Taylor has emphasized, *Geist* for Hegel is essentially embodied in a twofold sense. First, *Geist* must have its seat in embodied, living subjects: in rational animals, human beings. Second, *Geist* must be expressed in an external medium (e.g., language, custom, institution). Taylor calls this requirement, the "principle of necessary embodiment."[1] *Geist* is actual (*wirklich*) only as embodied. *Geist* comes to be embodied – comes to be actual – through its own activity. *Geist* is self-actualizing (VG, 74/64). And *Geist* actualizes itself by expressing its self-conception in an objective (spatiotemporal) medium. Thus, in Hegel's view, the spiritual is not to be identified with 'the internal' or 'the inward'. On the contrary, *Geist* is a self-objectifying (EG, §387R), self-manifesting (EG, §383), self-actualizing (EG, §381R) entity. Self-consciousness, for Hegel,

1 Taylor 1975, 83.

is to be understood as a process of internalization and appropriation. He maintains that *Geist* first expresses, embodies, and objectifies its self-understandings through its actions and then attains self-consciousness by becoming aware of and subjectively appropriating these objectively expressed self-understandings.

The word 'spirit' may also have the disadvantage of suggesting 'the spiritual' *as opposed to* 'the worldly'. Hegel, however, regards such worldly institutions as the market and government as genuinely and essentially spiritual – as expressions of human (and ultimately divine) self-understandings. It is crucial to Hegel's view that *Geist* expresses, objectifies, manifests, and actualizes itself *in the world*. Only by doing so does *Geist* become fully actual. Thus Hegel's conception of 'the spiritual' is unabashedly worldly.

These disadvantages of the term 'spirit' may be offset by Hegel's use of *Geist* to mean 'spirit' in the sense of principle. In Hegel's view, the spirit of a people (its *Volksgeist)* consists in a principle (the set of ideas and values) that expresses its self-conception. Hegel maintains that every people is characterized by its own unique *Volksgeist* (VG, 64/55) that is expressed, inter alia, in its customs, laws, art, religion, judiciary, and modes of commerce. This sense of spirit clearly derives from Montesquieu, as Hegel himself acknowledges (VG, 121/102). It is the sense in which Montesquieu used the word *esprit* in *De l'esprit des lois*. Hegel further contends that there is a single principle (the *Weltgeist*) expressing the self-conception of the human species that is articulated, developed, and actualized through the course of world history. A second offsetting factor is that Hegel uses *Geist* to mean 'spirit' in the sense of animating force or power. He maintains, for example, that human societies exhibit a basic drive to develop and express their own conception of the human being (VG, 122/102) and that human history can be understood in terms of a basic drive of the human species to attain a fully adequate understanding of itself and to form a social world that corresponds to this understanding. Hegel combines the idea of *Geist* as principle and *Geist* as force by speaking of *Geist* as an activating principle. Thus the spirit of a people (its *Volksgeist)* is the activating principle of that people, and the spirit of world history (the *Weltgeist)* is the activating principle of world history.

2. *Geist* is 'self-interpreting'.[2] We need to be clear about what this claim comes to. This means, first, that *Geist* is capable of forming

2 The phrase 'self-interpreting' comes from Taylor 1985b.

an interpretation of itself, of the kind of entity it essentially is, and of the needs, aims, and goals it essentially has. Thus this claim is an elaboration of the basic idea that *Geist* is self-conscious. Self-interpretation is an essential activity of *Geist* because every activity of *Geist* is, inter alia, an expression of its (possibly implicit or tacit) self-interpretation (EG, §377Z) and because the basic aim of *Geist* is to know itself. Thus Hegel writes: "The sole endeavor of spirit is to know what it is in and for itself, and to reveal itself to itself in its true form. It seeks to create a spiritual world in accordance with its own concept, to fulfil and realise its own true nature, and to produce religion and the state in such a way that it will conform to its own concept and be truly itself or become its own Idea" (VG, 61/53). *Geist,* Hegel contends, attains self-knowledge by developing successively more adequate interpretations of itself, that is, a series of increasingly more coherent interpretations accounting for an increasingly wide range of its activities.

Second, the proposition that *Geist* is self-interpreting also means that *Geist* is (at least partially) 'defined' or 'constituted' by its self-interpretations. We can approach this rather obscure idea by observing that for Hegel spiritual phenomena (e.g., social and cultural practices) are defined as *spiritual* phenomena because they express human self-understandings. They are constituted as the specific spiritual phenomena they are by the particular self-understandings they express. Thus, for example, the (ancient) Greek world was constituted by the specifically Greek self-understanding. In order to grasp the spiritual character of a spiritual phenomenon, we must view it as a mode and expression of a self-interpretation. Grasping 'the spirit' of a particular spiritual phenomenon consists in grasping the self-understanding it expresses.

The idea that *Geist* is defined or constituted by its self-interpretations is *not* to be understood as the claim that *Geist* consists of mental stuff (e.g., Cartesian mental substance) rather than physical stuff. As we have seen, *Geist* is actual (is *wirklich*) only as expressed and actualized. And Hegel insists that the expression of *Geist* must (metaphysically) have a physical seat (the activities of people – physical beings in a physical world – and their products). Geist is 'constituted' (in the sense of actualized) by human beings engaging in the social, political, and cultural practices of their community.

Also involved in the idea that *Geist* is defined or constituted by its self-interpretations is the notion that *Geist* actualizes itself in a wealth of stages and 'shapes' (*Gestalten*). According to Hegel, the various stages in world history (e.g., the Greek and Roman stages) represent different stages in the development of *Geist*. In Hegel's view, *Geist* has also taken shape in a variety of attitudes or cultural configurations, such as the "Unhappy Consciousness" described in the *Phenomenology of Spirit* (PhG, 163–77/126–38). The central point is this: Each of the shapes and stages through which *Geist* actualizes itself expresses a determinate understanding of the nature of *Geist* and is defined as the shape or stage of *Geist* it is by the specific understanding it expresses. Thus *Geist* can be said to be defined or constituted by its self-interpretations in the sense that the various shapes and stages through which it actualizes itself are defined or constituted by its self-understandings.

But in maintaining that *Geist* is defined or constituted by its self-interpretations, Hegel does not mean to suggest that *Geist* is whatever it happens to take itself to be. Hegel holds that *Geist* has a true nature, or true essence (VA, 1:129/1:93) – a *Begriff* (concept) – that is in an important respect independent of what *Geist* takes itself to be. Hence, *Geist*'s self-understanding can be one-sided and inadequate. The less closely its self-interpretations correspond to its *Begriff*, the less adequate they are. And conversely, the more fully its interpretations correspond to its true *Begriff*, the more adequate they are.

It must, however, be pointed out that Hegel does not think that *Geist* has a fixed essence that is given fully articulated from the start. He maintains, rather, that *Geist*'s true *Begriff* is itself subject to a developmental process. (In this respect Hegel's view of essence differs from the traditional view, according to which essences are by their very nature fixed and immutable.) *Geist*'s *Begriff* becomes fully determinate only through *Geist*'s struggle to articulate and actualize itself.[3] Thus *Geist*'s development is not only a process through which its articulations and actualization of its *Begriff* develop but also a process through which its *Begriff* develops. *Geist*'s 'true Begriff' is that form of its *Begriff* which would eventuate from an ideal process of development. This *Begriff* attains its true and final form *only at the end* of *Geist*'s developmental process.

A corollary of this point is that although *Geist* aims from the start to actualize itself as the kind of entity it is, the kind of entity that it

---

3   What precisely it *means* to say, on the one hand, that *Geist* has a true essence and, on the other hand, that this essence is subject to a developmental process – how Hegel can coherently make both claims – is one of the fundamental interpretive questions concerning Hegel's conception of *Geist*.

is, is something that can be fully specified only at the end of *Geist*'s developmental process (see PhG, 24/11). It is only when *Geist* has completed its process of development that it can understand what it was doing. It is only when *Geist* has arrived at its goal that it can understand where it was going. This is why Hegel insists that *Geist*'s self-understanding is inherently retrospective.

3. Hegel contends that human beings are essentially *Geist* in two distinguishable respects.

(i) Human beings are essentially *Geist* in that they are essentially spiritual beings.

(ii) Human beings are essentially *Geist* in the sense that they are essentially vehicles of *Geist*.

Let us consider each of these ideas in turn.

(i) In saying that human beings are essentially spiritual beings, Hegel is making a metaphysical claim. He is saying that they are beings of a particular kind and that the specification of this kind specifies what they *really are*. But what does this claim come to?

To say that human beings are essentially spiritual beings is, first of all, to say that they are essentially self-interpreting. In Hegel's view, human beings have the (spiritual) capacity to form an interpretation of the kind of beings they are and the (spiritual) goal of coming to understand the kind of beings they are and of objectifying this self-understanding in their social arrangements and culture. The activity of self-interpretation is characteristic of the kind of beings they are, and the aim of self-knowledge is an aim they have because they are the kind of beings they are. Moreover, *as* spiritual beings they are defined or constituted by their self-understandings. Their 'spiritual reality' (*geistige Wirklichkeit*) consists of the self-understandings that are expressed in their form of life.

To say that human beings are essentially spiritual beings is also to say that human beings are essentially social and cultural. Hegel maintains that human beings are essentially social and cultural in the sense that they can actualize themselves as spiritual beings only as the result of being raised and socialized within a human community and only by actively participating in a human community. Thus he says: "Man owes his entire existence to the state [i.e., the politically organized community] and has his essence within it alone. Whatever worth and spiritual reality he possesses are his solely by virtue of the state" (VG, 111/94, translation modified). Considered purely as natural or biological beings, human beings are not yet spiritual. A normal human infant raised within a human community will become a spiritual being, but unless a human being has been socialized, unless it has gone through a *Bildungsprozeß* – a process of education and acculturation – it has not actualized itself as a spiritual being. This is part of what Hegel is getting at when he says: "Man can only fulfil himself though education and discipline; his immediate existence contains merely the possibility of self-realisation (i.e., of becoming rational and free) and simply imposes on him a vocation and obligation which he must himself fulfil" (VG, 58/50).

The idea of human beings as social and cultural beings is closely connected with the idea that they are self-interpreting. In Hegel's view, human beings come to acquire their core self-understandings as the result of being raised within the social and cultural practices of their (national) community. "The individual does not invent his content [i.e., his core self-understanding], but merely activates the substantial content which [comes from the community and] is already present within him" (VG, 95/81).

One further respect in which human beings are essentially social and cultural, according to Hegel, is that their deepest and most important needs and goals are socially and culturally formed. Hegel does not think that the human being is a conative tabula rasa whose needs are fully constituted by her socialization. He recognizes that human beings enter the social and cultural world with a variety of biologically given desires, needs, and drives. But he holds that these drives, needs, and desires are then shaped and channeled by cultural and social institutions and that these culturally shaped and channeled drives, needs, and desires reflect the self-understandings embodied in these institutions. Hegel also holds that the deepest needs and ends that human beings have consist in participating in certain forms of social and cultural life; in the modern world, the relevant forms of social life are to be found in the family, civil society, and the state, and the relevant forms of cultural life are to be found in art, religion, and philosophy.

Hegel also believes that human needs and goals vary – culturally and historically – with the self-understandings that are expressed in the arrangements of different national communities. "Each individual, at any given moment, finds himself committed to some essential interest of this kind; he exists in a particular country, with a particular religion, and in a particular constellation of knowledge and attitudes concerning what is right and ethically acceptable. All that is left for him to do is to select particular aspects of it with which he wishes to identify himself" (VG, 52-3/46). And he claims, famously: "Each individual is . . . *a child of his time*" (PR, ¶13). Hegel's conception of the human being is thus radically cultural and historical.

It is not, however, historicist. Hegel thinks that there is a constellation of needs and goals of the human being *as such* – a constellation of needs and goals that could be thought of as defining *the* human good. This constellation consists of the needs and goals that human beings would come to acquire as the result of being raised in a social world that had attained the final and correct understanding of the human being.

(ii) Hegel's claim that human beings are essentially *Geist* in that they are essentially vehicles of spirit can be understood as consisting of two related subclaims:

(a) Human beings are essentially vehicles of finite *Geist*.
(b) Human beings are essentially vehicles of absolute *Geist*.

(a) In saying that human beings are essentially vehicles of finite *Geist*, Hegel means that they are essentially vehicles of the national communities of which they are a part. Hegel thinks that national communities are spirits, first of all, because they exhibit self-consciousness. As we have seen, Hegel claims that every national community has a national principle – a *Volksgeist* – realized in its institutions and practices, which expresses its self-conception, which is to say, its self-consciousness. Second, Hegel maintains that national communities are spirits because he thinks that each national community is a collective subject that cannot be reduced to an aggregate of individual subjects.

The third reason why Hegel holds that national communities are spirits turns on an aspect of his conception of *Geist* we have not yet considered. Hegel's basic conception of *Geist* (discussed in section 1) actually has two crucial elements. The first, as we have seen, is subjectivity. The second is substantiality. Hegel conceives of *Geist* as both subject and substance. Indeed he thinks that we only grasp *Geist* as *Geist* when we grasp it as both subject and substance. *Geist* is a substantial subject and a subjective substance (see PhG, 22-3/14). By 'substance' (*Substanz*) Hegel means, very roughly, an entity that exists through itself, that depends upon nothing other than itself for its own existence. Thus *Geist* is self-subsisting subject. The third reason Hegel has for regarding national communities as spirits, then, is that he takes them to be substantial. He thinks that they are substantial in that they are self-reproducing. They maintain and reproduce themselves by raising their members to behave and understand themselves in such a way that will reproduce their arrangements.

In saying that human beings are 'vehicles' of the national communities of which they are a part, Hegel means that it is through them that their national communities maintain and reproduce themselves. We can approach the basic idea here by considering a smaller group: the family. In Hegel's view, the family maintains and reproduces itself by raising its members to have a complex set of motivations that will lead them to marry and form families. The individual human beings who marry and form families are 'vehicles' of the family in the sense that it is through them that the family reproduces itself. Hegel also thinks that human beings are the vehicles of their national communities in the sense that the national community becomes conscious of itself through their activity.

Hegel is committed to what could be called 'the principle of the indispensability of individual self-consciousness'. Although he thinks that there can be collective subjects, he denies that there can be a free-floating social subject whose consciousness is not rooted in the subjectivity of its members. He holds that the only way in which a collectivity can attain self-consciousness is through the consciousness of its members. Hegel contends that a national community attains self-consciousness (and so becomes a subject) when its members come to identify with its institutions and practices, regard its national principle as expressive of their own self-understanding, and regard its *Volksgeist* as constitutive of their spirit.

Hegel contends that human beings are *essentially* vehicles of their national communities in two key respects. First, it is only by acting as vehicles of their national community – only by maintaining and reproducing its arrangements and identifying with the self-understandings these arrangements express – that they can actualize themselves as spiritual beings, which is to say, actualize themselves as the kind of beings they really are. Second, serving as vehicles of their national community constitutes a fundamental component of their vocation (*Bestimmung*) as spiritual beings.

(b) Before we can understand what Hegel means by saying that human beings are essentially vehicles of absolute *Geist*, we must have some understanding of what he means by this notion. Absolute *Geist* is defined by Hegel as that form of *Geist* which is totally self-transparent and totally self-sufficient. It depends on nothing, needs nothing, and is bound by nothing. Absolute *Geist* is fully self-actualizing and fully actualized in the world. It is that form of *Geist* which perfectly expresses and objectifies the true *Begriff* of *Geist*. Moreover, in absolute *Geist,* the split between subject and object is fully overcome (EG, §381). Absolute *Geist* is that subject that knows itself to be the whole of reality: 'the absolute'. It is through absolute *Geist* that the absolute comes to know itself as spirit.

A form of *Geist* is *finite* if it is less than totally self-transparent or less than totally self-sufficient. The form of *Geist* that is realized in human societies and history – that is, 'objective spirit' (*objektiver Geist*) – is *epistemically* finite because it does not grasp itself as the whole of reality, and it is *ontologically* finite because it is dependent on nature.

Hegel identifies absolute *Geist* with (the Judeo-Christian) God (EG, §§564–71). This should come as no surprise inasmuch as properties of *absolute Geist* could not possibly be exhibited by anything short of God, and anything that exhibited all the properties of absolute *Geist* could plausibly be thought of as God. Moreover, Hegel's conception of absolute *Geist* clearly derives from the Judeo-Christian conception of God, and he clearly takes himself to be referring to this God when he talks about absolute *Geist*. But since Hegel's conception of absolute *Geist* differs from the Judeo-Christian conception in a number of important respects, it would perhaps be more accurate to say that Hegel maintains that the Judeo-Christian God, properly understood, is absolute *Geist*.

Considering the differences between Hegel's conception of absolute *Geist* and the Judeo-Christian conception of God will enable us to sharpen our understanding of Hegel's concept of absolute *Geist*. In the Judeo-Christian tradition, God is an infinite transcendent subject whose existence is independent of both humanity and nature. Hegel maintains that this tradition is right in maintaining that God is a subject distinct from humanity and nature but wrong in maintaining that he is a transcendent being whose existence is independent of mankind and nature. Absolute *Geist* does not exist outside the spatiotemporal world. His existence depends on mankind and nature, for he is constituted (in the sense of actualized) by nature and human beings. In Hegel's view, God (absolute *Geist*) exists only as actualized in nature and becomes self-conscious only through the consciousness of human beings. On the other hand, absolute *Geist* cannot be reduced ontologically to mankind and nature. Human beings are finite spirits and nature is not spirit at all (or, more precisely, it is spirit that is not aware of itself as such).

Hegel maintains that the Judeo-Christian account is correct in maintaining that God is infinite (ontologically unlimited and unrestricted) but wrong in explaining God's infinity in term of transcendence. God's infinity is rather to be explained by reference to his immanence within the world as a whole. Nature and mankind, properly understood, are manifestations of God. God, properly understood, is wholly manifested in nature and through mankind. The complex formed by God-as-manifested-in-nature-and-through-mankind (which is to say: absolute spirit) is identical to both the world-as-a-whole insofar as it expresses God and God as manifested or realized. God (absolute *Geist*) is infinite, then, in that everything that exists is a manifestation of his existence. There is nothing other than God that limits or restricts him because there is nothing *other* that could limit or restrict him (see WL, 1:149–66/137–50). Absolute *Geist* depends on nothing, needs nothing, and is bound by nothing in the sense that it depends on, needs, and is bound by nothing that is *other than itself.*

Human beings are *vehicles* of absolute *Geist*, then, in that it is through them that absolute spirit actualizes itself and attains self-consciousness. They are *essentially* vehicles of absolute spirit in the sense that actualizing absolute *Geist* constitutes their highest vocation.

II. The *Doppelsatz*

The *Doppelsatz* (or double dictum) – "What is rational is actual, and what is actual is rational" (PR, ¶12) – is one of Hegel's most famous, most provocative, and most discussed philosophical slogans.[4] Its two brief lines provide an extraordinarily provocative, memorable, and condensed formulation of three crucial aspects of Hegel's philosophical point of view. They encapsulate Hegel's basic (1) conception of reason, reality, and their relation, (2) methodological approach, and (3) normative outlook. Because of this, the *Doppelsatz* provides a wonderful device for exploring Hegel's thought. Not surprisingly, the dictum also poses a number of interpretive diffi-

---

4 See, e.g., Haym 1857, 365–9; Rosenzweig 1920, 2:77–80; Fackenheim 1969–70, 691–8; Löwith 1941, 153–62, 1964, 135–50; Henrich 1983, 13–17; Wood 1990, 10–11. The term *Doppelsatz* belongs to Henrich 1983.

culties. Written in Hegel's technical vocabulary, it is extremely abstract and compressed, richly ambiguous, and, furthermore, exists in a number of different formulations. These difficulties can, however, be turned to our advantage, for working through them will help us gain access to Hegel's thought. My discussion will be loosely organized around the three aspects of Hegel's philosophical point of view mentioned above.

1. Before turning to the first of these three aspects (Hegel's conception of reason, reality, and their relation), I want to make a few remarks about the two main terms of the *Doppelsatz*: 'rational' (*vernünftig*) and 'actual' (*wirklich*).

'Rational', as Hegel uses the term, has both an epistemic and a normative aspect; roughly speaking, it means both rationally intelligible and reasonable or good.[5] In ordinary speech 'actual' (*wirklich*) and 'existing' (*existierend*) are often used interchangeably, which can give rise to the (false) impression that the *Doppelsatz* asserts that everything that exists – including, in particular, every existing state – is reasonable or good. Read in this way, the *Doppelsatz* expresses a horrifically conservative doctrine, one that rules out the possibility of criticizing existing social institutions and practices altogether. But in Hegel's technical vocabulary, the words 'existing' (*existierend*) and 'actual' (*wirklich*) are not interchangeable. Indeed, Hegel draws a sharp distinction between the two. He defines *Wirklichkeit* ('actuality', 'reality') as the "unity of essence [*Wesen*] and existence [*Existenz*]" (EL, §142). The essence of things (taking 'things' here in the broadest possible sense) consists, roughly speaking, in their inner or underlying rational structure. (Hegel's assertion that things, generally speaking, have an inner or underlying rational structure represents one of the respects in which his view is idealistic.) Things are actual (*wirklich*) only to the extent that they express, manifest, realize, and correspond to their inner essence. What makes them actual – to the extent that they are actual – is not that they exist but rather that they exist *and* express their inner essence. Thus, in Hegel's terminology, not everything that exists is actual. To the extent that things fail to live up to their essence, they fall under the categories of 'mere appearance' (*bloße Erscheinung*) and 'illusion' (*Schein*).

Although Hegel recognizes that the philosophical distinction he draws between 'existence' and 'actuality' is technical, he contends

5 See Inwood 1983, 497.

that it has roots in educated speech, which, he maintains, declines to give the name real (*wirklich*) poet or real (*wirklich*) statesman to a poet or statesman who can do nothing really meritorious or reasonable (EL, §142Z). Hegel also holds that his technical sense of 'actuality' corresponds to what he calls the 'emphatic sense' of the ordinary word. This reflects his general view that philosophy captures the 'speculative content' of ordinary language. In any case, the upshot of all this is that the *Doppelsatz*, properly understood, does not affirm the rationality of everything that exists. The dictum makes the far more restricted claim that what is *actual* is rational. Hegel says quite explicitly: "everything which is not rational must on that very ground cease to be held actual" (EL, §142Z, translation modified). And so the *Doppelsatz* does not entail that existing political states are rational merely because they exist. It is worth pointing out that Hegel does provide a criterion for distinguishing those features of the modern state that are actual from those that are not.[6] It consists in the account of the underlying rational structure of the modern social world provided in the *Philosophy of Right*. To the extent that institutions conform to the arrangements described in the *Philosophy of Right*, they are actual. To the extent that they fail to conform, they are not.

Now as we have seen, the German word *Wirklichkeit* can be translated as either 'actuality' or 'reality', and *wirklich* can be translated as either 'actual' or 'real'. 'Actuality' has quite appropriately become the standard translation for *Wirklichkeit*, as Hegel uses it, and 'actual' the standard translation for his use of *wirklich*. One reason for this is that 'actual' preserves the contrast with potential and undeveloped that is central to Hegel's conception of *Wirklichkeit*. A thing is *wirklich* to the extent that it has developed its potential. Another reason for translating *wirklich* with 'actual' is to respect Hegel's general practice of using the term *Realität* to mean something rather different from *Wirklichkeit* (e.g., to contrast with 'negation' or 'ideality'). If one has to choose one single word to represent *Wirklichkeit*, 'actuality' is the word to pick.

But things are not quite as tidy as this suggests. Hegel does, after all, often use 'realize' (*realisieren*) and 'realization' (*Realisation*) interchangeably with 'actualize' (*verwirklichen*) and 'actualization' (*Verwirklichung*). And he explicitly recognizes the possibility of employing *Realität* and *real* in a sense that is virtually identical to

---

6 Cf., for a differing view, ibid., 502.

his use of *Wirklichkeit* and *wirklich* (EL, §91Z). Moreover, whereas *Wirklichkeit* is a perfectly ordinary German word – like 'reality' in English – the English word 'actuality' is specialized and learned. It is far more idiomatic to speak of a real statesman than an actual statesman. Moreover, 'reality' not 'actuality' is the honorific term in English. We may or may not care whether things are actual, but we do intuitively care whether they are real. 'Actuality' lacks the intuitive force – the ring – of 'reality'.

The most important limitation of the standard translation of *Wirklichkeit*, however, is that it obscures the crucial fact that when Hegel talks about *Wirklichkeit*, he means to be talking about what *we* would call *reality*. I do not mean to suggest here that Hegel's conception of *Wirklichkeit* captures our commonsense conception of reality, but rather that he thinks of his philosophical conception of *Wirklichkeit* as providing a philosophical account of the ordinary notion of reality. One point the *Doppelsatz* makes is that what is rational is *real* and what is *real* is rational – a point that cannot conveniently be expressed without rendering *wirklich* as 'real'. And so, although I will usually follow the standard practice of translating *Wirklichkeit* with 'actuality' and *wirklich* with 'actual', I will at times use 'reality' and 'real' as alternative translations. Doing so will make it possible to see that *reality* is one of the many things the *Doppelsatz* is about.

One might doubt this, for one might doubt whether the *Doppelsatz* is about anything other than the use of words. The claim that what is real is rational can be read as an explication of Hegel's use of 'real' (*wirklich*) – and hence as analytic.[7] After all, his definition of *Wirklichkeit* establishes a definitional connection between what is real and what is rational. Within Hegel's technical vocabulary, things are *by definition* real to the extent that they fulfill their essence. The essence of a thing is *defined* as its underlying *rational* structure. And so it follows immediately from Hegel's definition of 'reality' and 'essence' that things are rational to the extent that they are real. For this reason, Hegel's claim that what is real (or actual) is rational has often been held to be an empty tautology. And by the same token someone might contend that nothing is gained by speaking of reality rather than actuality: since Hegel stipulates that 'real' should be used in the way he does, no substantive claim is being made. The *Doppelsatz* does not say anything about reality after all. All that is at issue here is *words*.

7 Cf. Haym 1857, 368.

But this reading of the *Doppelsatz* is mistaken. Although it is true that Hegel defines *reality* in such a way as to establish a definitional connection between what is real and what is rational, his definition of 'reality' is philosophically subsequent to his philosophical conception of reality. The real philosophical work is done by the conception (a conception that Hegel defends in the *Science of Logic* and throughout his system as a whole), not the definition. Hegel's purpose in *defining* the word 'reality' is simply to express his philosophical conception in a convenient terminology. The point of the *Doppelsatz* is not to establish a *definitional* connection between the words 'real' and 'actual' but rather to assert a *metaphysical* connection between reality and reason. And so Hegel's claim that the real is rational is not empty. It instead provides a summary statement of his philosophical conception of reality and as such makes a substantive claim – a claim about the nature of the real, which, as we shall see, has important normative implications.

2. I turn now to Hegel's conception of reality. The key fact here is that this conception ascribes an intrinsically normative or teleological dimension to the real. Things are *real*, in Hegel's view, to the extent that they live up to their own underlying norm or end – their essence or concept. This conception of reality differs from the commonsense view, according to which things can be perfectly real despite being defective or imperfect. Hegel maintains that to the extent that things fail to correspond to their essence they lack reality, and he holds more specifically that to the extent that an existing political state fails to correspond to the essence of the state, it is not a real state in the relevant sense of the term. Moreover, the defects and imperfections of existing political states lack reality in his view. They exist and may cause suffering, but they are not real. What makes things real – to the extent that they *are* real – is the fact that they exist and correspond to their essence. This, then, is the conception of reality that Hegel's definition is meant to capture.

It may be helpful to think of Hegel's conception of reality as reflecting both a step toward and a step away from Platonism. Hegel takes one (obvious) step toward Platonism in refusing to identify the real with what is "palpable and immediately perceptible" (EL, §142Z, translation modified) and in consigning much of what is given in experience to the metaphysical status of "transitory *existence*, external contingency, opinion, appearance without essence, untruth, deception, etc." (PR, §1R). The disdain Hegel sometimes shows for what merely exists certainly has a Platonic feel. But Hegel also takes another (and somewhat less obvious) step *away* from Platonism in insisting that what is real *must* be externally realized. Things are real only to the extent that they have an external, spatiotemporal existence.

Hegel's conception of reality is thus Janus-faced: one side looks toward the ideal; the other side looks toward existence. In responding to the objection that he claims that everything that exists is rational, Hegel emphasizes the side of his conception of reality that faces the ideal. But it is crucial not to overlook the other side, the side that looks to what exists. The whole point of Hegel's conception of reality is to bridge the gap between what is ideal and what exists. As Hegel understands it, reality is to be identified neither with the essence of things considered apart from their existence nor with the existence of things considered apart from their essence. The reality of the state consists in the essence of the state insofar as it is realized in existing states and existing states insofar as they realize the essence of the state. Reality, for Hegel, is the *unity* of essence and existence. It is also the unity of "the inward" (inner rational structure) and "the outward" (the external embodiment of that structure) (EL, §142).

Thus, for Hegel, reality is immanent within the phenomenal world. The phenomenal world is not identical with reality, for it contains much that is not real. A large portion of this world consists of mere appearances: appearances that fail to live up to their essence and appearances that have no essence. But the real is not a Platonic, ontological "beyond" (*Jenseits*) either. It is not a realm of ideas that are not realized in this world. Nor is the real a Kantian, epistemic "beyond": a thing in itself that lies beyond the bounds of human cognition. The real has external existence in the phenomenal world and is accessible to human cognition. One grasps the reality of things by seeing how their existing features express and embody their essence and how their essence is expressed and embodied in their existing features.

Hegel contends that the final and correct way of comprehending reality is to grasp it as what he calls "the idea" (*die Idee*) (EL, §236). 'The idea', in Hegel's technical vocabulary, consists of the concept (*der Begriff*) (singular) – the underlying rational structure of the world as a whole – together with its actualization (*Verwirklichung*) in nature, history, and the social world. In his view, 'the idea' is real, indeed fully and completely real, and in fact is the only true reality. The upshot of all this is the familiar point that Hegel's basic conception of reality is idealistic. It is not idealistic in denying the existence of matter or in taking the world to be a posit of the mind of the individual. It is idealistic in at least the three following respects: (i) it attributes an intrinsically normative or teleological dimension to reality; (ii) it maintains that things are real only to the extent that they fulfill their inner essences; and (iii) it contends that 'the idea' is the only true reality. It is this idealistic conception of reality that makes it possible for Hegel to say that "the true ideal [*das wahrhafte Ideal*, i.e., 'the idea'] . . . is what is real [*wirklich*], and the only real" (VGP, 2:110/2:95).

From the standpoint of philosophically informed common sense, the philosophical account of the modern social world that Hegel provides in the *Philosophy of Right* will appear to represent an idealized characterization of the institutions and practices with which Hegel was familiar because many of the features it includes were absent in particular cases. Prussia, for example, lacked a constitutional monarchy, a representative bicameral assembly, and public jury trials. But it should be clear from the account of Hegel's conception of reality just provided that Hegel does not regard the *Philosophy of Right* in this way. To characterize an account as *idealized* is to suggest that it is an abstraction, that it abstracts from reality in certain important respects. And although Hegel recognizes that the *Philosophy of Right* abstracts from various *existing* features of the modern social world, he emphatically denies that it abstracts from its reality (*Wirklichkeit*). He would insist that the discrepancies between his philosophical account of the social world and particular existing institutions do not reflect the failure of his account to capture reality but instead the failure of those institutions to realize their essence. Treating Hegel's account of the modern social world as an idealization may represent a fruitful, *deflationary* way of reconstructing his approach – one that enables us to take his investigation seriously while ignoring his philosophical conception of reality. But we cannot understand what Hegel is doing in the *Philosophy of Right* unless we appreciate the truly remarkable fact that he genuinely takes his philosophical account of the modern social world to be thoroughly realistic.

3. Hegel's conception of reason has two closely related elements: (i) an account of the conditions of normative validity and (ii) a view of reason as an active force or power. Hegel's conception of normative validity reflects his general commitment to the principle of

internal criticism: the idea that criticism must be given in terms that appeal to principles or practices to which the agents to whom it is addressed are already committed. He maintains that norms ('oughts,' ideals, principles) are valid only if they are rooted in the essence of the things to which they apply. A norm that is rooted in the essence of a thing can be said to have a foothold in the thing's "own rationality" since, in being rooted in the thing's essence, it is rooted in the thing's rational structure. Roughly speaking, a norm is 'rooted' in the essence of a thing if it figures centrally in the characterization of the thing's kind and plays a central explanatory role in accounting for the thing's normal operation, that is, activities through which it realizes its essence. Thus to say that the ideal of providing mutual love, understanding, and support is rooted in the essence of the family – a view Hegel holds – is to say that having this end is part of what it is to *be* a family and that, by realizing this end, families realize themselves *as* families. A family *has* the end of providing mutual love and so forth if it is "organized around" this end. It is organized around this end if it exhibits an underlying structure that, if ideally realized, would realize it. Norms that are not rooted in the essence of things to which they are applied are *mere* oughts or ideals, in Hegel's view. Being alien to the essence of things to which they are applied, such norms lack any rational grip or force.

It should be noted that Hegel's claim that norms are valid only if rooted in essences entails that norms must be rooted in the actual in order to be valid. By 'essences' Hegel means *realized* (or actualized) essences: his general view being that essences must be actualized in existing features of the things whose essence they are. But the realized essence of things constitutes their actuality (*Wirklichkeit*). And so, for Hegel, actuality (or reality) is the source of valid norms. One sense, then, in which the rational is actual is that valid norms are rooted in the real.

Hegel's conception of normative validity is illustrated by the distinction he draws between what he calls "ideals of imagination" (*Ideale der Phantasie*) and "ideals of reason" (*Ideale der Vernunft*) (VG, 75/65). *Ideals of reason* are so called because they are rooted in the reality of things. It is precisely because they are rooted in the real (existing rational practices) that they are genuine and "binding upon reality at large" (VG, 76/65). *Ideals of imagination* derive their name from the fact that they are grounded solely in individual imagination or fantasy. Hegel holds that ideals of imagination are *mere* ideals – ideals that lack any genuine claim to be satisfied and whose nonfulfillment does not constitute an objective wrong. Ideals of reason, on the other hand, are genuine, or true, ideals. They have a "genuine claim to be satisfied" and their nonfulfillment constitutes "an objective wrong" (VG, 76/66). This distinction allows Hegel to recognize that there is a class of ideals that are *not* rooted in reality (a fact that gives rise to the general impression that there is a fundamental split between what is ideal and what is real) while also maintaining that there is another class of ideals that *are* rooted in reality (a fact that shows that there is no fundamental split between the ideal and the real).

Now in conceiving of valid norms as rooted in the essence or reality of things, Hegel already conceives of reason as a force or power. In order for the ideal of mutual love, understanding, and support to be rooted in the essence of the family, existing families must realize this end at least to some degree. In order to *be* families, they must be organized around this end, and in order to be *organized around* this end, they must have some success in realizing it. If it were literally true that a family failed utterly to realize this end, it could not be said to be a family at all. Thus, in Hegel's view, valid norms are not powerless. The very conditions that make them valid guarantee that the things to which they apply will exhibit at least some tendency to realize them. Another sense in which the rational is actual, then, is that valid norms are realized at least to some degree. None of this is to say that the validity of a norm guarantees its *ideal* satisfaction – that is, that the things to which it applies realize the norm in a perfect and complete way. Even if the ideal of mutual love and so forth *is* rooted in the family, no existing family will perfectly realize this ideal, and some existing families will diverge radically from the ideal. The Karamazov family represents a real possibility, but the Waltons and Huxtables are fantasies of television.

Now, obviously enough, the claim that valid norms will be realized to *some* degree is both vague and weak. How well must a family actualize the ideals of the family in order to be said to realize this ideal 'to some degree'? A possible answer would be: well enough to be properly called a family. Deciding whether a given family actualizes the ideal of the family well enough to be properly called a family is a matter of judgment. And there may be cases – say, with extremely dysfunctional families – in which it is not clear whether a given 'family' really is a family. But, presumably, most families actualize the ideal of the family well enough to be families properly so called. The vagueness of the idea of realizing a norm to some degree is perhaps somewhat less threatening than might first appear.

The worry about weakness is more serious. Whatever the minimal level of success may be, it must be very low, for, presumably, it is a level that even the Karamazovs can satisfy. There are highly dysfunctional families that are still families. And so the worry is that the minimal level of success is so minimal as to make the standard it provides empty or to divest this standard of all value. If the minimal level of success is a standard even the Karamazovs can satisfy, one might well wonder whether the standard is worth taking seriously.

Here it must be pointed out that Hegel also maintains that things will generally realize those norms that are rooted in their essence to a *significant degree*. This idea is obviously vague, but it may be possible to clarify its force by giving some sense of the range of cases within which it falls. A family that realized the ideal of mutual love, understanding, and support *only* to the minimal degree required in order for it to be a family would not realize this ideal to a significant degree. The Karamazovs provide a literary example of a family of this sort. But a family could be said to realize this ideal to a significant degree without realizing it perfectly and completely. A family does not have to be just like the Waltons or the Huxtables to be properly said to realize the ideal to a significant degree. Nor must a family realize this ideal on the whole. But a normal family – a family that could properly be called normal – would realize the ideal to a significant degree. Although it might exhibit serious problems and difficulties, it would, nonetheless, embody the ideal of mutual love, understanding, and support in a real and substantial way.

In any case, the idea that things will generally realize those norms that are rooted in their essence to a significant degree flows out of Hegel's conception of normative validity. Hegel is committed to the view that there is a nonaccidental connection between 'normal' in the sense of 'conforming to norm' and 'normal' in the sense of 'what generally transpires'. He thinks that in order for a norm to be in place – to be valid – the pattern of action the norm prescribes must generally (but not universally) take place. Part of what it *means* for a pattern of action to constitute a thing's 'normal operation' is for that pattern to be a pattern that things of its kind generally exhibit. Thus the ideal of providing mutual love, understanding, and support would not be a norm rooted in the essence of the family if families did not generally realize this ideal to a significant degree.

Another sense in which the rational is actual is that valid norms are realized to a significant degree.

Turning briefly from Hegel's conception of reason back to his conception of actuality, it is worth noting that Hegel contends that existing things exhibit a tendency to realize valid norms. His conception of the actual entails that, to the extent to which things are actual, they will realize – or tend to realize – those norms that are rooted in their essences. Hegel conceives of essences as rational tendencies: tendencies to realize the structures in virtue of which things are rationally intelligible, reasonable, and good. And so to say that norms must be rooted in the essences of things to which they apply is to say that they must be rooted in things that are so constituted as to exhibit a tendency to realize them. Hegel maintains that reality is essentially rational in the sense that it displays an *inherent tendency* to realize valid norms.

In order to appreciate this point, it is crucial to realize that Hegel offers two distinct lines of argument. One line flows out of his conception of normative validity:

> In order for the rational to be rational (i.e., in order for norms to be valid), the actual must be rational; it must provide the foundations for valid norms and realize these norms to some, and indeed a significant, degree.

The other line flows out of his conception of the actual:

> Since essences are tendencies to realize structures in virtue of which things are intelligible, reasonable, and good, the actual will necessarily exhibit a tendency to be intelligible, reasonable, and good.

Although the first line entails that we cannot specify the content of valid norms without looking to the reality of the things in question, the second line maintains that – quite apart from the question of determining what the content of valid norms is – we can say that, insofar as things are real, they are constituted so as to realize valid norms. Thus the *Doppelsatz* allows of both an epistemic and a metaphysical reading. On the epistemic reading, the *Doppelsatz* maintains that what is actual is rational because what is rational is actual: the fact that the conditions of normative validity are met provides an epistemic guarantee that the actual will be rational. On the metaphysical reading, the *Doppelsatz* maintains that what is rational is actual because what is actual is rational: The nature of actuality provides a metaphysical guarantee that the rational will be actual.

4. Having now considered Hegel's conception of reason and reality, we are now in a position to consider variant formulations of the *Doppelsatz*. In his 1817–18 Heidelberg lectures, Hegel stated:

> What is rational must happen, since on the whole the constitution is only its development. (VPRW, 157)

Then, in the Heidelberg lectures he gave in the following year, Hegel asserted:

> What is rational becomes actual, and the actual becomes rational. (VPRHN, 51)[8]

On the face of things these two formulations (which I will refer to rather inelegantly as the 'development' and the 'becoming' versions) seem rather different from (what I will call) the 'canonical' formulation we have been considering up until now.

To begin with, the word 'actual' (*wirklich*) is completely absent from the development version, which might be taken simply to refer to what exists. Thus one might think that the development version baldly proclaims that the existing constitution (*Verfassung*) – that is, the de facto arrangement of the state – is the development of the rational. But this reading is not plausible. Quite apart from the fact that it involves attributing a claim to Hegel that is absurd by any reasonable standard, it clearly runs against the grain of his thought. The distinction he makes between existence (*Existenz*) and actuality (*Wirklichkeit*) is after all a central feature of the 1812–13 *Science of Logic* (WL, 2:186–217/541–53). In any case, the development version does not provide a blanket affirmation of what exists. It does not say that *the constitution* is the development of the rational, period. What it says is that the constitution is the development of the rational *on the whole* (*überhaupt*). The qualification is absolutely crucial, for it reflects the Hegelian distinction between existence and actuality. Those aspects of the constitution which *do not* represent a development of the rational are merely existent. Those aspects which *do* represent a development of the rational are actual. Only those aspects of the constitution that are actual are held to be a development of the rational. Hegel may not have used the *word*

8 Wood's translations (1990, 13).

'actual' (*wirklich*) in the development version, but his *conception* of actuality is there all the same. As far as this point goes, there is no fundamental difference between the development and canonical versions of the *Doppelsatz*.

Now, like the canonical version, the becoming version of the *Doppelsatz* does use the word 'actual' (*wirklich*). But the use to which it puts this word might suggest that, unlike the canonical version, it identifies the philosophical categories of actuality and existence. After all, it is clear that part of Hegel's point in saying that "what is rational becomes actual" is that what is rational *comes into existence* and that part of his point in saying that "the actual becomes rational" is that *what exists* becomes rational. Nonetheless, we should not conclude that the becoming version identifies existence and actuality in any serious way. Hegel is deliberately speaking loosely in this version of his dictum so as to make his point maximally provocative and forceful. He is using the word 'actual' to mean 'existent', and hence violating his own self-imposed linguistic strictures, but he is *not* identifying the existent with the actual. This verbal looseness also allows him to suggest a thesis that gives the becoming version much of its force: namely, that in coming into existence, the rational (the underlying rational tendencies of things) becomes actual and that in becoming actual the existent becomes rational. Things are complicated somewhat by the fact that in the becoming version, Hegel also means 'actual' (in his technical sense of the term) by 'actual'. Part of his point in saying that what is rational becomes actual is that what is rational becomes *more actual* in the sense of coming to be more adequately realized in existing things. And part of his point in saying that what is actual becomes rational is that what is actual becomes *more rational* in the sense of coming to fulfill its essence in a more adequate way.

This leads us to the truly striking difference between the two variants and the canonical version. Whereas the two earlier versions speak of what must *happen*, what *develops*, and what *becomes*, the final version speaks of what *is*. The rhetorical effect of this contrast is enormous. And the contrast might well seem philosophically fundamental. Unlike the canonical version, which can so easily be read as flatly proclaiming the rationality of the present, the development and becoming versions seem to suggest that the future – not the present – is the true locus of rationality. And unlike the canonical version, which seems to present the rationality of the actual as a static state of affairs, both the development and the becoming versions clearly represent the rationality of the actual as a *process*. Moreover, considered from the perspective of Hegel's immediate political circumstances, the development and becoming versions can be read as expressing Hegel's optimism in the Prussian reform era. Similarly, the canonical version can be read as endorsing the Prussian restoration. Furthermore, the development and becoming versions can easily be read as generic expressions of political reformism – as suggesting quite generally that social change is necessary and rational – and the canonical version can easily be read as a generic expression of political conservatism – as suggesting quite generally that the status quo is fine as it is.

But striking as these differences are, their philosophical significance is, I think, easily exaggerated.[9] The canonical version is not meant to deny that rationality or actuality is to be understood in terms of processes. The canonical version assumes that the actuality and the rationality of social institutions are both realized by the processes through which the institutions maintain and reproduce themselves. The family, for example, maintains and reproduces itself by raising its members to act in such a way (fulfilling their duties as family members) that they will maintain and reproduce the family. Hegel believes that it is precisely because social reproductive processes are taking place that the rational *is* actual and the actual *is* rational. And although the canonical version does not emphasize this point, it does presuppose it. The development and the becoming versions may be forward-looking in a way in which the canonical version is not, but neither version flatly denies the rationality of the present. The view that the present is not rational but the future will become rational is fundamentally un-Hegelian. Hegel is deeply opposed to any suggestion that the rational (or the ideal or the divine) is to be found somewhere other than in the present – in some *Jenseits*, or beyond. The development and the becoming version do express a certain optimism about the future, but this optimism must be understood to be rooted in a basic faith in the present. The underlying image here is not the Marxian one of the present age containing the seeds of its own destruction (like capitalism) but of the present containing the seeds of it own development. The outlook is reformist rather than revolutionary. And although the *language* of the canonical version may be static, the *conception* of reason that underlies it is no less dynamic than the

9 Cf. Henrich 1983, 13–17; Wood 1990, 11–14.

conception of reason that is expressed in the development and becoming versions.

Indeed the basic conception of reason at work in the development, becoming, and canonical versions of the *Doppelsatz* is the same. Reason is, among other things, the basic tendency of the social world to become more rational. One crucial respect in which the social world becomes more rational, in Hegel's view, is that its arrangements come to reflect an increasingly more adequate conception of the human spirit.

Hegel contends that this transformation takes place through the process of historical development he calls "world history" (*Weltgeschichte*). Each stage of world history is represented by a determinate national principle (*Volksgeist*), expressed in the particular ordering of the family, economy, and government and in the particular forms of art, religion, and philosophy, that corresponds to the highest level of self-understanding available to human beings at the time (VG, 74–5/64). That nation whose principle corresponds to the highest level of self-understanding available to human beings at the time will become historically dominant (see VG, 59/51–2). Its world historical task consists in the development of its national principle (VG, 67/58); in developing this principle, it furthers the self-understanding of the human spirit. Once a historically dominant nation has fully developed its national principle, it enters a period of decline, and the task of developing a more adequate conception of the human spirit transfers to another nation (VG, 69/60). The succession of stages of world history corresponds to the succession of increasingly more adequate conceptions of the human spirit, developed by a succession of historically dominant nations. The basic tendency of the social world to become more rational consists, then, in its tendency to develop social arrangements that correspond to increasingly more adequate conceptions of the human spirit. It is this tendency that Hegel has in mind when he characterizes reason as an "infinite power" (VG, 28/27). One of the many senses in which the rational is actual, then, according to Hegel, is in its tendency to actualize itself in increasingly more adequate ways through the course of world history.

Both the development and the becoming version of the *Doppelsatz* express this conception of reason more or less on their face. In saying that the rational must happen in the development version, Hegel means that it must happen in the course of world history. By the development of reason, he means a development that occurs in world history. Similarly, when Hegel says that what is rational becomes actual and what is actual becomes rational in the becoming version, he is thinking of world history as the arena of these transformations. Although the canonical version makes no explicit reference to the dynamic character of reason and so may *appear* static, it is clear that Hegel is thinking of reason as a developmental power in this version as well. He clearly believes that the circumstance of the present the canonical version describes, in which the rational *is* actual and the actual *is* rational, is the result of the historical process through which the rational has *become* actual and the actual has *become* rational: the process of world history. Historically speaking, the fact that the rational is actual (the fact that the social world has exhibited a tendency to become more rational) explains why the actual (the present) is rational. Although the canonical version, in contrast to the development and becoming versions, does not emphasize the developmental character of reason, this is a difference of emphasis, not doctrine. The upshot of all this is that the development, becoming, and canonical versions of the *Doppelsatz* do not offer competing accounts of the fundamental nature of reason, reality, and their relation. Rather they express a common fundamental conception and differ only in the particular aspects of this common fundamental conception they happen to emphasize. The real value of looking at the different versions is that doing so enables us to see what these aspects are and so better appreciate the richness of Hegel's view.

Before going on to the methodological implications of the *Doppelsatz*, there is one further aspect of Hegel's conception of the social world's becoming more rational that I would like to explore. The final way in which, according to Hegel, the social world has become more rational is that the existing institutions of the modern social world realize their essence to a far greater degree than the institutions of the ancient world realized theirs. World history, in Hegel's view, is marked by a closing of the gap between the ideal and the existent. Indeed, Hegel's conception of world history can be understood as the story of the process through which this gap becomes progressively smaller.

I would like to approach this point by turning to one extremely illuminating context in which Hegel addresses it: namely, his discussion of the status and limitations of Plato's *Republic* in the Preface to the *Philosophy of Right*. It is in the Preface that Hegel makes his famous and remarkable claim that the basic character of the

Republic and the *Philosophy of Right* are the same: each of these works is *"its own time comprehended in thoughts"* (PR, ¶13). Far from being an "empty ideal," as is commonly thought, the *Republic* is "essentially the embodiment of nothing other than the nature of Greek ethical life" (PR, ¶12, translation modified). Commentators have understandably had difficulty in taking this claim seriously,[10] for two main reasons. First, this interpretation is radically at odds with Plato's own understanding. It is generally recognized that Plato took the *Republic* to represent a repudiation of the polis of his time. Second, the social world Plato describes in the *Republic* diverges radically from the existing Greek polis of his time. It is, for example, a social world without marriage, a world in which the two upper classes lack private property, and a world in which no one enjoys freedom of occupation. And so the question that naturally arises is: How could Hegel have seriously maintained that the *Republic* was its own time comprehended in thought? Presumably, the difficulties that make Hegel's interpretation problematic are too obvious for him to have overlooked them. How then could Hegel have seriously maintained that the *Republic* was "its own time comprehended in thoughts" *given* that he recognized that his interpretation faced these difficulties?

Hegel himself does not provide an explicit answer to this question, but I believe it is possible to construct the sort of reply he would give. Hegel would presumably concede that his account of the real import of the *Republic* is radically at odds with Plato's self-understanding, but he would argue that his understanding of what Plato was doing in the *Republic* is superior to Plato's. Hegel follows Kant in thinking that it is possible to understand a philosopher better than that philosopher has understood himself, and he would note that he, Hegel, has the advantage of writing at a time when philosophy has come to a full understanding of its own historical nature. Although for Hegel philosophy has always been historical – all philosophy is its own time comprehended in thought – it is only in the present age (in Hegel's time) that the historical character of philosophy has come to be recognized. Hegel would also concede that the arrangements of the social world Plato presents in the *Republic* differ radically from the existing institutions of Plato's time. Indeed, the word 'concede' here is something of a misnomer since this is a point that Hegel wants to assert. In any case Hegel would –

10 See, e.g., Inwood 1984, 53–4.

and, in effect, does – argue that this discrepancy is, in the first instance, a reflection of the defects of the *Republic* and, ultimately, a reflection of the defects of the Greek social world of Plato's time. This point bears elaboration.

Let us begin by observing that Hegel rejects the common view that the reason the *Republic* radically diverges from existing social arrangements is that the social arrangements it depicts are too good for the world. Writing in the *Lectures on the History of Philosophy*, Hegel maintains that the *Republic* is a chimera "not because excellence such as it depicts is lacking to mankind, but because it, this excellence, falls short of man's requirements" (VGP, 2:110/2:95). That Hegel should judge that the Platonic ideal is defective should come as no surprise, given his understanding of the actuality of the rational. Indeed his criticism of this ideal flows from his conception of the actuality of the rational. "The true ideal," Hegel maintains, "is not what [merely] *ought* to be real [*wirklich*], but what *is* real, and the only real; if an ideal is held to be too good to exist, there must be some fault in the ideal itself, for which reality [*Wirklichkeit*] is too good" (VGP, 2:110/2:95, translation modified). But how can Hegel both maintain that the ideal provided in the *Republic* was defective because unrealizable and maintain that the *Republic* is a reflection of the substance of Greek ethical life?

Before we can answer this question, we need to look more closely at the reasons Hegel gives for maintaining that the ideal the *Republic* offers is defective. In addition to holding that this ideal is defective because it is unrealizable, Hegel also maintains that it is defective because it fails to include the "principle of self-subsistent particularity." And, indeed, he contends, these two defects are related. It is precisely because Plato's ideal state fails to include the principle of self-subsistent particularity that it cannot be realized.

We can begin to get a grip on the idea that the *Republic* is a reflection of the substance of Greek ethical life if we recall that Hegel maintains that the social arrangements of ancient Greece provided no room for human subjectivity or particularity. Indeed, he contends that, from the standpoint of Greek ethical life, "the principle of self-subsistent particularity, which had suddenly overtaken Greek ethical life in [Plato's] time" (PR, §185R), could appear "only as a destructive force" (PR, ¶12). Hegel maintains that the *Republic* represented Plato's response to the appearance of this "deeper principle." Plato, Hegel tells us, "absolutely excluded [this principle] from his state, even in its very beginnings in private property . . . and the family, as well as in its more mature form as the subjective will, the choice of a social position and so forth" (ibid.).

Now Hegel holds that *this* response was fundamentally conditioned by the character of the social world in which Plato lived. It was because the principle of self-subsistent particularity could only appear as a destructive force from the standpoint of Greek ethical life that Plato regarded it as a threat. And it is because Plato regarded it as a threat that he felt the need to exclude it. Moreover, the underlying ideal of the Greek world, according to Hegel, was that of a "purely substantial state" (i.e., a state that provided no room for subjectivity and particularity), and it was *this* ideal that Plato captured in the *Republic*. Indeed, Hegel contends that it is precisely the *Republic*'s success in capturing this ideal that accounts for its "deep and substantial truth."

This brings us to the key point. Hegel contends that the ideal that the *Republic* captures – the ideal that was in fact embedded in ancient Greek life – was a defective ideal. It was defective precisely because it provided no room for the principle of particularity. And so, according to Hegel, the deep reason why Plato's ideal was defective was that it *reflected* the actuality of his social world – a world whose arrangements provided no place for human subjectivity or particularity. In Hegel's view, the strengths and weaknesses of Plato's *Republic* reflect the strengths and weaknesses of the social world within which he lived. The strengths of the state described in the *Republic* are the strengths of a purely substantial state, and the weaknesses exhibited by the *Republic* are the weaknesses of a purely substantial state. Thus, Plato's state *was* its own time comprehended in thought.

We can now return to the point that motivated this excursus. Although Hegel maintains that the *Republic* and the *Philosophy of Right* are alike in that both capture the underlying aspirations of the social worlds they depict, they differ in the following respect: The gap between the arrangements described in the *Philosophy of Right* and the institutions that existed in Hegel's time was much narrower than the gap between the arrangements described in the *Republic* and the institutions that existed in Plato's time. The gap between the *Republic* and the existing social world was enormous; the gap between the *Philosophy of Right* and the existing social world was small. Hegel holds that there is a substantial degree of correspondence between what he calls "the more advanced [*ausgebildeten*] states of our time" (by which he means the most advanced European states of his time) and the structures described in the *Philosophy of Right* (PR, §258Z; VPRG, 632; VGP, 2:36/2:25-6). He thinks that these states *on the whole* do fulfill the aspirations of the modern state.

According to Hegel, the closing of the gap between ideal and existing social arrangements is to be explained in part by the development of the ideals of human social life embedded in social arrangements over the course of world history. The ideal that was rooted in the arrangements of Plato's time – the ideal of a purely substantial form of social life – was defective. It failed to meet "man's requirements" because it provided no room for human subjectivity. And this defect led to the decline of ancient Greece. World history is, among other things, the story of the development of an ideal that meets human requirements, incorporating subjectivity and unifying it with substantiality. Thus Hegel says, "The principle of the modern state has enormous strength and depth because it allows the principle of subjectivity to attain fulfillment in the *self-sufficient extreme* of personal particularity, while at the same time *bringing it back to substantial unity* and so preserving this unity in the principle of subjectivity itself" (PR, §260). We shall return to this extremely suggestive passage in Chapter 6.

5. Let us now turn to the methodological implications of the view of reason and reality the *Doppelsatz* expresses. Hegel presents the dictum in the context of a discussion of the proper aim of philosophical investigation and the relation of philosophy to actuality: "It is *this very relation of philosophy to actuality* which is the subject of misunderstandings, and I accordingly come back to my earlier observation that, since philosophy is *exploration of the rational*, it is for that very reason the *comprehension of the present and the actual*" (PR, ¶12).

The starting assumption of this passage is that the aim of philosophy, including, in particular, social philosophy, is to explore "the rational." Hegel's concern is to explain why, since social philosophy has this aim, the philosopher is committed to comprehending what is present and actual in the social world. The *Doppelsatz* provides a summary statement of his answer: it is because what is rational is actual and what is actual is rational that social philosophy must look to the actuality of the social world. "To comprehend *what is* is the task of philosophy, for *what is* is reason" (PR, ¶13).

But what does comprehending "what is" come to for Hegel?

It is *not* a matter of grasping the existing world as such. To the extent that existing social institutions or their existing features fail to manifest the underlying rational essence of the social world, they are of no philosophical interest. Considered in themselves, the "infinite wealth of forms, appearances, and shapes" that surround "its [rational] core are not the subject-matter of philosophy" (PR, ¶12). This might give the impression that comprehending "what is" amounts to comprehending the inner essence of things as such, and ignoring existing arrangements. But Hegel rejects this position as well. He contends that philosophy is concerned with the rationality of the social world insofar as it is actualized in existing institutions and practices. Hence philosophy *does* care about existing arrangements; it cares about them *as* manifestations of the rational. For Hegel, comprehending "what is" is a matter of grasping the inner essence of the social world insofar as it is manifest in existing institutions and grasping existing institutions insofar as they manifest the essence of the social world. It is in this way that one grasps what is actual.

As to how concretely the philosopher is to grasp the actuality of the social world, Hegel has fairly little to say. His general approach is to look to those features of the social world (i.e., the modern social world) that are most central and reasonable (e.g., the most reasonable features of "the more advanced" modern European states) and to construct an account on the basis of the results of this investigation. His background conception of reality guarantees that in identifying the most central and reasonable features of the present age (i.e., those corresponding to the most adequate available self-understanding of the human spirit) one will thereby identify the actuality of the present. The philosopher identifies what is actual by looking reasonably at the world.

Hegel's research program, if we can call it such, then, is surprisingly empirical. Although he maintains that we know more or less a priori that the actual social world is rational, he contends that the only way in which we can ascertain the details of its rationality is by *looking to* the social world. Moreover, he thinks that we have only comprehended [*begriffen*] the rationality of the social world when we have grasped these details. And while discerning the actuality hidden within existing social institutions and practices does require the employment of norms – the goal is, after all, to identify those features of the social world that are most *reasonable* – the norms we are to employ are norms that are rooted in the social world. We are not to approach the social world from the standpoint of our own individual and private "ideals of imagination" but from the standpoint of "ideals of reason" – ideals that are rooted in existing institutions and practices. And to find these ideals we must look to the social world. Thus the normative dimension of Hegel's research program is itself empirically grounded. But it would be a mistake to conceive of this program as purely empirical. In his view, grasping the rationality of the actual also involves grasping the *Zeitgeist* (the spirit of the age), that it, the historically dominant social and political trends and the historically available possibilities. And this, in turn, requires interpretation. Thus, the sort of investigation Hegel proposes also includes a central and indispensable hermeneutic component.

It is worth emphasizing that Hegel's philosophical approach is fundamentally historical. Hegel contends that "since philosophy is the *exploration of the rational*, it is for that very reason the *comprehension of the present*" (PR, ¶16). This reflects his view that reason has an essentially historical dimension: what is rational becomes actual and what is actual becomes rational. As we have seen, the rational structure that underlies the social world is subject to a process of historical development through which it comes to reflect an increasingly more adequate conception of the human spirit. This structure actualizes itself through a series of historical stages. These stages constitute the actuality of the rational. At any given time, the rational is actual only as actualized in the social arrangements of that time. Grasping the rational, then, is a matter of grasping the historically specific form of the rational structure of the social world that has become actual in the present.

When Hegel says that philosophy "is *its own time comprehended in thoughts*" (PR, ¶13), he means that philosophy consists in the activity of comprehending in thought the (actualized) rational structure of the central social institutions of its own historical period. The reason philosophy cannot "transcend its contemporary world" is that the rational is available to cognition and actual only to the extent that it is actualized in the present. Hegel does not, however, conclude from this that philosophical accounts of the social world can never lay claim to any absolute standing, that they are "true" only relative to the historical situation in which they are written. He maintains that there is a form of social life that reflects the final and correct understanding of the human spirit and is realized in human history: the form of social life that is realized in the modern social world (see PR, §273R).

Hegel's philosophical approach involves a self-conscious blurring of the categories of the descriptive and the normative.[11] It is neither purely descriptive nor purely normative. It is not purely descriptive, first of all, because articulating the norms that are rooted in the modern social world is a fundamental component of comprehending its actuality. The *Philosophy of Right* is, among other things, an account of the underlying ideals and normative aspirations of the modern social world. Moreover, inasmuch as the *Philosophy of Right* is supposed to provide an account of the norms that are rooted in the actuality of the modern social world, it also provides an account of how the modern social world ought to be. But, of course, Hegel's approach is not *purely* normative. He maintains that the norms that the *Philosophy of Right* articulates are rooted in the existing structures of the modern social world and substantially realized. Hence the *Philosophy of Right* does "distance itself as far as possible from the obligation to construct a *state as it ought to be*" (PR, ¶13) in the sense of providing an account of the state as it ought to be that is different from what the (actual) state is. It purports to show how the social world *ought to be* by showing what the actuality of the social world *is*. Hegel's approach, then, is both descriptive *and* normative. It flows out of his normative conception of the real (the actual is rational) and his realistic conception of the normative (the rational is actual). Let us turn now to the basic normative outlook the *Doppelsatz* expresses.

6. The *Doppelsatz* maintains that the modern social world is as it ought to be. There are two key respects in which this is supposed to be so. First, the modern social world is 'as it ought to be' in that its essence or underlying rational structure is as it ought to be. Its essence is as it ought to be, and, indeed, is *absolutely* as it ought to be, because it reflects a correct understanding of the human spirit. By contrast, the essence of Plato's social world was as it ought to be merely *relative to its stage in world history* because it reflected the most adequate understanding of the human spirit available at the time, one that recognized the importance of "substantiality," or community. It was as it ought to be *merely* relative to its stage in world history because the most adequate understanding of the human spirit available at the time was limited, inasmuch as it failed to recognize the importance of subjectivity. Strictly speaking, the essence of both Plato's and Hegel's social worlds were as they ought to be relative

11 Cf., for a differing view, Walsh 1969, 7–8.

to their stages in world history, for both reflected the most adequate understanding of the human spirit available at the time. What was special about the essence of Hegel's social world was that it was as it ought to be both relative to its stage in world history *and* absolutely. Hegel holds that it was as it ought to be in these two respects because the most adequate understanding of the human spirit available at his time was correct: it recognized the importance of both substantiality (community membership) and subjectivity. Second, the modern social world is 'as it ought to be' in that its essence is substantially realized: the more advanced states in modern Europe conform to it on the whole. This is one of the features that Hegel takes to distinguish the social world of his time from the social world of Plato's time.

It will come as no surprise that the claim that the modern social world is as it ought to be is grounded in Hegel's conception of actuality. His conception of actuality entails that, to the extent that things are actual, they are 'as they ought to be' in the sense of conforming to their essence. Reality, in Hegel's view, is necessarily as it ought to be in that there is an intrinsic, metaphysical connection between reality and goodness (things being as they ought to be). Indeed, Hegel holds quite generally that the actuality of the social world is necessarily good. Obviously, this is a strong and provocative claim. What is less obvious is that it is extremely abstract. In particular, the claim abstracts from the question of how "mature" or well developed the essence of the social world is at any given point in history. It also abstracts from the question concerning how well at any given point in history the social world realizes its essence. The answers to *these* questions cannot be derived from an analysis or explication of the concept of actuality. And so Hegel's claim that the essence of the modern social world reflects the correct understanding of the human spirit and that this essence is substantially realized transcends what can be said on the basis of his conception of actuality. It derives from his philosophically informed investigation of the state of his social world, which involves, among other things, a detailed political assessment of the more advanced states, that is, the more advanced European states.

Hegel's claim that the essence of the modern social world is substantially realized because the more advanced European states conform to it on the whole bears comment. Hegel does *not* think that all existing or even most existing states must conform on the whole to the essence of the modern social world in order for that essence to be substantially realized. He instead maintains, somewhat counter-intuitively, that *all* that is required for the essence of the social world to be *substantially* realized is that there be some existing states that correspond to this essence on the whole. Thus, the claim that the essence of the modern social world was substantially realized is compatible with the claim (which Hegel himself believed) that the essence of the modern social world was not substantially realized in vast portions of the globe (the 'less advanced' European nations, North and South America, Africa, and Asia) in his time.

But how can Hegel say this? How can the mere fact that the more advanced European states correspond on the whole to the essence of the modern social world make it the case that the essence of the social world is realized to a substantial degree? Why isn't it necessary that all or most existing states conform on the whole to the essence of the modern social world?

To answer these questions, we must consider how Hegel understands the prior question concerning whether the essence of the modern social world is substantially realized. He does not regard this question as being, in the first instance, a question about *existing* institutions but instead takes it to be a question about the *essence* of the modern social world, or the pattern of social life that corresponds to it. Rather than starting with existing states generally and asking, Do they, on the whole, realize the essence of the modern social world? Hegel starts with the essence of the modern social world and asks: Are there any existing states that, on the whole, realize this pattern of life? For Hegel, the key issue is whether the essence of the modern social world is substantially realized some-place or other. What he is asking is: Is the essence of the modern state substantially realized *at all*?

Accordingly, Hegel maintains that if there are *some* existing states that on the whole correspond to the essence of the modern state, the essence of the modern social world *is* substantially realized. It is substantially realized *in those existing states* that conform to it on the whole. From this perspective, then, the fact that the essence of the modern social world was not substantially realized outside the more advanced states of Europe in Hegel's time would not count against the claim that the essence of the modern social world was substantially realized then. If the more advanced states of Europe conformed to it on the whole, that would be enough.

Hegel maintains that if the essence of the modern social world is substantially realized in a few existing states, then the modern social world can *itself* be said to substantially realize its essence. He contends that those states that substantially realize the essence of the modern social world constitute the actuality of the modern social world. Thus, the *modern social world* could be said to realize substantially its essence in the more advanced states of Europe.

From all that has been said, it is clear that Hegel thinks that the proposition that the modern social world is as it ought to be is compatible with the fact that no existing institution ideally realizes its essence – that no existing institution realizes its essence in each and every respect. In claiming that the modern social world is as it ought to be, Hegel is not saying that every existing institution conforms to its essence on the whole. Nor is he saying that those existing institutions that do conform to their essence on the whole conform to their essence in each and every respect. Thus Hegel states: "The state is not a work of art; it exists in the world, and hence in the sphere of arbitrariness, contingency, and error, and bad behavior may disfigure it in many respects" (PR, §258Z; VPRG, 663). The point I want to bring out at this juncture is that it is part of Hegel's basic normative conception that existing institutions will *inevitably fail* to realize their essence in certain respects.

Hegel maintains that such failure is inevitable because existing institutions exist in the finite sphere of "arbitrariness, contingency, and error" constituted by human action, and anything existing in this sphere will necessarily exhibit defects and imperfections and inevitably be marred by human wickedness. He maintains, quite generally, that "where there is finitude, there opposition and contradiction always break out again afresh, and satisfaction does not get beyond being relative" (VA, 1:136/1:99). Imperfection is a necessary condition of actuality. Everything that is actual – everything that is part of the world of finitude and contingency – will be defective in some respect or other.

Hegel does not think that particular institutional defects or imperfections are to be explained by reference to the general fact of imperfection. The fact that *this* state deviates in *this* way from the essence of the state is to be explained by reference to its particular circumstances and history. Similarly, the fact that *this* family fails to conform to the essence of the family in *these* respects is to be explained by reference to *its* particular circumstances and *its* particular history. But the *general* fact that particular institutions or groups display defects and imperfections is to be understood as the general fact of imperfection, which in turn is to be explained by reference to the conditions of actuality and the nature of the world of finitude and contingency.

Perhaps the most striking conclusion that Hegel draws from his understanding of the relation between actuality and imperfection is that imperfection is a necessary condition of the social world's being as it ought to be. In order for the social world to be as it ought to be, its essence must be realized in existing institutions. But the price of realization in existing institutions is imperfection. And so, for Hegel, imperfection is the price of the social world's being as it ought to be. Accordingly, Hegel denies that the inevitability of institutional imperfection counts against the claim that the social world is as it ought to be. In the first place, as we have just seen, imperfection is, for Hegel, a condition of the social world's being as it ought to be. The general fact of imperfection, which appears to be a bad thing, turns out to be, if not a good thing, something we can accept or live with because it is a necessary condition of the realization of the essence of the social world and hence the realization of the human spirit. In the second place, to the extent to which existing institutions exhibit defects and imperfections, they fail to conform to their essence, and hence lack actuality.

Although Hegel recognizes that existing institutions do fail to conform to their essence in various respects and so recognizes the *existence* of defects and imperfections, he denies that these defects and imperfections are *actual*, except, perhaps, to the extent that they further the realization of the rational. Hegel's second line of argument is that institutional defects and imperfections do not count against the claim that the social world is as it ought to be since they are not actual and hence not part of the actuality of the social world. But it is important to note here that in denying the actuality of defects and imperfections, Hegel does not mean to deny that they have causal powers. Hegel clearly recognizes that the defects and imperfections of existing institutions and groups (e.g., particular states and particular families) do have causal powers and indeed are a fundamental source of human suffering. His conception of actuality allows him to claim that institutional defects and imperfections are not actual despite the fact that they have causal powers.

7. I close this discussion of Hegel's basic normative outlook and conclude this chapter by considering the role that his normative outlook assigns to criticism. The first thing to remark is that his normative outlook does not preclude it. We have just observed that, as Hegel understands it, the claim that the modern social world is

as it ought to be is not only compatible with the claim that existing institutions will exhibit defects and imperfections but actually presupposes it. And Hegel's view entails that to the extent that existing institutions fail to live up to their underlying essence, they are subject to criticism. The account of the central arrangements of the modern social world – the family, civil society, and the state – that he lays out in the *Philosophy of Right* purports to specify what this essence is.

Now there are various passages in which Hegel seems to suggest that the only sort of legitimate criticism is that which is directed to relatively superficial features of those institutions. Thus he says, "When understanding turns this 'ought' [i.e., the critical 'ought to be'] against trivial external and transitory objects, against social regulations or conditions, which very likely possess a great relative importance for a certain time and special circles, it may often be right. . . . for who is not acute enough to see a great deal in his own surroundings which is really far from being as it ought to be?" (EL, §6). But this restriction is not supported by Hegel's own general theoretical position, for the claim that the modern social world is as it ought to be is compatible not only with the claim that *trivial and transitory features* of existing states may fail to conform to the essence of the modern state but also with the claim that certain *core features* of existing states fail to conform to the essence of the modern state. Hegel's general view allows the possibility that even those states that do on the whole conform to the essence of the modern state may fail to correspond to this essence in certain nontrivial ways. Thus, for example, while Hegel held that although Prussia did, on the whole, conform to the essence of the modern state, he also recognized that Prussia lacked a constitutional monarchy, and he supported the attempts of Stein and Hardenberg to transform the Prussian monarchy along constitutional lines. Hegel's position is, I think, seen in its best light as allowing criticism not only of trivial and superficial features of existing states but also of those core features of existing states that fail to conform to the essence of the modern state.

There are, however, a number of key respects in which criticism *is* limited in Hegel's view. The first, which flows from his conception of normativity, is that criticism of existing institutions must be 'internal'. Hegel contends that criticism of existing institutions is valid only if it is grounded in norms that are rooted in the essences of the institutions to which it is applied. The general methodological corollary of this position is that in assessing existing institutions, we must look to the ideals they 'aspire' to realize – the ideals they are organized around. Institutions cannot be rationally criticized for failing to live up to our personal 'ideals of the imagination', only for failing to live up to 'ideals of reason' – ideals that are rooted in their own structure. Nor, according to Hegel, can institutions be criticized for failing to conform to 'transcendent' standards, unless those purportedly transcendent standards are actually rooted in the essences of those institutions. Hegel maintains that criticism which is not rooted in the essences of institutions to which it applies is, at best, mere moralizing. Thus, one respect in which Hegel's basic normative outlook limits criticism is that it rules out 'external criticism', criticism that is not based on norms rooted in the essences of the institutions to which it is applied.

There is an important respect in which Hegel's view precludes radical criticism. In his view, the central social institutions of civil society, the modern family, and the state have a kind of 'absolute standing', for he takes these institutions to constitute the practical realization of the correct understanding of the human spirit. He maintains that although one can, in principle, legitimately criticize particular features of particular families, civil societies, and states – including features that may be deeply rooted – one cannot legitimately criticize modern societies for being organized around these institutions. Thus Hegel would, for example, oppose feminist proposals for the elimination of the family, Marxist proposals for the elimination of private ownership of the means of production, and anarchist proposals for the elimination of the state.

Moreover, Hegel also holds that there are important limits on the respects in which existing families, civil societies, and states can be legitimately criticized. Although existing families can be criticized for failing to live up to the essence of the family, existing forms of civil society can be criticized for failing to live up to the essence of civil society, and existing states can be criticized for failing to live up to the essence of the state, the underlying rational structure of the family, civil society, and state (the features described in the *Philosophy of Right*) cannot themselves be criticized. What this means, practically speaking, is that in the modern social world legitimate criticism will inevitably be reformist. For Hegel, legitimate social change in the modern social world will always be a matter of bringing existing arrangements into line with the essences of the family, civil society, and state, rather than transforming the essential underlying structures of these arrangements. Although this conception of the limits of criticism *is* clearly grounded in Hegel's general commitment to the principle of internal criticism, it also grounded in his view that the essence of the modern social world represents the correct understanding of the human spirit. Returning to the language of the *Doppelsatz,* we could say that, for Hegel, criticism of the modern social world must be reformist both because the rational is actual (because the essence of the modern social world provides the sole valid source of institutional criticism) and because the actual is rational (because the more advanced European states correspond on the whole to the essence of the modern social world).

Finally, Hegel maintains that the activity of criticism is of secondary importance. This is not to say that Hegel maintains that criticism is of secondary importance to philosophy. As we have seen, Hegel does not regard criticism as belonging to the business of philosophy at all. The task of philosophy is to "comprehend what is," where "what is" is understood as what is actual. The only context in which Hegel regards criticism as being appropriate is practical – the context of relating to the social world – and it is in this context that he holds that the importance of criticism is secondary. Hegel maintains that the *central* task in relating to the social world is to grasp its rationality and to act on the basis of one's understanding. This is why he says that "such instruction as [the *Philosophy of Right*] may contain cannot be aimed at instructing the state on how it ought to be, but rather at showing how the state, as the ethical universe, *should be recognized*" (PR, ¶13; my emphasis). The point here is not that one ought not to criticize existing arrangements, but rather that doing so is less important than coming to understand what the underlying rational structure of the modern social world is and how it is manifested in its existing arrangements. Hegel assigns primary practical importance to 'comprehending what is' because he believes that comprehension of the actuality of the modern social world can help individuals (i) find satisfaction in their participation in the family, civil society, and state; (ii) fulfill their ethical duties (which he maintains flow out of the rational structure of these institutions); (iii) realize themselves as spiritual beings; and (iv) attain reconciliation.

Hegel regards criticism as of secondary importance, first, because he holds that the 'more advanced' European states, which are those states with which he is primarily concerned, conform on the whole to the essence of the modern social world. Although he recognizes that these states do stand in need of criticism and reform, he maintains that the fact that they do conform on the whole to the essence of the modern social world is the basic fact about them – the fact that is of the greatest practical importance. At the level of concrete political activity, Hegel is far more concerned about the consequences of people failing to recognize the positive features of their social world than he is about the consequences of their failure to recognize its defects. And, as we have seen, he thinks that the defects of the social world will be evident enough and that the difficult thing is to 'grasp the affirmative'.

Second, Hegel does not regard the critical examination of society by individuals as a fundamental mechanism of social change. He was far more likely to place his confidence in change from within the system, promoted by progressive governmental ministers and civil servants, than change brought about by intellectual critics outside the system. And so Hegel would not be inclined to promote the sort of social changes he thought necessary by emphasizing the importance of criticism.

Third, Hegel has grave doubts concerning the possibility of philosophically informed criticism. The point of his famous dictum that "when philosophy paints its grey in grey, a shape of life has grown old" (PR, ¶16) is that providing a philosophical account of a social world's underlying rational structure only becomes possible when that social world has completed its process of development and faces historical decline. This is why Hegel says, concerning "the subject of *issuing instructions* on how the world ought to be," that "philosophy, at any rate, always comes too late to perform this function. As the *thought* of the world, it appears only when actuality has gone through its formative process and attained its completed state" (PR, ¶16). Although it is clear that these remarks are meant to show that philosophy can never be in a position to provide guidance concerning fundamental social change, it is not so clear that they are supposed to indicate that philosophy can never be in a position to support reformist political change. Nonetheless, they obviously convey a general outlook that would not lead one to emphasize criticism.

The idea that criticism is of secondary importance to comprehension is deeply rooted in Hegel's thought. But it is perhaps worth pointing out that it is possible to accept this ordering and still emphasize criticism to a greater extent than Hegel does. One might believe that the basic fact about one's social world was that it conformed to the essence of the social world on the whole *and still* be committed to criticism and reform. Criticism of existing institutions can be the expression of a deep commitment to and confidence in the underlying rational structure of one's social world. One can engage in criticism in order to promote the process through which "the rational becomes actual" and "the actual becomes rational" in one's society. Such criticism can provide a way of combining appreciation of the affirmative aspects of one's social world with recognition of its defects. Criticism of this sort *can* be emphasized within a Hegelian framework.

3

THE CONCEPT OF RECONCILIATION

Reconciliation is the basic concept of Hegel's project. My purpose in this chapter is to provide a preliminary account of what this concept is. The chapter consists of six sections. Section I discusses the ordinary concept of reconciliation and compares the English word 'reconciliation' with *Versöhnung*, the German word it represents. Section II explores the attitude of reconciliation. In section III, the role that conflict plays within reconciliation is explored. Hegel's philosophical concept of reconciliation is the topic of section IV. Section V provides a characterization of alienation, the polar opposite of reconciliation. The relation between reconciliation, revolution, criticism, and reform is briefly discussed in the sixth section.

For reasons to be discussed, Hegel himself never made the concept of reconciliation the topic of extended independent discussion. The account this chapter provides represents an abstraction from his general theory of reconciliation. More specifically, it represents an abstraction from Hegel's conception of the relationship between individuality and social membership, the subject of Chapter 5, and from his account of the structure of the modern social world, the subject of Chapter 6. As such, the account of the concept of reconciliation presented here cannot be completely self-standing. This chapter is meant to provide access to the concept of reconciliation and not to provide the foundation of the theory.

I. 'Reconciliation' and 'Versöhnung'

The word 'reconciliation', as it is ordinarily used, is systematically ambiguous as between the *process* of reconciliation and the *state* that is its result. The process may be variously described as a process of overcoming conflict, division, enmity, alienation, or estrangement; the result, as the restoration of harmony, unity, peace, friendship, or love. The concept of reconciliation contains within it something like a story: two parties begin as friends, become estranged, and become friends again. The basic pattern is thus one of unity, division, and reunification. This pattern is exemplified by the Christian teaching (which provides the religious background of Hegel's conception of reconciliation) that Christ reconciles man to God. According to this doctrine, man had, through sinfulness, become estranged from God. But then Christ overcame God's enmity by sacrificing his life on the cross and thereby restored the state of harmony between God and man.[1]

'Reconciliation' is the English word I am using to represent the German word Hegel uses, namely, *Versöhnung*; it is also the standard translation of the term. But since the English differs from the German in a number of respects, we need to be aware of what these differences are.[2] One minor difference is that whereas 'reconciliation' is a fairly neutral and commonly used word, the word *Versöhnung* is loaded and much less frequently used. German is more inclined to use the expression *sich (wieder) vertragen* to speak of reconciliation in a neutral way.

Also, in contrast to 'reconciliation', *Versöhnung* strongly connotes a process of transformation. When two parties become genuinely *versöhnt*, they do not resume their old relationship unchanged. They become *versöhnt* by changing their behavior and attitudes in fundamental ways. Parties who have attained *Versöhnung* do not have to decide to get along together; their getting along together is, instead, the natural result of their being in a new, transformed state. The unity of their new relationship may be described as 'higher' in the sense of being more flexible, complex, and stable than the unity that preceded it. Although the word 'reconciliation' does not deny that a transformative process of this sort takes place, it does not convey *Versöhnung*'s positive suggestion that it *does* take place.

---

1 See *The New Catholic Encyclopedia*, s.v. "reconciliation."
2 I am indebted to Gisela Striker for discussion of these matters.

Unlike 'reconciliation', *Versöhnung* tends to sound churchy. Grimm's *Deutsches Wörterbuch* tells us that Luther used *versöhnen* "unusually often" in his translation of the Bible.[3] The root of *Versöhnung* is *Sühne*, which means 'expiation' and 'atonement'. The notion of *Sühne* figures centrally in the Christian story of *Versöhnung*, according to which man's separation from God was brought about by human sin and overcome through an act of expiation and atonement on the part of Christ. Although the semantic connection between *Sühne* and *Versöhnung* is generally considered obsolete, the connection still colors the ordinary use of the latter word. Even today one can hear echoes of *Sühne* in *Versöhnung*. *Versöhnung* is not, however, related to *Sohn* (son). There is no etymological connection between the Christian doctrine that God's son (*Sohn*) is the reconciler (*Versöhner*) and the composition of the word *Versöhnung*. Nor is there any etymological connection between *Sühne* (whose Middle High German forms include *süene* and *suone*) and *Sohn*.[4]

The main difference between the English and the German words is that, in its ordinary use, the English 'reconciliation' can mean *submission* or *resignation*. This may suggest that the real aim of Hegel's project is surrender and acquiescence – something that would, of course, be objectionable.[5] If reconciliation is a matter of submitting to the powers-that-be or resigning oneself to the status quo, who wants it? Better to be alienated than to submit or resign. But in fact the features of 'reconciliation' that give this impression are not shared by *Versöhnung*. As we saw in Chapter 1, *Versöhnung* simply does not mean 'submission'. Nor does it mean 'resignation'. One can become *reconciled* to a circumstance that is completely contrary to one's wishes, but one cannot (grammatically) become *versöhnt* to it. German does have a word for this sense of 'recon-

---

3 *Deutsches Wörterbuch*, s.v. "versöhnen."
4 Ibid., s.v. "Sühne."
5 The negative tone of 'reconciliation' is especially clear when the verb is used with the preposition 'to', a usage that suggests that the process of reconciliation is asymmetrical and that the object of reconciliation is a state of affairs that is viewed in a negative light. One becomes reconciled *to* the loss of a child. The use of the preposition 'with', on the other hand, suggests that the process is symmetrical and that the object of reconciliation is a person who is viewed in a positive light. I become reconciled *with* my friend. Nonetheless, I propose to use (the negative sounding) 'reconciliation to' to render (the more positive) *Versöhnung mit*. I will speak of people as becoming reconciled *to* the social world *without* meaning to suggest either surrender or resignation. I adopt this nonstandard and possibly misleading usage because it sounds much more natural to speak of people as becoming reconciled *to* the social world than of their becoming reconciled *with* the social world.

ciliation' – reconciliation as resignation – but it is *abfinden*, not *versöhnen*. Think of it this way: if *Versöhnung* is possible, resignation is unnecessary.

So *Versöhnung* is different from resignation. To be *versöhnt* to the social world is to view it in a positive light. *Versöhnung* involves something like complete and wholehearted acceptance. In contrast to 'resignation', *Versöhnung* contains a very strong element of affirmation. Thus Hegel speaks of "*das versöhnende Ja*" (the reconciling yea; PhG, 494/409). One is *versöhnt* only when one is in a position to say yes to one's situation, and one becomes *versöhnt*, in part, by saying yes to it. Indeed in some respects, Hegel's use of the term *Versöhnung* may be even more positive than its ordinary use, since for him *Versöhnung* is more than a matter of acceptance, even full acceptance: to be *versöhnt* to something is to *embrace* it. There is nothing, then, in the word *Versöhnung* that suggests that Hegel's project is invidiously conservative or that its aim is surrender or acquiescence. It is crucial that we remember that the English word 'reconciliation' carries baggage the German word does not.

II. The attitude of reconciliation

Let us consider more closely what sort of attitude reconciliation – now understood as *Versöhnung* – is. We have just seen that the crucial contrast between 'reconciliation' and 'resignation' is that the former essentially involves an element of affirmation. This contrast also distinguishes reconciliation from the attitude that might be called 'pure acceptance'. By 'pure acceptance' is meant an outlook in which one accepts things as they are without judging or evaluating them. This attitude is encouraged by certain forms of Stoicism that maintain that the crucial thing is simply to register how things are and act in accordance with the realities of the situation. If the situation contains elements that are painful, those elements are simply accepted as a part of the situation without evaluation.

Reconciliation is also to be contrasted with consolation (*Trost*).[6] The two words are, it is true, very close in meaning. Indeed, if we

6 Freud might usefully be thought of as a resignation–consolation theorist. In *Civilization and Its Discontents*, he attempts to persuade people to *resign* themselves to the discontents that inevitably result from the conflict between the instincts and the demands of society and to find *consolation* in sublimation. He argues, in effect, that this conflict generates a split between people and the social world that makes anything that could be properly called reconciliation impossible. See Freud 1930.

speak loosely, we may use them interchangeably. Consolation, like reconciliation, is a response to a prior disappointment, and like reconciliation, involves a form of acceptance. Nonetheless, the two attitudes are distinct. Consolation is fundamentally a matter of providing relief, comfort, or solace for some loss or pain. One's spouse dies, but one takes consolation in the continuing existence of one's children. Their existence does not negate the loss, but it does provide comfort and solace. If, however, one is truly reconciled – reconciled in the sense of *versöhnt* – one has no need for consolation, because one has fully accepted the situation. One regards it as necessary and good.

Let us consider two slightly different forms that consolation can take. The first essentially involves substitution (VG, 78/67). The world generates the need for this type of consolation when it fails to live up to a deeply rooted expectation. One becomes consoled by finding a partial substitution for one's loss. But the fact that one needs consolation shows that one has not fully accepted the situation: one regards it, instead, as a "misfortune which ought never to have happened in the first place" (VG, 78/67). The notion of a 'consolation prize' (*Trostpreis*) reflects this idea. One receives a consolation prize when one loses; it provides comfort because it offers a substitute for what one really wanted, namely, to win.

The second form consolation can take essentially involves compensation (EL, §147Z). The need for this form of consolation may arise when the present situation is one of misery, pain, and suffering. One becomes consoled by the prospect of future compensation. Thus, for example, medieval Christianity sought to provide consolation for what it regarded as the inherent misery of life in this world by promising satisfaction and fulfillment in the hereafter. The Christian renounces his or her aims and interests (concerning this life) in the hope of receiving a reward in the next life. Christianity's emphasis on consolation led Hegel to call it "the religion of consolation" (EL, §147Z). One might suggest that Christians who found consolation through compensation genuinely *accepted* their situation and argue that this blurs the distinction between reconciliation and consolation. But the thing to note here is that the sense in which they accepted their situation is a very special and limited one: they accepted life as a stage leading to future satisfaction – satisfaction in some 'beyond' (*Jenseits*). Reconciliation, on the other hand, crucially involves accepting the present in its own right, not merely as a stage to something else. To be reconciled is to find satisfaction in the present. (See PR, ¶¶7, 14.) Hegel says, "Philosophy is . . . not consolation; it is more; it reconciles" (VG, 78/67; my translation).

There is a form of reconciliation that closely resembles consolation (or even resignation). Becoming reconciled can in some circumstances turn essentially on abandoning certain antecedently held expectations. If one is prevented from accepting a situation that (as a matter of fact) is genuinely good solely by the unreasonableness of one's expectations (e.g., the expectation that the world will respond favorably to one's each and every idiosyncrasy), then abandoning those expectations will be the *sine qua non* of reconciliation. This form of reconciliation may look like consolation since the situation one becomes reconciled to is contrary to one's original wish. But consolation involves essentially coming to terms with the failure of satisfaction of expectations that one *still* regards as reasonable (i.e., even after one has found consolation). Attaining reconciliation, on the other hand, turns on freeing oneself of expectations that one has justifiably come to regard as unreasonable. People who seek consolation regard the nonsatisfaction of their expectations as a genuine loss for which some kind of replacement or compensation is due. People who attain reconciliation come to see that the fact that their unreasonable expectations were not fulfilled does not constitute a real loss at all. It should be pointed out, however, that this form of reconciliation is not simply the result of recognizing the irrationality of one's original expectations alone. It is not a form of adaptive preference formation, or adaptive preference change.[7] Rather we are supposing that the situation one becomes reconciled to is genuinely good. The role that recognizing the irrationality of one's original expectations plays in this form of reconciliation is that of making it possible to grasp the goodness of one's situation, which in turn brings about a state of reconciliation.

Reconciliation is not a matter of thinking that everything is wonderful. Hegel's celebrated rich and suggestive claim that reconciliation consists in recognizing "reason as the rose in the cross of the present" (PR, ¶14) illustrates this point. The image of the cross of the present is a metaphor for the suffering and wickedness that are an inevitable part of human life, the problematic features of human

---

7 The terms 'adaptive preference formation' and 'adaptive preference change' were coined by Elster (1983, 110).

social life, and alienation. Its importance for Hegel's conception of reconciliation can hardly be overemphasized. As we have seen, Hegel maintains that it is possible *both* to be genuinely reconciled *and* to recognize (i) that the fundamental features of the modern social world include divorce, poverty, and war, and (ii) that particular families, civil societies, and states will inevitably exhibit defects and imperfections. "The state is not a work of art," Hegel tells us, "it exists in the world, and hence in the sphere of arbitrariness [*Willkür*], contingency [*Zufalls*], and error [*Irrtums*]" (PR, §258Z; VPRG, 633). Reconciliation, as Hegel understands it, is thus compatible with recognizing that the social world exhibits features that are genuinely problematic.

Indeed, to say that Hegel thinks that becoming reconciled is *compatible* with recognizing that the social world contains problems is at best an understatement, for he thinks that recognizing and accepting this fact is integral to the process of reconciliation. One cannot become genuinely reconciled by putting on rose-colored glasses; reconciliation is instead a matter of accepting the social world *as* a world that contains problems. Hegel would insist one cannot recognize "reason as the rose *in* the cross of the present" (one cannot grasp the rationality of the modern social world) without also seeing the *cross* in which the rose is placed. And although finding reason as the rose in the cross of the present is supposed to make it possible to "delight in the present" (PR, ¶14), the cross of the present, together with its attendant pain, remains. In Hegel's view, the delight that is internal to reconciliation must coexist with full appreciation of the suffering for which the cross stands. Consequently, reconciliation, as Hegel understands it, will inevitably be shadowed by a mood or feeling that could be characterized as melancholy.[8]

This response is not, however, to be confused with resignation. Hegel does not maintain that the basic situation is *defined* by the cross of the present (that it is exclusively, fundamentally, or primarily a situation of pain or alienation), a circumstance that *would* call for resignation. He maintains, on the contrary, that it is possible to find reason as the rose in the cross of the present (to see that the modern social world is fundamentally rational) and, as a result, to delight in the present. And he holds that because *this* is possible, it is

---

8 I indebted to Victor Gourevitch for reminding me of the importance of this side of Hegel's conception of reconciliation.

also possible to fully accept the basic situation: a situation in which metaphorically the present *is* the cross, but the cross *contains* the rose of reason.

One might think that the continuing presence of melancholy means that what Hegel calls reconciliation is not reconciliation at all. But this reaction turns on the mistake of thinking that reconciliation can contain no component of negativity, that it must be free of any admixture of sadness. Reconciliation is not, however, the transformation of the negative into something joyous. What Hegel is characterizing as reconciliation *is* a form of reconciliation. So long as we insist on asking, Is reconciliation really positive (in the sense of being wholly and unadmixedly positive) or is it essentially negative? we will not be in a position to understand what the attitude of reconciliation is. Although reconciliation *is* a positive attitude – a genuinely positive attitude – it is a positive attitude that contains within it a moment of negativity.

Hegel's recognition that reconciliation includes a moment of negativity is part of what makes his conception attractive, for it provides one possible answer to the question, How can full acceptance of the world be combined with clear-eyed recognition of its defects? Hegel answers that they can be combined *if* full acceptance is accompanied by a sense of melancholy. Melancholy represents a way of registering the clear-eyed recognition of the defects of the world that is compatible with full acceptance. Obviously, the idea here is not that one first accepts the world and then cultivates a sense of melancholy as a way of addressing the problems posed by its defects. The thought is rather that the sense of melancholy is an integral component of one's acceptance of the world: a human response to the recognition of imperfection, wickedness, and suffering.

Of course, it might be argued that a sense of melancholy cannot be combined with full acceptance. The two are simply incompatible. If acceptance is complete, there is no room for melancholy; if any sense of melancholy remains, the acceptance is not full. But this seems wrong. The sort of attitude Hegel has in mind is not debilitating depression; it is instead compatible with full and even enthusiastic participation in the arrangements of social life. It is also compatible with taking delight in the present. Acceptance, delight, and melancholy can all coexist in one mind. Although extremely complex, the psychological state of reconciliation is coherent.

Clearly, Hegel's conception of reconciliation requires something like a balancing act. When the objective conditions warrant the attitude of reconciliation, there will be a natural tendency to slide into resignation (as one attends to the problematic features of the social world) or joyous affirmation (as one attends to the social world's positive features). No one would suggest that maintaining the synthesis of affirmation and realism internal to reconciliation will be easy. But it is one thing to say that the attitude of reconciliation is difficult to maintain and another to say that it is impossible. I believe that the considerations Hegel brings forth support the thesis that the attitude of reconciliation can in principle be maintained. Reconciliation is a possible attitude toward the social world.

Much of the interest in Hegel's theory consists in his attempt to show that there could be a world that is worthy of reconciliation and to show that the modern social world is in fact such a world, but it would be a mistake to think that the interest of his theory consists *solely* in this. In providing an account of the *attitude* of reconciliation, Hegel provides an account of something that is philosophically interesting in its own right.

III. Reconciliation and conflict

We have seen that reconciliation, as ordinarily understood, is among other things, a process of overcoming conflicts. This is certainly true of Hegel's understanding of reconciliation as well. But it is important to see that Hegel does not conceive of reconciliation as a state of 'perfect harmony', a circumstance in which no conflicts whatsoever remain.

We might first observe that, even as ordinarily understood, reconciliation need not be a state of perfect harmony. The process through which two individuals become reconciled may involve their coming to recognize that conflict can be a part of a healthy relationship and coming to accept their conflicts as a healthy part of their relationship. In a similar vein, Hegel maintains that conflict is an integral component of reconciliation with the social world. He contends that people will inevitably come into conflict with the modern social world, even if it is well ordered and even if they are reconciled (PR, §§149, 150R). More precisely, they will experience conflicts between the separate and particular interests they have as individuals and the obligations they have as family members, members of civil society, and citizens. There will be times when parents will not want to stay at home with their children, when workers will not feel like going to work, and when citizens will have no desire to pay their taxes.

That such conflicts will occur is no accident. Hegel argues that, in a well-ordered modern social world, people will be raised to have separate and particular interests, some of which will inevitably come into conflict with the demands of their social roles (PR, §§189–208; VPRHO, 488). He also allows that the obligations people have, say, as family members will occasionally come into conflict with the obligations they have, say, as members of civil society: sometimes the demands of work and family will collide. A well-ordered social world is a world that will generate conflicts.

In Hegel's view, being reconciled essentially involves accepting – indeed, embracing – these tensions. His social theory is supposed to show us that the ongoing tensions between our separate and particular interests and the demands of the social world are a necessary by-product of our individuality. We are also supposed to see that the conflicts between the demands of the family, civil society, and state are necessary by-products of the social differentiation required for the complete unfolding of the human spirit. Human beings need separate institutional spheres in which they can find intimacy, actualize their individuality, and enjoy political community. But conflict is the price of differentiation. Thus conflict and antagonism are internal to Hegel's conception of reconciliation.

They are not, however, final. What is crucial, Hegel maintains, is that there be no *fundamental* conflicts between the interests people have as individuals and the demands of the family, civil society, and state (PR, §§147, 151). Hegel takes this fundamental unity to be a hallmark of a well-ordered modern social world. In such a world, people will be raised to identify with the roles of family member, member of civil society, and citizen (PR, §§187, R; VPRHN, 125). And they will be taught to embrace the norms internal to these roles and regard them as the "substantial" (*substantiell*) component of their self-conception and take the good of their family, civil society, and state to constitute the "substantial" component of their own individual good (EG, §515; PR, §145Z; VPRHO, 484). At the same time, in a well-ordered social world, the family, civil society, and state will function so as to promote and foster the individuality of its members and provide them with both intimacy and political community (PR, §260; VA, 1:136/1:98). Hence it will be *reasonable* for its members to embrace the norms internal to its institutions and to regard the good of its institutions as part of their own good. Also, the demands of the family, civil society, and state in a well-ordered modern society will be organized in such a way that no tragic conflicts between them can occur (PR, §150R): no members of a well-ordered modern social world will face the predicament of Antigone and Creon (see PhG, 327–42/266–78). Moreover, the demands of a well-ordered modern social world will be sufficiently well integrated as to allow its members to lead coherent and nonfragmented lives. The members of such a world will be free of the painful personal and psychological division Schiller took to be characteristic of modernity.[9] If they *do* experience division of this kind, it will be possible for them to overcome it through a process of philosophical reflection.

Hegel's conception of reconciliation is thus one that understands itself as preserving conflict at one level and overcoming it at another. Both elements are attractive. The fact that it seeks to preserve conflict is attractive because the idea of a perfect harmony is both utopian and dangerous: utopian because unrealizable, dangerous because invidiously anti-individualistic. The fact that Hegel is willing to embrace conflict makes his thought quite appealing. He is far too often placed in the camp of the enemies of conflict.[10] In fact, Hegel, in contrast, say, to Marx, is one of the great friends of conflict.[11] Nonetheless, Hegel's attitude toward conflict is not Nietzschean. He does not regard the existence of conflict as something to be celebrated in its own right. It is important that Hegel argues that, at the most fundamental level, conflicts are overcome because, in so doing, he secures the status of his conception as a conception of reconciliation. Furthermore, unfashionable though it may be, the idea that there might be a conflict-embracing form of unity is actually quite appealing (VA, 1:82/1:55). The search for a conflict-embracing higher unity may turn out to be in vain, but it is far from obvious that a form of unity of this sort is an unreasonable thing to look for. Let us turn now to Hegel's philosophical concept of reconciliation.

9 Schiller 1801.   10 Cf. Nussbaum 1986, 51–84; Williams 1981, 72.

11 Marx did, it is true, think of class conflict as a fundamental motor of human history and to that extent affirmed conflict. But the world the revolution was to bring about was to be essentially free of conflict. The point I have just been urging is that, according to Hegel, the social world at which world history 'aimed' – the modern social world – was a world that included conflict.

IV. The philosophical concept of reconciliation

'Reconciliation' in Hegel's technical sense of the term refers to both a *process* (VA, 1:81/1:55) and a *state*. The process is that of *overcoming alienation* from the social world, and the state, that of *being at home in the social world*, which is its result. Hegel says, for example, that reconciliation is "the movement that makes estrangement [*Entfremdung*] disappear" (VPRJ, 5:107/3:172), and he characterizes the final stage of *Geist*'s reconciliation as that in which it "is reconciled with itself in the object [*in dem Gegenstand versöhnt bei sich selbst*]" (VPRJ, 3:85/1:177). Being at home in the social world (*Beisichsein, Zuhausesein*), then, is the linchpin of Hegel's theory.[12] It is the concept out of which the concepts of both reconciliation and alienation are constructed.

The idea that reconciliation, understood as being at home in the social world, provides the answer to alienation is quite intuitive. The feeling of alienation can be understood as the feeling of being 'split' from the world, of not fitting in there; it is the feeling of not being at home in the social world. Contained within this feeling is a wish: the wish to be at home in the social world. And contained within *this* wish is another wish: the wish that the social world be a home. We might say that the ideal of reconciliation is contained within the felt experience of alienation.

My discussion in this section has two parts. I first examine the idea of what it is to be at home in the social world and then consider what it is for the social world to be a home.

1. According to Hegel, people – modern people, anyway – are fully at home in the social world if and only if

 (i) the social world is a home,
 (ii) they grasp that the social world is a home,
 (iii) they feel at home in the social world, and
 (iv) they accept and affirm the social world.

Being at home in the social world (and hence reconciliation) is both an objective *and* a subjective matter. It is not wholly subjective, since there is an objective condition the social world must meet – that of being a home – if people are to be at home there.[13] There is more

---

12 I discuss Hegel's use of *Beisichsein* to refer to freedom in section 2c below.

13 This point is worth emphasizing because many people, Marx being the most famous, have maintained that for Hegel reconciliation is purely subjective. The

to being at home in the social world than holding a certain attitude, or even than holding a certain *warranted* attitude. It is, among other things, a matter of standing in a particular *objective structural relation*: that of being in a social world that is in fact a home. But being at home in the social world is not wholly objective either, since there is a set of subjective conditions (conditions ii through iv) that people must satisfy in order to be at home.

Let us look more closely at what these subjective conditions come to. By 'grasping that the social world is a home' is meant coming to know or truly believe that the social world is a home. Presumably, it is possible to grasp this fact at different levels. Thus, the ordinary person might grasp this fact at the level of ordinary consciousness and the intellectual might grasp it in a philosophically adequate way (cf. PR, §147R) and both can be at home (PR, ¶¶7, 14). 'Feeling at home' in the social world is a matter of feeling connected to its central arrangements. It involves feeling that one 'fits into' the social world and feeling that one 'belongs there'. By 'accepting the social world' is meant accepting that the social world is arranged as it is, not denying that its central arrangements are as they are, not fixing one's thoughts on other ways in which it might ideally be arranged or dwelling on its shortcomings. 'Affirmation' is stronger and more positive than 'acceptance'. In 'affirming the social world' I consent to its central arrangements. 'To affirm the social world' is to say yes to it and the way it is arranged. 'Affirmation' also involves endorsing and embracing the social world's central institutions.

We can see from this that the process of coming to be at home – and hence the subjective process of attaining reconciliation – is a matter of *subjective appropriation*.[14] It is by grasping that the modern social world is a home and then coming to feel at home there and accepting and affirming these arrangements that people become reconciled to the modern social world.

basic mistake people make in thinking about the idea of being at home in the social world is that of conflating it with the idea of *feeling* at home in the social world; the basic mistake people make in thinking about reconciliation is that of conflating it with the idea of *feeling* reconciled to the social world.

14 In this respect, Hegel's philosophical concept of reconciliation is analogous to the traditional Christian conception, according to which human beings have been objectively reconciled to God through Christ but must, nonetheless, subjectively appropriate Christ's deed through a personal act of reconciliation. (See VPRJ, 3:249–50/1:349–50; and the *New Catholic Encyclopedia*, s.v. "reconciliation.")

In order fully to understand Hegel's conception of being at home in the social world, we need to understand what it is for the social world to be a home. But before turning to this topic, I would like to ward off a number of possible misunderstandings. Hegel's philosophical account of reconciliation as being at home in the social world is intended neither as an *analysis* of the ordinary concept nor as a *stipulative proposal*. Hegel thinks of his account as capturing the "speculative content" of the ordinary term. In his view, the ordinary word *Versöhnung* contains within it the roots of the correct philosophical conception of reconciliation. The development of this implicit philosophical content, like the development of the philosophical content of other philosophically rich ordinary words (such as *Wirklichkeit*), involves extending the notion beyond its ordinary use and transforming it in various ways, but never wholly abandoning its original sense. This reflects Hegel's general view that "ordinary consciousness" represents a fundamentally sound but blurred understanding of an underlying truth, and that philosophy has the task of giving this understanding clear conceptual formulation. Now, since Hegel's account is meant to capture the speculative content of an *ordinary word*, it is not to be understood as a *revision* of our present conceptual scheme, that is, of the standard use of this term. Nor is it simply stipulation. On the other hand, since his account is supposed to capture the *speculative content* of the ordinary word, it cannot be understood as descriptive analysis either. Thus Hegel's account of reconciliation blurs the familiar distinction between *descriptive analysis* and *conceptual revision*.[15] To insist on forcing Hegel's approach into either of these two categories will only produce confusion.

One might attempt to relate Hegel's philosophical concept of reconciliation and the ordinary concept by appealing to another familiar philosophical distinction: that between *concept* and *conception*.[16] This distinction can be illustrated by saying that the concept of justice is defined (very roughly) as the appropriate terms of sharing the benefits and burdens of social cooperation and interactions, whereas different conceptions of justice might consist in various specifications of what the appropriate terms are. People who share the same concept of justice might disagree about what the appropriate conception of justice is. Some might hold a Rawlsian con-

15 See Strawson 1959, 9–11.   16 See Rawls 1971, 5.

ception of justice, others a libertarian conception, and still others a utilitarian conception. Accordingly, one might suggest that Hegel employs the ordinary *concept* of reconciliation and try to explain the differences between his talk of reconciliation and our ordinary understanding of reconciliation by suggesting that he is offering a novel *conception* of reconciliation. But this suggestion fails. Hegel's understanding of reconciliation as being at home in the social world is simply too far removed from the ordinary concept for this proposal to be plausible. More important, Hegel himself rejects the possibility of drawing any interesting distinction between his concept and his conception of reconciliation. This reflects his general rejection of any sharp distinction between concepts and theories, which is part of his radical holism. Indeed, largely because he rejects the concept-theory distinction, Hegel provides no extended independent account of the concept of reconciliation.[17]

My point here is not to deny that it might be possible to represent Hegel's view and the ordinary view as different conceptions of the same abstract concept. Nor is it to say that there is nothing to be gained by using the concept/conception distinction in thinking about Hegel. If nothing else, this distinction makes it possible to say clearly that for Hegel there is no sharp or interesting distinction between the philosophical concept and the philosophical conception of reconciliation. I simply want to say that insisting on accounting for the relation between Hegel's philosophical concept and the ordinary concept in terms of the concept–conception relation will result in confusion.

Fortunately, for our purposes it is not necessary to establish the relation between Hegel's concept of reconciliation and the ordinary concept in any precise way. And so rather than trying to provide a precise philosophical specification of their relation, I propose to sidestep the issue. Accordingly, I will remain agnostic about the relation between Hegel's philosophical concept of reconciliation

17 It may be worth pointing out that proponents of the concept–conception distinction need not be committed to the view that the distinction is terribly sharp. What is interesting about this point is that to the extent that they take this line, they move in Hegel's direction: in the direction of concept–theory holism. And once we recognize that one can speak of concepts in this more flexible manner, that is, use the notion of concept in such a way that there is no sharp distinction between concepts and conceptions, then it becomes clear that we can speak of Hegel's 'concept' of reconciliation without violating the core features of his methodological outlook, for in speaking of his concept of reconciliation we are not speaking of something that is supposed to be sharply distinguished from his conception, or theory, of reconciliation.

and the ordinary concept. I propose to treat Hegel's philosophical concept of reconciliation as being closely related to but different from the ordinary concept – without, however, taking a philosophical stand on this point.

2. Hegel's conception of what it is for the social world to be a home contains a number of different strands. These strands include the idea that the social world is a home if it is not 'other than' its members; that it is a home if it is good; and that it is a home if it constitutes a world of freedom. Each of these strands plays an important role in Hegel's thinking about reconciliation, and they are given different emphases in different places. But there is also another strand in this conception: the social world is a home if and only if it makes it possible for people to actualize themselves as individuals and as social members. It is on this strand that I will focus.

My discussion in this section has three parts. The first part lays out what it means to say that the social world makes it possible for people to actualize themselves as individuals and social members. The second examines the relation between this idea and the other strands of Hegel's conception of what it is for the social world to be a home. In the third part, the significance of the social world's being a home is discussed.

i. Two brief preliminary remarks are relevant here. First, I have said that Hegel maintains that the social world is a home if and only if it makes it possible for people to actualize themselves as individuals and as members of society. It would be somewhat more precise to say that he maintains this for *modern* people or that the *modern* social world is a home, if it meets this condition. Hegel does not believe that the ancient social world had to make the actualization of individuality possible in order to be a home. As we shall see in Chapter 5, Hegel contends that people in the ancient world were not individuals, in the relevant sense of the term, and so did not need a social world that allowed for the actualization of individuality. But as Hegel's views concerning the ancient world are not of central relevance to us here, I will not belabor the point. Let me simply stress that this chapter will concentrate on the relation between *modern* people and the *modern* social world. Second, although we will eventually need a clear and systematic understanding of what Hegel means by 'individuality' and 'social membership', I do not want to try to define these terms here; at this point in the discussion I will simply clarify the way in which I am using the terms as I go along. A more precise specification of these terms will be provided in Chapter 5.

Let us turn to the idea that the modern social world must make it possible for people to actualize themselves as individuals and social members. The basic intuition behind this idea is that people – modern people – are both individuals *and* social members, and indeed are in some sense 'essentially' both. The corollary of this point is that a modern social world in which it is not possible to actualize oneself either as an individual or as a social member would be a *world of alienation.*

Consider, for example, the social world Plato describes in the *Republic.* Hegel thinks that it provides an instance of a world of alienation of one particular kind: a social world that is alienating (or that would, in any case, be alienating for modern people) because it does not allow for the actualization of individuality. As Hegel represents him, Plato sought to exclude from his state private property, the family, and the free choice of a career. Hegel argues that these institutions or institutional features are all essential to the actualization of individuality (PR, §185R). Let us consider why.

First of all, Hegel contends that private property is essential to the actualization of individuality at both an abstract and a concrete level. At an abstract level, it is through the possession of property that one actualizes oneself as a bearer of individual rights (PR, §45; VGP, 2:126/2:111). In order to actualize oneself as a bearer of rights one must be recognized by others as a bearer of rights (PR, §71, R). The paradigmatic way in which others recognize one as a bearer of rights is by recognizing those external things that are one's property *as* one's property (i.e., an external embodiment of one's will) (PR, §71, R). At a more concrete level, the possession of property is a necessary precondition of the development and pursuit of separate and particular interests (PR, §189). In order to realize one's separate and particular interests, one must have the financial resources to do so. Moreover, the realization of one's separate and particular interests will typically involve the acquisition of property, both as means for the pursuit of these ends (the various commodities one needs to pursue one's interests) and as separate and particular interests in themselves (the commodities one wants for their own sake).

Hegel also contends that if people are to actualize themselves as individuals, they must be able to marry and form families (VGP, 2:126/2:112). If property is essential to the external actualization of individuality, marriage and the family are essential to the realization of its internal, subjective aspects. People must be able to marry if they are to have an institutional setting within which they can realize the ideal of romantic love, which Hegel regards as a crucial component of what he calls "the right of the subject's particularity to find satisfaction" and "the right of subjective freedom." They must also be able to marry (and form families) if they are to have an institutional setting within which they can find love and acceptance (a kind of recognition) as the particular persons they are, a condition that Hegel claims must be satisfied if people are to fully actualize themselves as individuals. In Hegel's view, the family provides the only institutional sphere within which one finds emotional acceptance of one's particularity (PR, §158).

Finally, Hegel argues that the free choice of social position (*Stand*) is a third necessary condition of the realization of individuality (VGP, 2:123/2:109–10). It is precisely by choosing one's social position (i.e., pursuing a freely chosen career or occupation) that one realizes one's own separate and particular interests. The upshot of all this is that, in excluding private property, the family, and the free choice of career, Plato excluded the "very beginnings" (PR, §185R) of individuality and in so doing provided the blueprint for a world of alienation: a social world whose arrangements would make it impossible for people to actualize themselves as individuals.

Hegel maintains that the Roman Empire provides an example – a real example – of a world of alienation of a different sort, one that was alienating because it made it impossible for people to actualize themselves as social members (PhG, 355–9/90–4; VPG, 380–5/314–18). The specific form of social membership it excluded was membership in a political community, which is to say: citizenship.[18] Free men in the Roman Empire were neither citizens nor slaves. They were recognized as persons, as bearers of legal rights, and were able to actualize themselves as private persons in that they were able to pursue their own separate and particular interests. But they could not regard themselves as part of a political community. They had no effective role in government nor could they lead a "general life" – a life devoted to their political community. From their standpoint, the state was an alien authority rather than an expression of their social being. Thus, Hegel characterizes the Roman Empire as a "soulless community" (*geistloses Gemeinwesen*)

18 See Plamenatz 1963, 162.

(PhG, 355/290). He holds that it was in response to the real, objective alienation of the Roman Empire that Stoicism, Epicureanism, and Skepticism developed. Each of these three schools represented a philosophical response to the fact that people could not "find themselves" in the Roman world.

Let us turn now to Hegel's conception of what it is for the modern social world to be a home: the idea that a modern social world is a home if and only if it makes it possible for people to actualize themselves as individuals (to actualize their individuality) and as social members (to actualize their social membership). This idea is extremely rich and can be thought of as containing five key components. By examining these components, we arrive at a preliminary understanding of Hegel's conception of what it is for the modern social world to be a home.

a. The first component is that a modern social world must contain a framework of institutional spheres within which it is possible for people to actualize their individuality and social membership. Actualizing oneself along these dimensions involves actualizing those capacities that are internal to individuality and social membership (e.g., the capacity to pursue one's separate and particular interests and the capacity to engage in domestic and political life). It also involves grasping that one is an individual (someone with separate and particular interests and individual rights) and that one is a social member (a member of a domestic group and a political community). To say that a social world must contain institutional spheres within which it is possible for people to actualize their individuality and social membership is to say more than that it must not prevent them (e.g., through legislation or informal social sanctions) from actualizing themselves in this way. It is also to say that it must provide them with an institutional context that enables them to do so. Plato's state lacked an institutional sphere within which people could realize themselves as individuals. And although the Roman Empire did include an institutional sphere – the family – within which people could realize one aspect of social membership (membership in a domestic group), it did not include a sphere within which people could actualize themselves as members of a political community, as citizens. Moreover, Hegel maintains that the Roman family was defective in various important respects. Unlike marriage in the modern social world, marriage in the Roman world was not a unity of feeling but instead a mere contract (VPG, 348/286). And the basic structure of the Roman family was one of domination: of husbands over wives and fathers over children. Consequently, it was not possible for people in the Roman world to fully actualize themselves as members of a domestic group; the requisite institutional structures simply were not available.

b. The second component (an elaboration of the first) is that in order to be a home a modern social world must be organized in such a way that people can actualize their individuality and social membership by participating in its central social institutions. The basic idea here is that it is not enough for people to be able to actualize themselves as individuals and social members by engaging in marginal forms of association, for example, the sort of associations Robert Bellah calls "life-style enclaves."[19] A life-style enclave is an enclave within the larger social world formed by people who share a common private life-style – a shared pattern of appearance, consumption, and leisure activities. Hegel insists that in order for the social world to be a home, it must be possible for people to actualize their individuality and social membership within the *mainstream* of the social world.

What this means more concretely, in Hegel's view, is that people must be able to actualize themselves as individuals and social members within the family, civil society, and the state. Hegel has two main reasons for saying this. The first reason has to do with his understanding of what it is to actualize oneself as an individual and social member *in the social world*. As he understands it, participation in the social world consists in participation in its central institutions. The second reason is that Hegel thinks that nothing short of participation in the central social institutions will provide a context that allows the full actualization of individuality and social membership. He maintains that in order to actualize themselves fully as individuals and social members, people must have at their disposal the full range of structures that the central social institutions provide.

c. The third component is that in order to be a home a modern social world must be organized in such a way that people are able to actualize themselves as individuals and social members in the normal course of things. The actualization of individuality or social membership must not require unusual talent or aptitude or heroic endeavors. By the same token, the mere fact that a given person can actualize himself or herself as an individual in a particular social world through the exercise of individual virtuosity – as, for example,

19 Bellah et al. 1985, 71–5.

Hegel claims that Socrates did in the Greek world – does not show that that social world makes it possible for people to actualize themselves as individuals. In order for a social world to be a home, it must be possible for ordinary people to actualize themselves as individuals and as members of society by participating in that social world's central social institutions in the normal way.

d. A fourth (and closely related) component is that in order to be a home the social world must promote the actualization of individuality and social membership. The idea here is that it is not enough that the social world provides a set of social spheres within which the bare possibility of actualizing oneself exists. The social world must also be organized so as to encourage people to actualize themselves in each of the two ways. More specifically, its central social institutions must be organized so that its members will be raised to have the end of actualizing themselves as individuals and social members and be rewarded for pursuing these ends. Hegel contends that in a well-ordered form of civil society, people will be raised to have the goal of actualizing themselves as individuals and will be rewarded when they do so; they will characteristically acquire both wealth and prestige to the extent that they succeed in actualizing themselves as individuals. And Hegel maintains that in a well-ordered social world people will also be raised to be members of a domestic group and a political community. A well-ordered family will reward its members for actualizing themselves as members of a domestic group by providing them with love, intimacy, and understanding. A well-ordered state will reward its members for actualizing themselves as members of a political community by providing them with a form of life in which they can self-consciously pursue the shared general end of the good of the community and attain recognition as members of the political community.

e. The fifth component of the idea that a modern social world is a home if and only if it makes it possible for people to actualize their individuality and social membership requires some elaboration. The underlying intuition here is that a social world must do more than make it possible for people to actualize their individuality and social membership separately. That is, it is not sufficient for people to be able to actualize their individuality *apart* from their social membership and their social membership *apart* from their individuality. In order to be a home, a modern social world must make it possible for people to actualize their individuality *through* their social membership and to actualize their social membership *through* their individuality. Hegel maintains that the social world is a home only if its structures "unify" individuality and social membership in a fundamental way. It must be possible for people to regard their social membership as an "essential aspect" of their individuality and to regard their individuality as an "essential aspect" of their social membership.

Let us call this idea the Schiller Condition. One of Schiller's fundamental concerns about the modern social world was that its structures led to the fragmentation of the human being. He wrote, in the sixth of his Aesthetic Letters, contrasting the Greek and modern worlds:

> However high the mind might soar [in the Greek world], it always drew matter lovingly along with it; and however fine and sharp the distinctions it might make, it never proceeded to mutilate. It did indeed divide human nature into its several aspects, and project these in magnified form into the divinities of its glorious pantheon; but not by tearing it to pieces; rather by combining its aspects in different proportions, for in no single one of their deities was humanity in its entirety ever lacking. How different with us Moderns! With us too the image of the human species is projected in magnified form into separate individuals – but as fragments, not in different combinations, with the result that one has to go the rounds from one individual to another in order to be able to piece together a complete image of the species.[20]

Schiller's specific concern in this passage is that the conditions of modernity prevent human beings from actualizing themselves as 'wholes' by preventing them from fully actualizing their natural powers. He goes on to say:

> That polypoid character of the Greek States, in which every individual enjoyed an independent existence, but could, when need arose, grow into the whole organism, now made way for an ingenious clock-work, in which, out of the piecing together of innumerable but lifeless parts, a mechanical kind of collective life ensued. State and Church, laws and customs, were now torn asunder; enjoyment was divorced from labour, the means from the end, the effort from the reward. Everlastingly chained to a single little fragment of the Whole, man himself develops into nothing but a fragment; everlastingly in his ear the monotonous sound of the wheel that he turns, he never develops

20 Schiller 1801, 31–3.

the harmony of his being, and instead of putting the stamp of humanity upon his own nature, he becomes nothing more than the imprint of his occupation or of his specialized knowledge.[21]

What the fifth component idea takes over from Schiller is the general idea of personal unity and harmoniousness. The specific kind of fragmentation with which Hegel is concerned is that which results from splits between individuality and social membership. Hegel follows Schiller in thinking that in order for people to be at home in the social world, they must be able to actualize themselves as wholes. But he then redefines the central condition of wholeness as unity of individuality and social membership.

The idea that the social world must make it possible for people to actualize their individuality through their social membership and their social membership through their individuality in order to be a home is, I hope, suggestive. What precisely it comes to, however, is not altogether clear. The task of clarifying this idea will be taken up in Chapter 5. Nonetheless, a few brief remarks will give us a sense of the basic idea.

Hegel maintains that social membership (understood as member-ship in the family, civil society, and the state) constitutes an essen-tial component of modern individuality. Membership in these in-stitutions is not merely an aspect of who people are *as social members*; it is also a component of who they are *as individuals*. One can con-sider them apart from their membership in these institutions – as 'atomic' individuals – but in doing so one views them *abstractly*, since one ignores essential features of their individuality. To come to a *concrete* (detailed and realistic) understanding of the individuality of modern people, one must recognize that their membership in the family, civil society, and state constitutes an essential component of their individuality. This, very roughly, is the conception of social membership that lies behind the idea of actualizing individuality through social membership.

Hegel also contends that individuality constitutes an essential component of (modern) social membership. Understood as the pursuit of separate and particular interests and the exercise of individual rights, individuality is an essential component of mem-bership in the modern institution of civil society. It is precisely by pursuing their separate and particular interests and exercising their

21 Ibid., 35.

individual rights that people actualize themselves as members of civil society. And, individuality, understood as subjectivity (the capacity to abstract from and identify with one's roles), is an essential aspect not only of membership in civil society but also of membership in the family and the state. Part of what it is *fully* to actualize oneself as a family member, member of civil society, and citizen is to incorporate these roles into one's subjectivity (one's self-conception) – something one does by grasping that they constitute an essential component of one's individuality (see VPRHO, 496). This, very roughly, is the conception of individuality that lies behind the idea of actualizing social membership through individuality.

From what has been said so far it is clear that Hegel's conception of individuality and social membership places tremendous weight on the claim that the roles of family member, member of civil society, and citizen provide the content of modern individuality and social membership. And so it will come as no surprise to say that part of the task of showing that the modern social world is a home consists in showing that these specific roles constitute essential components of individuality and that individuality constitutes an essential component of these roles. These tasks will be taken up in Chapters 5 and 6.

Let me close this section by noting that Hegel's view that the social world is a home if and only if it makes it possible for people to actualize themselves as individuals and members of society figures centrally in his understanding of why his contemporaries needed reconciliation. He thought that the reason they regarded their social world as alien and hostile or indifferent to their needs – and hence the reason they were alienated – was that it did not *appear* to make it possible for them to reach these goals.

In Hegel's time, civil society represented a new and troubling social formation, distinct from both family and state (PR, §182Z; VPRHO, 565). It appeared to be anarchic and incomprehensible, on the one hand, and atomizing and fragmenting, on the other (PR, §§184Z, 238; VPRHO, 570). It seemed to sever people's connections to family and state and to transform them into isolated individuals who lacked psychological unity and personal harmoniousness.

During this period, largely as the result of the emergence of civil society, the state had taken on a new and problematic form. It had become a large bureaucratic structure that seemed to be insensitive to the claims of individuality. It appeared to have become too large and complex to allow any kind of meaningful participation. It was far from clear that ordinary people could be citizens in any meaningful sense of the term. Nor was it clear how people could possibly actualize themselves as individuals by supporting its structures.

The modern, bourgeois family, on the other hand, appeared all too traditional (PR, §164Z; VPRG, 436) and, like the state, seemed to provide no room for individuality. If anything, it seemed like entering into marriage required the abandonment of individuality – a point reflected, for example, in Schlegel's *Lucinde* (see PR, §164Z; VPRG, 436).

The upshot of these developments was that the modern social world appeared, for the most part, to make it impossible for people to actualize themselves as both individuals and social members. And to the extent that it did make it possible for people to actualize themselves as individuals and social members, it did not appear to make it possible for them to do so in any unified way. Neither civil society nor the state appeared to foster social membership. Neither the state nor the family seemed to promote individuality. And there appeared to be a fundamental tension between the roles of member of civil society and citizen. Even under ideal conditions, they seemed incompatible.

Hegel argues that this appearance (that the social world fails to make it possible for people to actualize themselves both as individuals and as social members) is false. The fact of the matter is that the family, civil society, and state form a single coherent intelligible system, each of whose components promote both individuality and social membership (PR, §§157, 260). This system makes it possible for people to actualize themselves both as individuals and as citizens and to do so in a unified and integrated way. Because of this the modern social world is a home. The central task of Hegel's theory of the modern social world is to make good on this claim.

ii. We have been focusing on the idea that the social world is a home if and only if it makes it possible for people to actualize their individuality and social membership. But as we have noted, Hegel conceives of what it is for the social world to be a home in other ways as well. He also maintains that the social world is a home if it is not 'other' than its members, if it is good, and if it constitutes a world of freedom. And so the question naturally arises: How are these ways of conceiving of the social world as a home related to the idea that the social world is a home if and only if it makes it possible for people to actualize their individuality and social membership? Let me suggest that these other strands can be understood largely in terms of the latter idea, which gives us something like the cash value of these other strands of Hegel's conception.

a. Let us start with the idea that the social world is a home if it is not 'other' than its members (see PhG, 263–7/211–15; VA, 1:136/1:98). This idea is highly evocative but extremely abstract. It is associated with the intuition that alienation is a form of being 'split' from the social world, that being at home in the world is the circumstance of not being split from it, and that reconciliation is a process of overcoming splits. The connecting thought is that to the extent that the social world is other than its members (i.e., separate from, different from, or alien to them) they are split from it and hence alienated. Now obviously, the issue here is not one of numerical identity. At issue is whether the essence of the social world – its underlying rational structure – is fundamentally other than the essence of its members. Hegel maintains that the social world is a home if its essence is not fundamentally other than the essence of its members.

This idea lends itself to interpretation in terms of individuality and social membership, for Hegel maintains that the essence of modern personality can be understood in terms of individuality and social membership. And so the question whether the essence of the social world is fundamentally other than the essence of its members can be thought of as turning on the relation between the essence of the social world and the individuality and social membership of its members. Now, according to Hegel, the essence of the modern social world consists in its central social institutions: the family, civil society, and the state. One natural way of interpreting the question is to take it to be asking whether the social world's central social institutions make it possible for its members to actualize themselves as individuals and social members. If its central social institutions *do* make this possible, then it cannot plausibly be regarded as fundamentally other than its members.

b. A second strand of Hegel's conception of what it is for the social world to be a home is that the social world is a home if and only if it is good. The sense in which Hegel maintains that the modern social world is good is that it is as it ought to be (PR, ¶¶12–14; EL, §6). This returns us to the basic normative outlook expressed in the *Doppelsatz*, which we considered in Chapter 2. As we saw there, Hegel thinks that the modern social world is as it ought to be in two main respects.

First, he holds that it is as it ought to be in that its essence, or underlying rational structure, is as it ought to be. Second, he holds that the modern social world is as it ought to be in that its essence is substantially realized. And so we need to ask how the idea that the social world is a home because it is good and the idea that it is a home because it makes it possible for people to actualize themselves as individuals and social members are connected.

Let us begin by considering the first component of the idea that the modern social world is as it ought to be: the claim that its essence, or underlying rational structure, is as it ought to be. We know that Hegel maintains that the essence of the modern social world is as it ought to be *relative to its stage in world history* because it reflects the most adequate understanding of the human spirit available at the time. And we know that he maintains that its essence is *absolutely* as it ought to be because it reflects the final and correct understanding of the human spirit. Now if we ask what this understanding of the human spirit is, Hegel would reply by saying that it is that human beings are both individuals *and* social members.

Hegel contends that the essence of the Greek world reflected an understanding of people as social members (as members of the family and the state) but lacked an understanding of people as individuals (as bearers of individual rights and subjects of individual moral conscience). In his view, the human spirit could be at home in the Greek world during a certain stage of its development – before it came to grasp "the infinite value of subjectivity" (EL, §147Z) – but once it grasped the value of subjectivity, it could no longer be at home there. Nor could the human spirit be satisfied with the Roman world, which allowed it to actualize its individuality without also providing it with the good of political community. Although the transition from the Greek to the Roman world represented progress in one crucial respect, it represented regression in another. To the extent that people (free men) were able to actualize themselves as individuals in the sense of private persons in the Roman Empire, it represented progress. To the extent that they were not able to actualize themselves as members of a political community, it represented regression. What the human spirit really needed was a set of social structures within which people could actualize themselves both as individuals (private persons and moral subjects) and as social members (members of a family and state) (PR, §§260, 261, R). Hegel claims this is what the human spirit has found in the modern social world.

The upshot of all this is that the idea that the social world makes it possible for people to actualize themselves as individuals and social members gives us the content of the idea that the essence of the modern social world is as it ought to be. Hegel maintains that the essence of the modern social world is as it ought to be in that it makes it possible for people to actualize themselves both as individuals and as social members.

Let us turn now to the second component of Hegel's claim that the modern social world is as it ought to be: the assertion that the essence of the modern social world is substantially realized. To say that the essence of the modern social world reflects an understanding of human beings as individuals and social members is to say that the modern social world is organized around the ideal of making it possible for people to actualize themselves as individuals and as social members. Accordingly, what the claim that the essence of the social world is substantially realized amounts to is the claim that *this ideal* is substantially realized. Hegel maintains that this ideal is substantially realized in the "more advanced states" of his time (PR, §258Z; VPRG, 632; cf. VGP, 2:36/2:25–6). He contends that these states conform on the whole to the structures described in the *Philosophy of Right* – its account of the family, civil society, and the state – and that because of this they generally make it possible for people to actualize themselves as individuals and social members.

c. A third strand of Hegel's conception of the social world's being a home is that the social world is a home if it is what we could call a 'world of freedom' (PR, §§4, 142; VG, 61–4/54–5, 73/63). For Hegel, to say that the social world is a world of freedom is, first of all, to say that its central social institutions promote subjective freedom. Subjective freedom (*subjektive Freiheit*), as Hegel understands it, involves the freedom of individuals to pursue their own separate and particular interests and actualize their own freely chosen life plans (PR, §§185R, 285R), to act in accordance with their own private consciences (PR, §§114, 136–7; VG, 64/55), and to assess their social roles and institutions from their own subjective standpoints (PR, ¶15, §132). Both *Willkür* (PR, §§15, 16), or purely preferential choice, and choice that is considered and reflective (PR, §20) constitute forms of subjective freedom. Subjective freedom is also exemplified when people subjectively assess their social institutions and roles. Interestingly, Hegel contends that subjective freedom requires not only the absence of governmental interference (what

Berlin calls "negative freedom")[22] but also the presence of various institutional structures as well, such as civil society (within which people can pursue their separate and particular interests), marriage (within which people can satisfy their need for love, intimacy, and sex), and the state (within which people can find political community).

Hegel maintains that, in order to be a world of freedom, the social world must do more than promote subjective freedom. It must also promote what he calls "absolute freedom" (*absolute Freiheit*) (PR, §§21–4). As Hegel's conception of absolute freedom is abstract and obscure, I want to avoid becoming embroiled in all its details. Still we need to have *some* idea of what Hegel means. It will suffice for our purposes to provide a rough indication of the main idea.

Absolute freedom, in Hegel's sense of the term, can be understood as the circumstance of not being limited by (PR, §22) or dependent on anything that is 'other' than oneself (PR, §23; EG, §382Z). It is also a matter of the self relating only to itself (PR, §23; VG, 55/48) and being self-sufficient (EG, §382). It is not immediately clear what these conditions come to, but one thing that stands out from the start is that Hegel's conception of absolute freedom has a negative and a positive side. Examining these two sides will help us understand his conception of absolute freedom.

Viewed negatively, absolute freedom consists in not being limited by, restricted by, or dependent on anything that is other than oneself. The basic idea is that to be faced with anything that is 'other' is to be limited, constrained, and thus unfree (VA, 1:134/1:97). But, although Hegel himself does not explicitly make this distinction, it would be more precise to say that the main idea is that to be faced with anything that is 'ultimately other' – anything that cannot *ultimately* (i.e., as the result of philosophical reflection) be seen as sharing or expressing one's 'essence' – is to be limited, constrained, and thus unfree. The central issue is not whether one is faced with *anything* that is other (anything that immediately presents itself as being other) (see EG, §386Z). It is whether one is faced with anything that is *ultimately* other.

Freedom, in Hegel's view, is *not* threatened by otherness as such. The only real threat to freedom is posed by that which is *ultimately* alien or other. The root intuition here is that the circumstance of being faced with something that is ultimately other is one of limitation, restriction, and constraint and thus counts as a circumstance of unfreedom. At the core of Hegel's philosophical conception of freedom, then, is the familiar idea that freedom consists in the absence of limitation, restriction, and constraint. If we view dependence as a form of limitation or constraint, we can subordinate the idea of dependence as unfreedom to that of limitation as unfreedom and maintain that dependence is a form of unfreedom because it is a form of constraint (see VG, 55/48). But it might be more natural to regard the idea of dependence as unfreedom as an independent component of Hegel's conception of freedom since the idea of freedom as independence itself represents a basic way of conceiving of freedom.

The positive side of Hegel's conception of absolute freedom flows naturally from the negative side. The first connecting thought is that *if* the self is unfree so long as it is limited, restricted, or constrained by anything ultimately other, the only way in which the self can be free would be for it to relate to itself (PR, §22; VG, 55/48). If being faced by anything that is ultimately other amounts to limitation, restriction, or constraint, then unless everything that the self relates to can in some sense be seen *as* the self (i.e., as sharing or expressing its essence), the self will inevitably be limited, restricted, or constrained. The second connecting thought is that if the self is unfree so long as it depends on anything that is ultimately other, then the only way in which the self can be free is if it depends on itself alone. Unless the self is autarchic (i.e., self-sufficient), it will be dependent on something else and hence unfree.

Hegel's conception of absolute freedom has its roots in both Kant's conception of autonomy and Spinoza's conception of substance. The idea that the self is unfree if it depends on anything other than itself represents a generalization of the Kantian idea that the self is heteronomous (i.e., not autonomous) if it is ruled by a law that is not grounded in its own essence (reason). And the idea that the self is free if it is self-sufficient borrows Spinoza's idea of substance as that which is completely self-sufficient. Hegel maintains that freedom understood as "not being dependent upon anything other" (the generalization of the idea of autonomy) requires an ontological correlate (something like Spinoza's conception of substance). The self can be free, in Hegel's view, only to the extent that it can actualize itself as a substance. It may be worth pointing out that such a self would be both a subject and a substance (see PhG, 22–3/9–10).

Hegel's shorthand expression for his conception of freedom is *Beisichsein (Beisichselbstsein)*, 'being with oneself' (PR, §23). The idea of freedom as being with oneself encapsulates his view that freedom is a matter of not being faced with anything that is ultimately other. The circumstance of being 'with oneself' is that of relating only to oneself, of being with oneself *as opposed to* being with something that is ultimately other.

The idea of *Beisichsein* also contains within it the suggestion of unity and coherence, for, as Wood has noted, the primary sense of the German preposition *bei* expresses spatial proximity, contact, or belonging.[23] One of the reasons that the self that is *bei sich* is free is that it is unified and coherent. To the extent that the self lacks psychological and personal unity and coherence, it contains aspects or components that are external, alien, or other to itself, and hence is unfree. Thus, unless the self is well integrated, it is not free.

As Hegel uses it, *Beisichsein* is an abbreviation for *Beisichselbstsein in einem Anderem*, 'being with oneself in an other' (see EL, §§158, Z, 159R). This longer expression encapsulates the Hegelian thesis that the only way in which the self can truly come to be 'with itself' (and hence the only way in which the self can come to be truly free) is by relating to something other than itself. The idea that being with oneself presupposes relating to an other flows from the idea that in order to be genuinely with itself the self must develop its potential, actualizing itself in the external world. To the extent that the self fails to actualize itself, it remains dependent on things external to itself and hence unfree. But actualizing oneself in the external world is necessarily a matter of relating to things that are other. The world in which one actualizes oneself is an *external* world. Hence, the only way in which one can attain freedom is by coming to be with oneself in the other to which one must relate. The characteristic way in which one does this is by coming to 'find oneself' in the other. And the characteristic way in which one comes to find oneself in the other is by coming to see the other as sharing or being an expression of one's essence.

We now need to consider what Hegel means by saying that the social world must promote absolute freedom in order to be a world of freedom. The first thing to be said is that Hegel does not think that the social world must fully realize the conditions of absolute freedom. It is enough for the social world to promote the aspects

23 Wood 1990, 45.

of absolute freedom that can be realized through a possible scheme of social arrangements. And Hegel maintains that the social world actualizes these aspects if and only if it makes it possible for people to actualize themselves as individuals and social members. To say that the social world is a world of freedom is to say that it makes the actualization of individuality and social membership possible.

Let us consider how the actualization of individuality and social membership can be viewed as aspects of absolute freedom. We can begin by observing that unless the social world makes it possible for people to actualize themselves both as individuals and as social members, its arrangements will limit, restrict, and constrain them in crucial respects. If the social world does not make it possible for them to actualize themselves as individuals, they cannot actualize one key aspect of their essence: their individuality. If the social world does not make it possible for them to actualize themselves as social members, they cannot actualize another key aspect of their essence: their social membership.

Unless the social world makes it possible for people to actualize their social membership *through* their individuality and actualize their individuality *through* their social membership, people will lack the coherence and unity that freedom, understood as *Beisichsein*, requires. They will not be able to regard their individuality as part of their social membership. They will not be able to regard their social membership as part of their individuality. Their 'identity as social members' will turn out to be ultimately other than their 'identity as individuals'. They will not be able to form a unified conception of themselves according to which they can pursue their separate and particular interests *and* be members of a family *and* be citizens of a state. They will, in a word, be split.

On the other hand, if the social world *does* make it possible for people to actualize themselves as individuals and social members, then it will not limit or constrain them, either as individuals or as social members. To be sure, they may be prevented from carrying out particular individual projects (if, e.g., those projects involve the violation of the rights of others), but they will, nonetheless, be able to realize themselves *as individuals* – to pursue their separate and particular interests and cultivate and develop their own life plans. They will also be able to actualize themselves as social members – to find satisfaction by participating in domestic and political life.

It is worth observing that the word Hegel uses for his conception of freedom and the word he uses for his conception of reconciliation (*Versöhnung*) are one and the same: *Beisichsein*. Hegel's use of *Beisichsein* to mean both freedom and reconciliation enables him to encapsulate the view that freedom and reconciliation are essentially the same. He maintains that people can be at home in the social world only if it is a world of freedom and that the way in which they become free is by coming to be at home. Reconciliation is a process of liberation. If we ask what the social world's being a world of freedom comes to for Hegel, his answer would be that it makes it possible for people to actualize themselves as individuals and as social members. The idea that the social world makes the actualization of individuality and social membership possible gives the content and explains the significance of Hegel's conception of the social world as a world of freedom.

iii. Having now considered the relation between the idea that the modern social world is a home if and only if it makes it possible for people to actualize their individuality and social membership and the other strands of Hegel's conception of what it is for the modern social world to be a home, we are now in a position to look more closely at the significance of this idea. Hegel maintains that *if* the social world is a home, if it makes it possible for people to actualize themselves as individuals and members of society, it will be worthy of acceptance and affirmation. Let us consider why.

If the modern social world is a home it will be worthy of acceptance and affirmation, first, because it will satisfy the basic need that (modern) people have to actualize themselves as individuals and social members. Second, it will be worthy of acceptance and affirmation because it will not be 'fundamentally other' than its members. People will not be split from it either as individuals or as social members but will instead be able to find themselves within its central arrangements both as individuals and as social members. Third, acceptance and affirmation will be warranted because the social world will be good in the sense of 'being as it ought to be'. Its essence will reflect the correct understanding of the human spirit: the idea that human beings are both individuals and social members. And this essence will be realized to a significant degree. Finally, acceptance and affirmation will be appropriate because the social world will be a world of freedom. People will enjoy both subjective freedom and the freedom of being with themselves.

This account of what it means for the social world to be a home suggests that the social world's being a home is a very good thing indeed. But if it is important to appreciate the value of the social world's being a home, it is also crucial to recognize that this does not mean that everything will be wonderful. For example, even if the social world is a home, there is no guarantee that people will be happy.[24] The fact that Hegel's conception allows for unhappiness is one of its most strikingly sober features.

I would suggest, however, that this is also one of the attractive features of his conception – not, of course, because unhappiness is desirable but rather because the fact that the conception allows for unhappiness shows that it is realistic. But one might ask: Why doesn't the fact that a social world fails to guarantee happiness show that it is not a home? Why shouldn't we build the assurance of happiness into our conception?

The first thing to be said is that Hegel's conception of what it is for the social world to be a home does not leave happiness out. Hegel contends that if a social world *is* a home, it will promote happiness. In order to be a home a modern social world must contain a social sphere – civil society – in which people can effectively pursue their own separate and particular projects and meet their material needs (PR, §§182–256). A well-ordered Hegelian social world will also include a system of public administration whose functions include the provision of welfare and the prevention of unemployment (PR, §242, R). And one of the central tasks of the state will be to maintain and support the sphere of civil society and so support its citizens' pursuit of happiness (PR, §§260, Z, 261, 287–8;VPRG, 635; VPRHO, 717–18). Moreover, a well-ordered Hegelian social world will be organized around families within which people can find love, understanding, and support – essential emotional ingredients of happiness (PR, §§158, 161, 164). Thus, in Hegel's view, happiness is *a* goal of a well-ordered social world.

---

24 Hegel generally follows Kant in thinking of happiness (*Glückseligkeit*) as the maximal satisfaction of desires. His conception of happiness is thus subjective in that it holds that (i) the content of an individual's happiness is determined by the desires of that individual (and not by the individual's particular talents and capacities or by the functions of the human being as such) and (ii) the content of happiness may vary from individual to individual. Hegel, however, does not hold the extreme subjectivist view that identifies happiness with a purely subjective state such as pleasure or euphoric feeling. In raising the issue of the place of happiness in Hegel's conception of what it is for the social world to be a home, I am operating with Hegel's subjective conception of happiness. On the subjective conception of happiness, see Wood 1990, 53–74. On the distinction between objective and subjective conceptions of happiness, see Kraut 1979, 167–97.

But to say that happiness is a *goal* is not to say that it is guaranteed. Even if the social world is a home, careers will still fail, friends will still leave, illness will still strike, children will still die. And so one might ask again: Why doesn't the fact that a social world does not guarantee happiness show that it is not a home?

Hegel could reply as follows: Happiness has an essentially individual aspect. It is also especially sensitive to luck. Whether people are happy is partly up to them – how well they manage their lives as individuals within the free scope the central social institutions allow them – and partly a matter of chance – whether they happen to suffer the accidents or misfortunes that are beyond the control of any scheme of social institutions, however well-organized. Since happiness depends partly on factors beyond the control of any scheme of social institutions, it would be unreasonable to demand that the social world guarantee it.[25] In Hegel's vocabulary, the idea of a social world that guarantees happiness may represent an ideal of imagination, but it is not an ideal of reason. The unhappiness that results from individual decision, accident, or chance – bad though it may be – does not reflect a defect of the social world. If one's misfortune results from either one's own decision or from accident or chance, one has reason to be dissatisfied with one's lot, but not with one's social world. Purely individual misfortune does not provide a reason for hating or rejecting the social world.

In any case, to say that the social world is a home is not to say that it meets our each and every wish. It is rather to say that it makes it possible for us to actualize ourselves as individuals and as social members. As we have seen, the social world is a home in Hegel's view if we are not split from it either as individuals or as social members. One can be at home in the social world despite the fact that one is unhappy.[26] Being at home in the social world and being

25 It is perhaps worth noting that Hegel's claim that the social world cannot guarantee happiness does not turn on the subjectivism of his understanding of happiness. Aristotle, who holds an objective conception of happiness (one that identifies human happiness with the fulfillment of the function of a human being), explicitly and famously recognizes that happiness (*eudaimonia*) is prey to a range of contingencies, such as the loss of wealth, honor, and friends.

26 Hegel recognizes, of course, that the person who is at home in the social world and happy is better off than the person who is at home in the social world and unhappy. He is not denying that happiness is a good or that it is a great good. But he wants to insist (i) that a person can be at home in the social world despite being unhappy and (ii) that the person who is at home in the social world possesses a good – indeed, a great good – despite being unhappy. It goes without saying that Hegel does not think that the sort of unhappiness that results from a *correct* understanding of the social world is compatible with reconciliation.

happy are simply different notions. The social world need not guarantee happiness in order to be a home. What it must guarantee is the possibility of being at home.

One might say: Fine, the social world *can* be a home without guaranteeing happiness. But if the social world's being a home does not guarantee my happiness – or the happiness of its members generally – what's so great about it?

What's so great about it is that it meets two vital human needs: the need to actualize oneself as an individual and a social member and the need to be connected to the social world. When people are at home in the social world, they meet these needs and enjoy a very great good. This view reflects Hegel's acceptance of the famous Aristotelian doctrine that the human being is a political animal (PR, §§4, 75Z; VPRHO, 266–7; Aristotle, EN, 1097b 8–11; Pol., 1253a 8–12). It is because human beings need to actualize themselves as individuals and social members and because human beings need to be connected to the social world that alienation is an evil.[27] Think of it this way: Happiness is not the only thing people care about. They also care about being at home in the social world. Being at home in the social world represents an important human good in its own right.

One final remark: Hegel maintains that *freedom* is the greatest good, and that freedom and that being at home in the social world are coextensive. He contends that people are free if and only if they are at home in the social world. And he thinks that freedom, unlike happiness, *can* be guaranteed by the social world. A social world guarantees the freedom of its members if and only if it satisfies the condition of being a home. The greatest thing about a world that is a home is that it is a world of freedom, and the greatest thing about a world of freedom is that it is a home.

V. Alienation

The account of being at home in the social world advanced in the last section provides the basis for a relatively precise characterization of *alienation*: people are alienated if and only if they are not at

---

27 This point requires qualification. Hegel thinks that humanity had to undergo a long period of alienation, extending from the collapse of the Greek polis to the emergence of the modern state, in order to develop fully its powers and attain complete self-knowledge. He also thinks that, in the modern world, alienation typically plays a role in the normal development of individuals. Viewed from *this* perspective, alienation is not a bad thing, but rather a good one. Within a Hegelian framework it is also possible to say that the felt experience of alien-

home in the social world. We can distinguish among three forms of alienation: objective, subjective, and complete.

People are *objectively alienated* if the social world is not a home. Objective alienation is an evil in its own right, apart from its contribution to the feeling of alienation, because, as we have seen, Hegel maintains that people have a deep and abiding need to inhabit a social world that is a home. If this need is frustrated, people suffer an evil whether they recognize it or not.

The members of the Frankfurt school (Horkheimer, Adorno, and Habermas) believe that under the circumstances of contemporary capitalism, people suffer from 'pure objective alienation', that is, objective alienation unaccompanied by feelings of alienation.[28] Because it is capitalist, the social world they inhabit is not a home, but because of the influence of ideology, they are blinded to this fact, and so they fail to see their true predicament. Under such circumstances, people do not need a theory of *reconciliation*. What they need is a theory of *ideology*, which will provide the enlightenment necessary to begin the task of transforming their social arrangements.[29]

The existentialists (Heidegger, Sartre, Camus) take the view that objective alienation (or something like it) is part of the human condition.[30] In their view, it is a metaphysical (fixed, nonempirical) fact

ation is the only authentic reaction to the objective circumstance of alienation. When the social world is objectively alien, it is fitting and appropriate to feel alienated.

28 Hegel himself may not have recognized the possibility of pure objective alienation. He may instead have thought that objective alienation would always somehow show up in (and for) the agent as what I shall call 'subjective alienation'. In any case, the notion of pure objective alienation plays no role in his thinking. On the other hand, it is clear that pure objective alienation represents a logical possibility within the structure of his conception of alienation. Moreover, the members of the Frankfurt school have presented compelling arguments for thinking that pure objective alienation (or, in any case, something close to it) may represent a real possibility. They raise the possibility that to the extent that our social world is not a world of felt alienation, it may be one of pure objective alienation. Let us say, then, that the idea of pure objective alienation, even if not strictly speaking Hegel's, is manifestly Hegelian, for it is clearly built into the logical structure of his thought. We can think of the Frankfurt school as having seen the logical space Hegel provided for this notion and having developed a theory of pure objective alienation (*Ideologiekritik*) that gave content to the notion and connected the notion to the world. For the observation that Hegel may not have recognized the possibility of pure objective alienation, I am indebted to Frederick Neuhouser.

29 For an excellent discussion of the concept of ideology and the idea of a critical theory, see Geuss 1981.

30 Heidegger 1927; Sartre 1943; Camus 1942. Whether Heidegger is properly placed among the existentialists is controversial. See Heidegger 1947.

that the universe (including, in particular, the social world) is not a home for us. Part of what it is to be 'authentic' is to grasp, accept, and, perhaps, even affirm this fact. For the existentialists, the task is not to overcome the feeling of alienation by seeing the world as a home but rather to have the courage to live in the clear consciousness of the fact that it is not.

People can be *subjectively alienated* both when the social world is a home and when it is not a home. If the social world *is* a home, people are subjectively alienated if they *fail* to grasp this fact. If the social world is *not* a home, people are subjectively alienated if they *grasp* this fact. They are also subjectively alienated if they fail to meet any of the other subjective conditions of being at home in the social world. In the standard case, these items go together: it is because people *believe* that the social world is not a home that they feel alienated and reject the social world.

Hegel thought his contemporaries suffered from 'pure subjective alienation'. People experience pure subjective alienation when they are subjectively but not objectively alienated.[31] Pure subjective alienation is possible in Hegel's view because the social world can appear to be alien despite the fact that it is a home. He maintains that part of the task of becoming reconciled consists precisely in grasping that the social world is a home – and accepting it – *despite* the fact that it is subjectively alienating.[32] Pure subjective alienation is, in his view, a persistent feature of modern social life. This is yet another respect in which Hegel's understanding of reconciliation incorporates conflict and antagonism.

Hegel recognizes the logical possibility that the concept of pure subjective alienation may be empty. He understands that he must *show* that the concept has content and that it applies, in particular, to his own historical situation. This is, in effect, the task of demon-

---

31 To say that people suffer from a form of subjective alienation that is pure is not to say that the form of alienation from which they suffer has no roots in the objective features of the world. Presumably, pure subjective alienation will be rooted in certain objective features of the modern social world (e.g., the scale of the modern state and the complexity of civil society). To say that the form of subjective alienation from which people suffer is pure is rather to say that none of the features in which their alienation is rooted are such as to make the subjective world objectively alienating.

32 To be sure, Hegel thought that once one grasped that the modern social world was a home, one would cease to be subjectively alienated. But he thought that it would nonetheless remain true that the social world would *tend* to be subjectively alienating for people generally.

strating that the modern social world is a home despite the fact that it appears to be alien. It is, in other words, the central task of the *Philosophy of Right*.[33]

People are *completely alienated* if they are both subjectively and objectively alienated. Hegel thought that people in ancient Rome and medieval Europe were completely alienated. Marx thought his contemporaries were.

It is worth emphasizing that Hegel does not take alienation to be a purely subjective phenomenon, for some thinkers, here again most notably Marx, have taken him to hold this view.[34] It is also worth observing that Hegel takes subjective alienation (including pure subjective alienation) to be a genuine form of alienation. This observation blocks the natural objection that instead of freeing people from alienation, the project of reconciliation shows people that they are not alienated. In Hegel's view, people who are subjectively alienated do not merely *think* they are alienated or merely *feel* alienated. They *are* alienated. If you are subjectively alienated, you are not at home in the social world; for, as we have seen, being at home in the world includes an essential subjective dimension, and not being at home in the world *is* what it is to be alienated.[35]

VI. Criticism, reform, and revolution

I close this chapter by turning briefly to the topic of the relation between reconciliation, criticism, reform, and revolution. It must be said that reconciliation, as Hegel understands it, is incompatible with certain forms of radical or revolutionary action. To be recon-

33 I do not think that Hegel would maintain that pure subjective alienation could be a prominent feature of an ideally realized social world, for he contends that such a world would contain institutions designed to foster understanding and integration. Thus, in the ideal case, civil society will include corporate groups that will enable their members to understand their place in the social world and to see that they are members of civil society (and not isolated social atoms) (PR, §§250–6). The state will include an assembly of estates whose public discussion of political affairs will enable citizens to gain insight into the workings of government and to come to view themselves as citizens (PR, §§314, 315). These institutions would serve to prevent or overcome pure subjective alienation and so function as devices of reconciliation. But Hegel clearly *did* think that pure subjective alienation could be a prominent feature of a world that was sufficiently well organized so as to be a home. Although he recognized that his social world was not ideally realized, he thought that it was sufficiently well ordered so as to be a home despite the fact that subjective alienation was a prominent feature of that world.
34 Marx 1843–4, 384–5; 1978a, 58–9.
35 I am indebted to Shelly Kagan for raising this concern.

ciled is, among other things, to believe that no fundamental social transformations are necessary; because to say that the social world is a home is to say that the basic arrangements of the family, civil society, and state (i.e., the arrangements described in the *Philosophy of Right*) are acceptable. To be reconciled is also to believe that the essences or underlying rational structures, of the family, civil society, and state are realized to a significant degree.

Being reconciled, however, *is* compatible with engaging in criticism. Reconciliation is not a matter of thinking that particular families, civil societies, and states ideally actualize their essences. One can be reconciled and also recognize that, to varying degrees, particular families, civil societies, and states fail to correspond to their essences. And to the extent that particular families, civil societies, and states do fail to correspond to their essences they are subject to criticism and reform. Hegel himself engaged in critical writing in such essays as "The German Constitution" (VD), "The Wurtemberg Estates" (W), and "The English Reform Bill" (ER). Since being reconciled involves believing that the central social institutions do on the whole correspond to their essences, people who are reconciled may elect not to commit themselves to social or political reform. But people who are reconciled *can* engage in social and political reform nonetheless. Doing so represents one authentic way of responding to the recognition of the defects of the social world. Reconciliation is thus compatible with taking a more or less activist relation to the social world. Although it does not require social activism, it allows it. Reconciliation need not amount to quietism.

II

THE PROJECT OF RECONCILIATION

4

THE ANATOMY OF THE PROJECT

In the preceding chapter, we considered the basic concept of Hegel's project. In this chapter we consider the project's basic elements and structure. This will involve gathering together elements considered in the previous chapters. The present chapter consists of five sections. Section I specifies the project's aim, who gets reconciled, and what they get reconciled to. Section II explains why the project is necessary. Section III clarifies how the project proceeds. Section IV explains how the project is possible. Finally, in Section V, we step back and consider how the project can be seen as involving a process of self-transformation.

I. The project's aim, its subject, and its object

I begin by considering the aim of Hegel's project, who gets reconciled, and to what.

1. The aim is, of course, reconciliation (*Versöhnung*). Hegel seeks to reconcile his contemporaries to the modern social world. He seeks to enable them to overcome their alienation and be at home in the social world.

One might wonder whether this aim is distinctive. After all, reconciliation can be understood in various ways. If it is understood in the *most* general way – as the aim of showing that modern institutions are worthy of acceptance – then almost every modern political philosopher (e.g., Hobbes, Locke, Rousseau, and Kant) can be regarded as implicitly committed to this claim. And so Hegel's project might not seem very different from the tradition of modern political philosophy.[1] But this similarity should not distress us. On the contrary, the fact that Hegel's project can be viewed in this general way shows that its concerns are not, as one might have feared, divorced from the tradition of modern political philosophy but instead fundamentally continuous with them.

Recognizing this continuity does not, however, undermine the distinctiveness of Hegel's project. His project is distinguished, first, by the centrality of its commitment to reconciliation. His was the first modern philosophy to claim explicitly that reconciliation is the proper aim of political philosophy. Nor had anyone before Hegel made reconciliation the central organizing category of his political thought. Hegel's project is distinguished, second, by its specific conception of reconciliation. It was Hegel who introduced to the modern tradition of political philosophy the idea of reconciliation as the process of overcoming alienation and coming to be at home in the social world.

Even if one concedes the originality of this conception, one might still question its value. At first glance, talk of the social world's being 'a home' might seem hopelessly metaphorical. Such talk might also appear utterly unconnected with the tradition. In Chapter 3, however, we saw that Hegel's specific conception of what it is for the social world to be a home – the idea that it is a home if and only if it makes it possible for people to actualize themselves both as individuals and as social members – gives real content to the idea of the social world as a home. What needs to be emphasized here is that his specific conception also connects the idea of the social world as a home to the central concerns of modern political philosophy.

The idea that in order to be a home the social world must make it possible for people to actualize themselves as *individuals* is naturally aligned with what Rawls identifies as the tradition associated with Locke. This tradition "gives greater weight to what Constant called the 'liberties of the moderns', freedom of thought and conscience, certain basic rights of the person and of property, and the rule of law." The idea that in order to be a home the social world must make it possible for people to actualize themselves as *social*

1 I am indebted to Robert Pippin for raising this concern.

members is naturally associated with what Rawls identifies as the tradition associated with Rousseau. This tradition "gives greater weight to what Constant called 'the liberties of the ancients', the equal political liberties and the values of public life."[2] And so we can regard Hegel's view that in order to be a home the social world must make it possible for people to actualize themselves as individuals *and* as social members as expressing an attempt to reconcile the liberties of the moderns with the liberties of the ancients and thus to settle a fundamental conflict within modern political thought.

2. We have already considered one answer to the question concerning who gets reconciled: namely, Hegel's contemporaries. But this answer needs to be specified more precisely. Let us return to a passage from the Preface of the *Philosophy of Right* we have already had occasion to consider.

> To recognize reason as the rose in the cross of the present and thereby to delight in the present – this rational insight is the *reconciliation* with actuality which philosophy grants to those who have received the inner call *to comprehend*, to preserve their subjective freedom in the realm of the substantial, and at the same time to stand with their subjective freedom not in a particular and contingent situation, but in what has being in and for itself. (PR, ¶14)

Here Hegel explicitly addresses the issue of who gets reconciled, suggesting that the people who attain reconciliation are reflective individuals. When he speaks of "those who have received the inner call to comprehend," it is clear that he has reflective individuals in mind. More specifically, Hegel is thinking of people who conceive of themselves *as* individuals (hence their concern with preserving their "subjective freedom in the realm of the substantial [i.e., the social world]"), who stand in an explicitly reflective relation to their arrangements (who step back from their social world and ask whether they can be at home within it), and who seek to grasp (*begreifen*) their social world philosophically. Thus, Hegel's answer

2 I owe the reference to Constant and the specific formulation of the conflict between the two traditions to Rawls, who uses the contrast between the tradition associated with the "liberties of the moderns" and the tradition associated with "the liberties of the ancients" to motivate his conception of justice as fairness. Rawls maintains that one of the aims of justice as fairness is precisely to "adjudicate between these contending traditions" (Rawls 1985, 227). It goes without saying that Rawls's concern to reconcile these contending traditions is one point of connection between his interests and Hegel's.

to the question concerning who gets reconciled can be specified still more precisely by saying: *philosophically* reflective individuals.

The extreme generality of the rubric 'philosophically reflective individuals' might lead one to wonder who exactly Hegel has in mind. Hegel is not very explicit about this matter, but he would presumably say that philosophically reflective individuals are for the most part male, bourgeois, and European. The rcasons for this are fairly straightforward. Hegel assumes that (modern) philosophically reflective individuals are the products of a very specific kind of social world, namely, the sort of social world characterized by the modern family, civil society, and state. And he thinks that these institutions are substantially realized in the European nations of his time (e.g., England, France, and Prussia) and not, for example, in nineteenth-century China or India (see VG, 176/144–5). Hegel maintains that philosophically reflective individuals will typically be men because he shares the extremely unattractive view, common in his age, that women by and large are not psychologically or intellectually equipped for philosophical reflection (PR, §166Z; VPRG, 441; VPRHO, 527). Finally, he believes that philosophically reflective individuals will characteristically be bourgeois because he assumes that they will for the most part be products of one or other of the two central social groups he calls estates (*Stände*) whose form of life promotes reflection: the "estate of trade and industry" and the "universal estate" (civil servants).[3] It is important to emphasize, however, that Hegel does not *stipulate* that the people who get reconciled will be male, bourgeois Europeans. His theory allows anyone to attain reconciliation if he or she is philosophically reflective. Those who are not male, bourgeois Europeans and attain reconciliation will, in his view, necessarily be exceptions, but such exceptions are possible nonetheless.

Contemporary readers might well be concerned by the fact that Hegel's account restricts the possibility of reconciliation to reflective individuals (and hence for the most part to male, bourgeois Europeans). Why Hegel is not bothered by this fact is a matter we will address when we consider why the project of reconciliation is

---

3 Although it is true that "the estate of trade and industry" as Hegel conceives of it includes members of both the proletariat and the bourgeoisie (just as his conception of the "substantial estate" includes both peasants and landowners), it is fairly clear that Hegel thought of reflective individuals as coming out of the bourgeois sector of that estate. Hegel's conception of the central social estates is discussed in Chapter 6, section II.

necessary. But before going further, it is crucial to point out that Hegel does not take the possibility of *being at home in the social world* to be restricted to reflective individuals.[4] He thinks that in order to be at home it must be possible for members of both sexes and of each central social estate (i.e., peasants and landowners, workers and capitalists, and civil servants) to be at home. Accordingly, his account of the modern social world – the *Philosophy of Right* – is designed to show that it is a home for modern people generally. There he argues that workers can be at home because they can simultaneously pursue their separate and particular needs and find social integration within civil society (PR, §§189–208, 250–6), that peasants can be at home because their rural and patriarchal way of life is based on "family relationship and on trust" (PR, §203), and that women can be at home because they find their "substantial vocation" (*Bestimmung*) within the family (PR, §166). Whether or not we ultimately accept this claim, it is essential to appreciate that his account is designed to show that the modern social world is also a home for women and peasants. In this respect, at least, his project is strikingly inclusive. But let us now turn to the question of what philosophically reflective individuals become reconciled to. What is the object of reconciliation?

3. As we know, Hegel's answer to this question is: the modern social world. Let us consider this idea more closely. Hegel defines 'the modern social world' as the form of society organized around the modern family, civil society, and the modern state. Extensionally speaking, this expression refers to the social world of modern (nineteenth-century) Europe, what Hegel, rather unappealingly, calls the Germanic world (*die germanische Welt*; VG, 254/206). The modern social world is thus realized by a number of different nations (*die germanische Nationen*; e.g., France, England, Prussia). Hegel thinks that these different nations can all be thought of as forming one world – *the* modern social world – because he takes them to constitute a family of nations, sharing one common underlying rational structure, the structure presented in the *Philosophy of Right*.

Hegel no more stipulates that the modern social world is the social world of modern Europe than he stipulates that the people who get reconciled are male, bourgeois Europeans. Although he main-

---

4 Although reconciliation is defined as a process of coming to be at home in the social world, an individual can be at home in the world *without* being reconciled. Reconciliation is a precondition of being at home in the social world only if one is alienated.

tains that modern Europe is the locus of the modern social world, he holds that the structures of the modern social world – the family, civil society, and the state – are themselves universal in at least two respects: they express the correct self-understanding of the human spirit and are realizable at least in principle in the world outside Europe. Hegel thinks that as nations come to actualize the modern form of the family, civil society, and state, they will join the modern social world. For Hegel, then, the fact that the modern social world is European is a matter of history, not definition.

Still, there is at least one respect in which Hegel's outlook could be described as Eurocentric. As we saw in Chapter 2, Hegel holds the controversial view that the forms of the family, civil society, and state realized in nineteenth-century Europe correspond to the final and correct understanding of the human spirit and, as such, have a kind of absolute standing. But it is important to stress, again, that Hegel does not hold that the modern family, civil society, and state have this standing because they are European. He holds that they have this standing because they correspond to the correct understanding of *the* human spirit. In other words, it is not Hegel's view that the modern state is special because it is European but rather that Europe is special because it is the locus of the modern state. One can, of course, question whether Hegel is not surreptitiously reading parochial European values into his understanding of 'the' human spirit. But to show this one would have to establish that the specific values he stresses, such as the realization of individuality and social membership (not to mention freedom), are merely parochial European values. And it is far from clear that these values are *merely* parochial.

It should also be emphasized that by the modern social world Hegel means the 'actuality' (*Wirklichkeit*) of the modern social world, or the modern social world insofar as it is actual (*wirklich*). We saw in Chapter 2 what this means. The basic idea is that the actuality of the modern social world consists in the essences of the modern family, civil society, and state insofar as these essences are realized in existing institutions and groups; and therefore, existing institutions and groups are actual insofar as they realize the essences of the modern family, civil society, and state.

Thus, for Hegel the object of reconciliation is *not* my family, simply as such (or my civil society or state). It is *the* modern social world – a set of universal arrangements concretely realized in a variety of particular institutions and groups. This is not, however, to say that

I do not become reconciled to my family (or my civil society or state), for, in Hegel's view, I do. He maintains that I can become reconciled to my family insofar as it realizes the essence of the family (and similarly with my civil society and state). I become reconciled to *my* family as a realization of *the* family.

Now, of course, my family, like any family, will fail to actualize the essence of the family in various ways. But part of what it is to become reconciled to *the* family is to accept the fact that every particular instantiation of its essence – including, in particular, that instantiation which is my family – will inevitably be defective. Hegel contends that once one recognizes this, one will be less troubled by the defects of one's family. One will be able to accept one's family as a (necessarily) imperfect realization of *the* family.

The crucial thing to appreciate, then, is that reconciliation, as Hegel understands it, is not, in the first instance, a relation between people and particular institutions but a relation between people and the modern social world. Indeed, one of the crucial steps in the process of becoming reconciled is to grasp that one's relation to the modern social world is prior to one's relation to any particular social institution or group.

II. The need for the project

Let us consider why Hegel's project is necessary. The specific problem the project is meant to address is pure subjective alienation, a point we touched on in passing in Chapter 3. Hegel maintains that in the modern social world, reflective individuals experience 'pure subjective alienation'. They are *subjectively* alienated because they feel estranged from its arrangements, which they regard as alien and hostile. But their subjective alienation is *pure* (unaccompanied by objective alienation) because, contrary to appearances, the world they inhabit is in fact a home.

Thus, Hegel's understanding of the modern problem of alienation differs dramatically from Marx's. Both thinkers take alienation to be the central problem of their respective social worlds. But Marx, in contrast to Hegel, takes the problem to be objective. He thinks that his social world is not a home because its mode of production is capitalist. Accordingly, he maintains that the form of alienation his contemporaries experience is "complete" (both subjective and objective). It is his view that their subjective alienation mirrors their true, objective condition.

A less obvious difference is the following: Marx believes that most of his contemporaries suffered from the felt experience of alienation. Hegel does not. It is fairly clear that Hegel thinks that most people in the modern social world accept their basic social arrangements and feel comfortable within them. Thus, for example, he writes of "those who live within the actuality of the state and are able to satisfy their knowledge and volition within it" and says that "there are many of them, more in fact than think or know it, for *basically* this includes *everyone*" (PR, ¶7). Indeed, Hegel seems to think that most people in the modern social world are at home within its arrangements.

This point bears emphasis because there is a very strong temptation to read Marx's conception of the scope of subjective alienation into Hegel and to suppose that Hegel takes the circumstance of subjective alienation to be universal – that all or most of his contemporaries are subjectively alienated. That Hegel does not helps explain why he was not troubled by the fact that his account restricts reconciliation to philosophically reflective individuals. His general view is that they are the only people who need reconciliation.[5]

Once we recognize this, it becomes natural to ask why he regards subjective alienation as so important. Why is it anything more than the psychological problem of a privileged elite? First of all, it is necessary to emphasize that Hegel takes subjective alienation, including *pure* subjective alienation, to be a genuine form of alienation. In his view, people who are subjectively alienated do not merely *think* they are alienated or merely *feel* alienated. They *are* alienated. People who are subjectively alienated are not at home in the social world; for, as we saw in Chapter 3, being at home in the social world includes an essential subjective dimension, and not being at home in the social world *is* to be alienated. The problem that the project of reconciliation addresses is not merely psychological. The form of alienation it seeks to free reflective individuals from is real.

But even if this point is granted, the question remains that if subjective alienation is just the problem of the few, why is it so important?

5 We shall see in Chapter 7 that Hegel's conception of the modern circumstances of poverty puts extreme pressure on this view, since it suggests that there will inevitably be a class of people in the modern social world (Hegel calls them the "rabble," *der Pöbel*) who will experience subjective (and objective) alienation. This point is also taken up in the Conclusion. But, for the moment, let us bracket the issue and focus on the basic features of Hegel's understanding of his project.

Hegel would reply that subjective alienation is not just the problem of the few. He would begin by observing that the modern social world has itself become reflective. Its institutions and religious traditions promote and encourage subjective reflection. Whereas Socrates' reflection was an expression of a singular individual temperament that put him at odds with his social world (see PR, §138Z; VPRHO, 436), the reflection of modern individuals is an expression of the general reflectiveness of their institutions and culture that connects them with the basic tendencies of their social world. Even their demand that the social world make it possible to actualize both individuality and social membership – the very demand that leads to their estrangement – is itself an expression of an aspiration internal to the structures of the modern social world. Hegel maintains that reflective individuals are the vehicles of the self-understanding of modern culture. He contends that it is through them that modern culture achieves consciousness of its own demands and aspirations. It is through them that modern culture recognizes the need for a demonstration of the fact that its arrangements constitute a home.

Hegel holds that the failure of his reflective contemporaries to understand the modern social world reflects modern culture's failure to understand itself, for he takes them to be the locus of modern culture's subjectivity. The fact that *they* are subjectively split from their central arrangements shows that *modern culture* is subjectively split within itself. It is this latter subjective split that Hegel takes to be of preeminent importance. He associates it with the proposition that the human spirit (*Geist*) is not at home in the modern social world.

There are two main reasons, then, why Hegel takes the subjective reconciliation of reflective individuals to be so important. First, he regards them as the vehicles through which modern culture can overcome its internal subjective split. Second, he regards them as the vehicles through which the human spirit can grasp that it is at home in the modern social world. Thus, it would be a mistake to think that Hegel's project is simply directed to the problems of reflective individuals. At a deeper level, it is addressed to a fundamental problem within modern culture – a problem of the human spirit – that manifests itself within the experience of reflective individuals.

III. How the project reconciles

The next question is: How does the project proceed? How is it supposed to reconcile philosophically reflective individuals to the modern social world? The short answer is: through theory. The project proposes to reconcile philosophically reflective individuals by providing them with a philosophical account showing that they – and modern people generally – can be at home in the modern social world. Hegel thinks one needs the apparatus of philosophy in order to grasp (*begreifen*) that the modern social world is a home. It is only through the aid of philosophy that one can see (i) that the modern social world is a home if it makes it possible for people to actualize themselves both as individuals and as social members and (ii) that the modern social world does in fact satisfy this condition. Hegel also holds that nothing short of a specifically philosophical account can satisfy "those who have received the inner call to comprehend" (PR, ¶14), that is, the philosophically reflective individuals the theory is meant to address.

That the project of reconciliation proceeds by providing a *philosophical* account explains why Hegel thinks that one must be *philosophically* reflective in order to become reconciled. Unless one meets this condition, one will not be in a position to understand the account that shows the modern social world to be a home. Here it is important to remember that Hegel holds that it is only "those who have received the inner call to comprehend" who need or want such an account. He maintains that the subjective conditions for needing the philosophical account the project provides and the subjective conditions for being able to make use of such an account are the same.

It is in fact crucial to his account that these two conditions be identical, for this (alleged) identity is what is supposed to guarantee that everyone who *needs* to be reconciled *can* be reconciled. But it is perhaps worth pointing out that it is not at all clear that the two conditions *are* identical. It would seem that one could be reflective enough to be alienated from the modern social world without being sufficiently philosophical to make use of a philosophical theory of reconciliation. Although Hegel may have been the first philosopher to appreciate the pervasively reflective character of modern social life, it is not clear that he recognized that its basic reflectiveness would make the subjective conditions of alienation more democratic.[6] Hegel sometimes writes as if one had to be philo-

---

6   The phrase 'pervasively reflective' belongs to Bernard Williams, who acknowledges that recognition of the reflective character of modern life derives from Hegel. Compare his discussion of the reflectiveness of modern life in Williams 1985, esp. 2–4, 163–4, 199–200.

sophically educated or, in any case, exhibit a "better will" (*bessere Wille*) (PR, §138R) or a "nobler nature" (*edlerer Natur*) (VG, 173/ 143) to experience subjective alienation. But the fact of the matter is (and surely this was already true in Hegel's own time) that ordinary people *are* sufficiently reflective to experience subjective alienation. The irony here is that the reason for this is to be found in the very feature that Hegel himself took such pains to emphasize: the pervasively reflective character of modern social life.

IV. How the project is possible

The suggestion that the project of reconciliation is supposed to reconcile through theory leads naturally to the question concerning how the project is possible. If the form of alienation reflective individuals experience is genuine, how could it be overcome through anything other than a transformation of their social arrangements?[7] On the face of things, the idea that alienation can be overcome through *theory* is quite implausible. And so, Hegel's proposed solution to the modern predicament of alienation may seem at best bizarre. But we have, in effect, already seen how Hegel would respond to this concern. He would point out that the specific form of alienation experienced by reflective individuals is pure subjective alienation, which is a genuine form of alienation, and he would explain that the reason they are subject to this form of estrangement is that they fail to understand their social world (and themselves).

This point is illustrated by the following passage from the Preface to the *Philosophy of Right*: "What lies between reason as self-conscious spirit and reason as present actuality, what separates the former from the latter and prevents it from finding satisfaction in it, is the fetter of some abstraction or other which has not been liberated into the concept" (PR, ¶14). By "reason as self-conscious spirit" Hegel means philosophically reflective individuals; by "reason as present actuality," he means the modern social world. In referring to the *separation* of reflective individuals from the modern social world, Hegel is thinking of the subjective split between reflective individuals and the modern social world, or, in other words, their subjective alienation. The "fetter of some abstraction

---

7 The reader will recall Marx's famous eleventh thesis on Feuerbach: "The philosophers have only *interpreted* the world in various ways; the point however is to *change* it" (Marx 1845, 7; 1978c, 145).

or other" is the fetter of their understanding of the social world or themselves. This understanding can be characterized metaphorically as a "fetter," a chain or shackle, because it divides them from the modern social world. And it can be described as "abstract" because it is one-sided and false. Were their understanding to be "liberated into the concept," were they to attain a correct philosophical understanding of their circumstances, they would grasp that their social world is a home and so find "satisfaction" in its arrangements.

Once Hegel's understanding of his historical situation is spelled out, his solution no longer seems bizarre. *If* his reflective contemporaries are alienated because they *fail to understand* their social world (or themselves) and if their social world (or if they) could not be understood without the aid of philosophical theory, then a *philosophical account* of the modern social world and modern people is precisely what they need. Such an account would allow them to grasp that their social world is a home, and by grasping (*begreifen*) this fact, they could become reconciled to its arrangements (PR, ¶14). Hegel's diagnosis of his reflective contemporaries' plight may have been wrong, but relative to his understanding of their plight, the solution he proposed is quite reasonable.

Many people, most famously Marx, have held that Hegel believes that reconciliation through theory is *always* possible.[8] What has not been sufficiently appreciated is that Hegel denies this. Although Hegel does think that theory *can* reconcile, he maintains that it can do so *only if* certain objective social conditions are in place: namely, those that make the social world a home.[9] Hegel takes world history (*Weltgeschichte*) to be the process that gives rise to these conditions.[10] He maintains that the social world was not a home during the time of the Roman Empire (PhG, 355–9/290–4; VPG, 380–5/314–18) or the Middle Ages (VPG, 440–91/366–411).[11] The Roman

---

8 Marx 1843–4, 384–5; 1978a, 58–9.

9 What is at issue here is *social* and not *religious* reconciliation. Hegel thinks that religious reconciliation – reconciliation with God – *is* possible during periods in which the social world is not a home. But he also maintains that religious reconciliation is no replacement for social reconciliation (VGP, 2:588/3:95–96).

10 Because Hegel believed that world history had changed the world (i.e., made it a home), he could maintain that the point in his time was to interpret it.

11 Hegel thought that the social world of the ancient Greeks was a home, albeit a primitive one. It was primitive because it provided no place for 'subjectivity', that is, the exercise of conscience and critical reflection on one's social roles and institutions. Hegel maintained that it was precisely because the Greek world was primitive that it had to be superseded and that humankind was forced to enter a long period of alienation, including the eras of the Roman Empire and the Middle Ages, ending only in the modern world.

world failed to provide community; the medieval world failed to allow for individuality. During those eras, any attempt to reconcile people to the social world through theory would have been pointless. What was needed then was not a transformation of people's consciousness but a transformation of their objective social arrangements.

Once we recognize that Hegel thinks that theory can reconcile only when the requisite objective social conditions are in place, we can better understand his relation to Marx, for then it becomes clear that the basic difference between them does not, as has commonly been thought, concern the importance of objective social conditions. This is actually a point about which they agree. Hegel, like Marx, thinks that *if* the social world is alien, its social arrangements must be transformed in order for it to become worthy of reconciliation. This is the thrust of his *Lectures on the Philosophy of World History*.[12] He also agrees with Marx in maintaining that the social world could not be made a home without a revolution.[13] But, unlike Marx, who thought that that revolution was still to come, Hegel thought it had already taken place – in France in 1789. The basic difference between them is that Hegel affirms and Marx denies the proposition that the modern social world is a home.

Now if we generalize the idea of the project of reconciliation, we can think of Hegel and Marx as being engaged in different forms of the same basic enterprise. We can say that Marx is engaged in the 'political' project of reconciliation and that Hegel is engaged in the 'philosophical' project of reconciliation.

The *political* project gets its start from the proposition that the modern social world is not a home. It seeks to secure the objective conditions of reconciliation by transforming the central social institutions to make them worthy of reconciliation. Instead of seeking to reconcile people to the social world directly, it seeks to change the social world to make it worthy of reconciliation. It is 'political' in that it seeks to make reconciliation possible through political change.

The *philosophical* project gets its start from the proposition that the social world is a home although it does not appear to be one.[14]

---

12 Marx 1843–4, 384–5; 1978a, 58–9.
13 For useful discussions of Hegel's views on revolution, see Habermas 1971, 1973b; Ritter 1965, 1982; Theunissen 1970.
14 This is not to say that Hegel simply *assumes* that the social world is a home, for, as we have seen, one of the central tasks of his social theory is precisely to *show* this. The point is rather the following. The ultimate justification of the claim that the best way to overcome people's alienation is to provide them with a philosophical theory is to be found in the philosophical theory the project provides.

The philosophical project is 'philosophical' in that it attempts to reconcile people by providing them with a philosophical account of their central social institutions that will allow them to see that their world is a home despite appearances. The project attempts to reconcile by providing *rational insight* (*vernünftige Einsicht*) into the true nature of the social world (PR, ¶14). There is of course *a* sense in which the philosophical project is 'political' too, since, in recommending reconciliation, it recommends a particular *political* attitude: one of acceptance and affirmation.

Marx takes the philosophical project of reconciliation to be inherently *ideological*; for he thinks that if the social world were a home, there would be no need for social theory.[15] To say that a project is 'ideological' is to say that it is or promotes a form of 'false consciousness' (a false account of the social world or its members that stabilizes or legitimizes oppression). Marx argues that the social world is a home only if its workings and the fact that it is a home are *transparent*. In his view, if you need theory to be at home, the world you inhabit is not a home. Hegel, on the other hand, has a strikingly different conception of what it is for the social world to be a home: a conception in which the social world can both be a home *and* be in need of theory. He maintains that the historical transformations that made the modern social world a home, which include the emergence of civil society and the modern state, also gave rise to the need for social theory. He also argues, more generally, that the very conditions of modernity, which include the scale and complexity of the modern state and the fact that reflective individuals demand 'rational insight' into their social arrangements, make theory indispensable.

V. The role of self-transformation

I close this chapter by considering how the project can be seen as involving a process of self-transformation. The first thing to point out is that reconciliation is not a matter of seeing that the social world fits one's antecedently given self-conception. Hegel thinks that reflective individuals in the modern social world tend to view themselves atomistically.[16] They characteristically conceive of themselves as individuals *rather* than as social members. They do, of course,

---

15 For an excellent discussion of this point, see G. Cohen 1978, 326–44.
16 For a useful discussion of the idea of an atomic individual, see Taylor 1985a.

recognize that they occupy social roles, but they typically regard these roles as fundamentally external to their 'identity', as not in any way 'constitutive' of who they really are. The prevalence of this self-conception helps explain the popularity of contractarian theories in the modern social world, for such theories can be regarded as presenting the social world as an aggregate of atomic individuals. Indeed, if one generalized the project of showing the modern social world to be a home, one could say that there is a central strand of traditional contract theory (i.e., that exemplified by Hobbes and Locke) whose aim is to show that the modern social world (or, in any case, the modern state) is a home for atomic individuals.

Hegel's project of reconciliation is not, however, designed to show that the modern social world is a home for atomic individuals. It seeks to show that the modern social world is a home for people who are both individuals and social members, who are what I shall call 'individual social members.' (The notion of 'individual social member' is elaborated in Chapter 5.) Part of the process of becoming reconciled, then, involves a transformation of consciousness through which one moves from an initial state in which one regards oneself as an atomic individual to a final state in which one regards oneself as an individual social member. One of the 'abstractions' dividing reflective individuals from the modern social world is precisely their conception of themselves as atomic individuals.

This way of presenting things needs to be qualified, however. Although it is true that Hegel contends that reflective individuals in the modern social world tend to *explicitly* think of themselves individualistically, as atomic individuals, he also thinks that there is another, less explicit level at which they tend to think of themselves in more communitarian terms, as social members. He would say that reflective individuals – and modern people generally – typically identify in some very strong sense with their family and country. Although their 'official' self-understanding is individualistic, the self-understanding they express practically, in their day-to-day life, contains an essential communitarian component. Moreover, the wish to be part of the social world, to fit in with its arrangements, lies at the heart of their felt experience of alienation. Not the least reason why reflective individuals tend to experience the modern social world as indifferent or hostile is that they want to be *at home* within its arrangements, where being at home is not just a matter of being able to exercise individual liberties but also a matter of being able to actualize oneself as a social member.

It is noteworthy that Hegel thus anticipates the conflict between contemporary liberals (e.g., Rawls), who emphasize the individualistic aspects of the modern self-conception, and contemporary communitarians (e.g., Sandel), who emphasize its communitarian aspects. He would regard their philosophical conflict as the expression and articulation of a real tension implicit within the self-conception of modern individuals: a tension between the conception of the self as individual and the conception of the self as social member. But the point I want to stress here is that Hegel's own philosophical project is specifically designed to address this tension. His understanding of the initial state of the people to whom the project is addressed could be formulated in the following way. Although reflective individuals in the modern world view themselves both as individuals and as social members, they conceive of individuality and social membership in such a way as to make it seem impossible to be both full-fledged individuals and full-fledged social members. Their self-understanding is thus 'split' between their conception of themselves as individuals and their conception of themselves as social members. Accordingly, the transformation of consciousness internal to the process of reconciliation turns out to be somewhat more complex than it initially seemed. The process involves coming to recognize both that one is essentially a social member – a member of a family, civil society, and state – and that one implicitly conceives of oneself as family member, member of civil society, and citizen. The process also involves coming to grasp that individuality and social membership are in fact compatible, that it is possible to be both a full-fledged individual and a full-fledged social member, and that it is possible to actualize one's individuality through one's social membership and conversely. (These points are taken up in the next chapter.)

Hegel would insist that in coming to view themselves as individual social members, reflective individuals come to understand who they really are, for it is part of his view that people in the modern social world are raised to be individual social members. He in fact maintains that the way in which the modern social world maintains and reproduces itself is by producing individual social members. Moreover, Hegel also thinks that the conception of the self as an individual social member reflects the final and correct understanding of the nature of the self. And so Hegel would reject the suggestion that in coming to view oneself as an individual social member, one adopts a self-conception whose sole virtue is that it makes it possible to fit into the arrangements of the modern social world. He would argue that in coming to view oneself in this way, one adopts a conception of oneself that is true. Thus, for Hegel, one of the essential components of becoming reconciled is coming to adopt a true conception of who one is.

5

INDIVIDUALITY AND
SOCIAL MEMBERSHIP

We saw in the preceding chapter that Hegel's project of reconciliation revolves around his conception of the relation of individuality and social membership. He maintains that the modern social world is a home because it makes it possible for people to actualize themselves both as individuals and as social members. Part of the project of showing the modern social world to be a home consists in demonstrating that its central social institutions are organized so as to make it possible for people to actualize themselves in both of these ways. This task will be taken up in the next chapter. Another part of the project of showing the modern social world to be a home consists in the task of demonstrating the theoretical possibility of being both an individual and a social member. The present chapter takes up this logically prior task.

One might wonder why establishing the compatibility of individuality and social membership is necessary. Isn't it obvious that modern people are both individuals and social members? Each modern person is, after all, a distinct human being who participates in the social world. And so isn't it also obvious that individuality and social membership *can* be combined? Why is there an issue here?

Not the least reason is that there is a natural tendency to think that individuality and social membership cannot be combined, or, in any case, that there is a basic tension between them. One might think that individuality is properly understood as 'atomic individuality', that 'who one is' as an individual is to be identified with 'who one is' apart from one's social roles, and so take one's social roles to be external to one's individuality. One might hold that individuality is properly understood in terms of idiosyncrasy or eccentricity and thus take one's social roles to lie outside one's individuality, since they are shared by other people. One might identify individuality with nonconformity and suppose that actualizing oneself as an individual necessarily involves breaking with the social world – that is, that the price of individuality is being an outsider. Or one might draw a sharp contrast between individuality and social membership, associating individuality exclusively with the pursuit of one's separate and particular interests, and social membership exclusively with participation in the family and the state, and therefore conclude that there is a basic split between one's identity as an individual and one's identity as a social member.

Hegel holds that these ways of understanding the relation of individuality and social membership are mistaken and belong to the 'abstractions' that separate modern reflective individuals from the social world (PR, ¶14). He would agree with the commonsense contention that it is true, even obvious, that modern people are both individuals and social members, but he thinks that there is more to modern individuality than being a distinct human being and more to modern social membership than participating in the social world. Hegel contends that modern people are, so to speak, both *full-fledged* individuals and *full-fledged* social members. It is the very richness of modern individuality and social membership that makes their compatibility problematic.

My aim in this chapter, which is divided into six sections, is to present Hegel's conception of the relationship of modern individuality and social membership. The guiding idea will be that modern individuality and social membership are not only compatible but also intertwined and inextricable and, indeed, that it is precisely *through* their social membership that modern people are able to actualize themselves as individuals and *through* their individuality that modern people are able to actualize themselves as social members. To simplify matters I will begin by considering Hegel's conceptions of individuality and social membership separately, in sections I and II, and then show how these conceptions fit together. The relationship between individuality and social membership is elaborated in a preliminary way in section III and then more fully in the last three sections. Section IV shows how, according to Hegel, modern social membership makes modern individuality possible. Section V characterizes the social dimension of modern individuality and explains Hegel's conception of modern individuality in the complete sense. Section VI presents the individual dimension of modern social membership.

One brief remark concerning the philosophical status of this chapter. Hegel himself offers no explicit theoretical account of the relation of individuality and social membership. He instead speaks of (objective) *Geist* (EG, §§483–552). His conception of objective *Geist* is designed, among other things, to make it possible to avoid the misunderstandings that naive reliance on the categories of the individual and society are bound to generate. This chapter is meant to provide a reconstruction of Hegel's conception of objective *Geist* that will give us access to the account of the relation of the individual and society implicit within it.

I. Individuality

The preliminary characterization of Hegel's conception of individuality with which I begin (*Individualität, Einzelheit*) proceeds in two stages. The first stage presents Hegel's conception of individuality in 'the minimal sense'; the second presents his conception of individuality in 'the strong sense'.

According to Hegel, people are individuals in the 'minimal sense' if they conceive of themselves as being distinct from other people in virtue of having particular traits and qualities that distinguish them from others. (I shall use the phrases 'conceive of oneself', 'think of oneself', and 'regard oneself' interchangeably.) Thus, for example, I might distinguish myself from one person by reference to certain physical features that I have and from another by reference to psychological traits.

This conception is minimal in at least three respects. First, it states a necessary condition of being a human individual. A person who did not regard herself as distinct from other people could not be said to be an individual at all. Such a person could, of course, still be regarded as an individual entity – a thing distinct from other things. And such a person would, of course, still be a member of the human species, distinct from other members of the species. But she could not be regarded as an individual *human* being in the relevant (normative) sense of the term, for she would lack a conception of herself as an individual human being; and, Hegel contends, part of the concept of human individuality is that to be a human individual is to conceive of oneself as being one.[1] One becomes a human individual as a result of a process of individuation through which one differentiates oneself from others, in particular one's parents and the members of one's community. Being a human individual essentially involves self-consciously differentiating oneself from other human beings.

The second respect in which the minimal conception of individuality is minimal is that it states something like the weakest conception of individuality that can still intuitively be regarded as a genuine conception of human individuality. One could imagine a still weaker conception, according to which people are individuals simply if they distinguish themselves from other entities but without distinguishing themselves from other human beings as such. It is far from clear, however, that this conception counts as a genuine conception of human individuality; for it is plausible to suppose that part of what it is to think of oneself as an individual human being is to think of oneself as an individual human being *as opposed to other* individual human beings.[2]

The third respect in which the minimal conception of individuality is minimal has to do with what it omits. It does not, for example, include the idea of viewing oneself as having separate and particular interests. Nor does it include the idea of viewing oneself as having individual rights. It also leaves out the idea of viewing oneself as having a conscience. Moreover, one could be an individual in the minimal sense without having a conception of oneself as someone who can step back from one's social roles and institutions and question them.

The minimal conception of individuality thus represents a form of individualism that makes no reference to the contrast between the individual and society. One might, therefore, be tempted to say that this conception is not really a conception of *individuality* at all. But not the least advantage of regarding it *as* a conception of individuality is that it allows us to accommodate the intuition that there must be *a* sense in which people who do not distinguish them-

---

1 My formulation of this point has been influenced by Lear (1990, 22). The underlying Hegelian view is the idea of the human being as a self-interpreting animal. See Chapter 1.
2 This idea plays a crucial role in Fichte's conception of individuality. See Neuhouser 1993.

selves from their social roles or social world are individuals while at the same time marking this form of individuality as significantly restricted. Let us turn now to Hegel's conception of individuality in the strong sense.

Hegel contends that people are individuals in the strong sense if they both conceive of themselves as individuals in the minimal sense and conceive of themselves as (1) selves (see PR, §§5–7), (2) bearers of separate and particular interests (PR, §§184, Z, 186, 187, Z; VPRHO, 580, 570), (3) possessors of individual rights (PR, §§36, 37, Z; VPRHO, 192, 209), and (4) subjects of conscience (PR, §§136–7). Let us examine these four components.

1. The expression 'the self' can be used in many ways. From a Hegelian standpoint, to be a 'self' is to conceive of oneself as independent of and distinct from one's social roles in the sense that one thinks of oneself as having the capacity to 'abstract' from any given social role (cf. PR, §5).

To *abstract* from a social role is to 'step back' from it in thought and to enter into a *reflective* relationship with it. A person *steps back* from a social role when, for example, he considers how he is to relate to it. To step back from a social role *is* to question or evaluate it. A person may ask whether a given role is suitable to his temperament and character and whether he *wants* to play it, or he may ask whether he accepts the values and norms that are internal to that role and whether he *ought* to play it. The capacity transcends the capacity to enter into a reflexive relation with oneself. Someone might in principle be able to enter into a reflexive relationship with himself (e.g., to ask himself what he wants to wear today) without having the capacity to step back from his social roles (e.g., to ask himself whether he ought to perform his duty as a citizen).

In asking whether one wants or ought to play a given social role, one entertains, at least implicitly, the possibility that one might choose not to play it. Whether or not one chooses to reject the role, however, one *distinguishes* oneself from it when one steps back. One regards it as something external to oneself: as a role one plays as opposed to what one 'is'. And one regards oneself as someone who plays that role as opposed to someone who 'is' that role.[3] One comes to conceive of oneself as a *self* by grasping that one has the capacity to step back from one's social roles and by coming to form a general conception of oneself as the kind of being that has this capac-

3 Cf. for similarities Trilling 1972, 1–25.

ity. It should be added that 'the self', as the term is being used here, does not refer to some kind of inner entity: to speak of the self is to speak of the person.[4] It is, more precisely, to speak of the person as having the capacity to step back from his social roles, to *grasp* that he has this ability, and to form a general conception of himself as the kind of being who has that ability.

2. To conceive of oneself as the *bearer of separate and particular interests* is to think of oneself as having interests that are *separate* from the interests of other people and the interests of the group, community, or social world. Such interests are *particular* in that they are interests one has as the particular person one is. They are to be contrasted with interests one has in virtue of being in a relationship (e.g., a friendship, romance, or marriage) or the interests one has as a member of a group or community (e.g., a family or country). If a person has interests that are separate and particular, it is possible that there may be something that would be good for her that would not be good for other individuals or the community as a whole.[5] Separate and particular interests thus are the sort of interests that can bring one into conflict with other individuals or the community.

3. To conceive of oneself as a *possessor of individual rights* (e.g., the right to life and the right to property) is to think of oneself as having rights as the separate and particular person one is – rights that do not derive from one's status as the bearer of a particular social role or from one's position in society. One views oneself in this way when one insists upon one's rights or complains that one's rights have been violated without appealing to the prerogatives of one's social role or position. Hegel's technical expression for someone who views himself or herself in this way is 'person' (*Person*) (PR, §36).[6] To view oneself as a person in this technical sense is to regard oneself in contrast to other individuals and society, separated from them by the rights one has. As a person, one has certain rights against other individuals and against the community. And, like separate and particular interests, the rights one has as a person may bring one into conflict with other individuals or into conflict with the community.

4. To conceive of oneself as a *subject of conscience* involves regarding oneself as an independent source of moral assessment and evalu-

---

4 I use 'person' in the ordinary, nontechnical sense to refer to a single human being.
5 Cf. for similarities Thomson 1990, 222.
6 This technical sense of 'person' is not to be superimposed on the way in which this word is generally used in this chapter.

ation. It involves regarding oneself as having the capacity and right to assess courses of actions, social roles, and institutions on the basis of one's own private, subjective judgment, even in defiance of accepted practice and custom (PR, §§136–7; VPG, 309–10/253). "*Conscience* expresses the absolute entitlement of subjective self-consciousness to know *in itself* and *from itself* what right and duty are, and to recognize only what it thus knows as the good; it also consists in the assertion that what it thus knows and wills is *truly* right and duty" (PR, §137R). Conscience can in principle bring one into conflict with one's community since it is always possible for the deliverances of one's conscience to run counter to its demands.

If it is plain that the minimal conception of individuality is a conception of individuality, it is clear that the strong conception of individuality is one as well. It is, I think, also clear that the strong conception of individuality deserves its name. It is strong, first of all, in comparison with the minimal conception. We observed that one crucial respect in which the minimal conception is minimal is that it makes no reference to the contrast between the individual and society. This contrast, however, figures centrally in the strong conception. Conceiving of oneself as a self involves stepping back from one's social roles. Regarding oneself as a bearer of separate and particular interests involves grasping that one has interests that are distinct from those of the social world of which one is a part. Thinking of oneself as a possessor of individual rights involves regarding oneself as having rights that can bring one into conflict with society. And conceiving of oneself as a subject of conscience involves thinking of oneself as a source of moral assessment that is independent of the norms and practices of society. Indeed, when we see everything that is included in the strong conception of individuality, it becomes clear that this conception *is* strong, not only in comparison with the extremely modest minimal conception but also in its own right.

It is, of course, possible to develop a still stronger – still more ambitious, still more demanding – conception of individuality than the one Hegel presents. Thus, for example, Nietzsche holds that a person is a genuine individual only if he undertakes to create his own values and live a life that is radically original and hence radically nonconformist.[7] Mill also holds a conception of individuality that is stronger than Hegel's. Although he denies that genuine in-

7 Nietzsche 1883–5, 65–8, 80–3; 1966a, 51–4, 62–3; 1886, 41–63; 1966b, 35–56.

dividuality requires originality or nonconformity, he contends that being a genuine individual requires determining for oneself which of the customs and traditions of one's social world are suitable for oneself and *choosing* one's own life plan, rather than simply doing what 'one' does.[8] But even though Hegel's conception of individuality is not as strong as either Nietzsche's or Mill's, it is still a strong conception of individuality. And, it would, I think, be plausible to say that someone who satisfied its conditions was a full-fledged individual.

Hegel thinks that modern people are individuals in the strong sense. Moreover, he maintains that individuality in the strong sense is a distinctively modern phenomenon, and he associates its emergence with the influence of Christianity and Roman law. He says "The principle of the *self-sufficient and inherently infinite personality* of the individual [*des Einzelnen*], the principle of subjective freedom . . . arose in an inward form in the *Christian* religion and in an external form (which was therefore linked with abstract universality) in the *Roman* world" (PR, §185R).

Hegel holds that the ancient Greeks – or more precisely, the ancient Greeks living in the period ending in the late fifth and early fourth centuries B.C.E., the period "when their culture was at its height" (VG, 71 /62) – were not individuals in the strong sense of the term (PR, §261Z; VPRHO, 719; PhG, 324–8/263–6). Before the appearance of the Sophists, in the fifth century, the ancient Greeks identified "immediately" (*unmittelbar*, 'spontaneously', 'unreflectively', 'directly') with their social roles (e.g., as family members and citizens; see VPG, 326/267; PhG, 354/289).[9] There was no 'psycho-

---

8 Mill 1859, 53–71.

9 One natural response to the claim that the ancient Greeks identified immediately with their social roles is that it *cannot* be right, because, after all, Socrates, the paragon of subjective reflection, was an ancient Greek. Accordingly, it is important to emphasize that the period of Greek culture that Hegel has in mind is pre-Socratic and indeed pre-Sophist. Hegel ascribes the introduction of subjective reflection into ancient Greek culture to the Sophists (VPG, 309/253) and contends that it was with Socrates (PR, §138R) that "the principle of subjectivity [*Innerlichkeit*] – of the absolute independence of thought – attained free expression" (VPG, 328/269). Indeed, Hegel claims that, prior to Socrates, the Greeks had "no real morality [*Moralität*]" (VG, 71/62). It was Socrates who first assigned "to insight, to conviction, the determination of men's actions" and "posited the subject as capable of final moral decision, in contraposition to country and to custom" (VPG, 329/269–70, translation modified). And it was Socrates who taught the Greeks (and the rest of humanity) that "the moral man is not he who merely wills and does that which is right – not the merely innocent man – but he who has the consciousness of what he is doing" (VPG, 329/269). It should also be stressed

logical distance' separated them from their roles. Indeed, in Hegel's view, the Greeks did not think of their social roles *as roles*. They lacked the reflective detachment that such a view presupposes.

Nor, according to Hegel, were the ancient Greeks disposed to assess their social roles and arrangements from the standpoint of subjective acceptability. Hegel maintains that the "habit of living for their country, without further reflection, was the principle dominant among them. The consideration of the state in the abstract – which to our understanding is the essential point – was alien to them" (VPG, 308/253). Hegel even goes so far as to say that with respect to "the Greeks in the first and genuine form of their Freedom [i.e., in the period before the Sophists came on the scene], we may assert, that they had no conscience" (VPG, 309/253; cf. VG, 71/62).[10] Hegel also claims, no less strikingly, that the ancient Greeks did not conceive of themselves as having separate and particular interests (VPG, 308/252).[11] The ancient Greeks immediately

that Hegel recognizes that there *was* a period in ancient Greek history – the period beginning with the appearance of the Sophists – in which people did reflect on their arrangements, but he contends that this was a period of decay and corruption (VPG, 309/252-3, 326-7/267-8). And he further holds that this decay was due precisely to the introduction of the principle of subjectivity, which, from the standpoint of Greek ethical life, represented a destructive force and corrupting factor (VPG, 309/252; PR, ¶12) that ultimately "plunged the Greek world into ruin" (VPG, 309/253; see VG, 250/203; PR, §185R). To the extent that Socrates, the Sophists, and others in ancient Greece engaged in subjective reflection, they acted contrary to the spirit of Greek ethical life (which was *essentially* unreflective) and undermined its foundations. Hegel's conception of Greek life is, of course, highly idealized, and his general picture of Greek history is very controversial. I should say that, although I want to ward off certain misunderstandings of Hegel's view of Greek antiquity, my aim is not to defend it but simply to present it as one component of a larger conception needed to understand Hegel's conception of modern individuality and social membership. For our purposes, it suffices to regard Hegel's conception of Greek life prior to the Sophists as a kind of *Gedankenexperiment* – an attempt at imagining what it would be like for agents not to conceive of themselves as individuals in the strong sense.

10 Hegel would deny that Antigone represents a counterexample. In his view, the crucial thing about her was precisely that she did *not* think of herself as a moral subject standing apart from her social roles. In deciding whether to fulfill the dictates of the state and leave her brother Polyneices unburied or to fulfill the dictates of the family and bury him, Antigone did not look into her own conscience but followed the principle of the family in accordance with her role as sister, with which she wholly and completely identified. Her absolute certainty of the correctness of her position was a reflection of this complete and total identification. For an insightful discussion of this point, see Shklar 1971.

11 Hegel contends that because the ancient Greeks did not conceive of themselves as having separate and particular interests, the interests of the community could be "intrusted to the will and resolve of the citizens," and the Greek constitution could – and indeed, *had* to – be democratic (VPG, 308/252).

identified their good with the good of their community (PhG, 324–42/263–78). Hegel also contends that the ancient Greeks did not think of themselves as having rights apart from the prerogatives attached to their social roles and, indeed, that they felt no *need* for the protection of individual rights.

Here it should be pointed out that, although Hegel denies that the ancient Greeks were individuals in the *strong* sense, he never denies that they were individuals in the *minimal* sense. It is the strong, not the minimal, conception of individuality that Hegel regards as distinctively modern. The point deserves emphasis because one persistent source of misunderstanding of Hegel's conception of the ancient Greeks consists precisely in the assumption that, in denying that they were individuals, he *must* have meant that they were not individuals in the minimal sense of the term.

II. Social membership

Turning to Hegel's conception of social membership, we can start by observing that Hegel maintains, quite generally, that human beings are essentially (*wesentlich*) social. He contends that they are essentially social in two key respects. First, they depend on society for the satisfaction of biological, social, and cultural needs. Second, they depend on society for the realization of their distinctively human capacities, such as thought, language, and reason. Human beings would not be able to realize themselves as the kind of beings they are – as spiritual and hence social and cultural beings – unless they were members of a society. This view might be thought of as an interpretation of Aristotle's doctrine that man is a political animal.

In addition to this general and familiar view, Hegel is also committed to the specific and distinctive claim that modern people are essentially members of the modern social world. Let us examine this claim more closely.

In saying that modern people are essentially members of the *modern social world* Hegel means that they are essentially members of a specific kind of society: a society organized around the modern family, civil society, and the modern state. This claim is much stronger than the familiar Aristotelian position, which simply says that human beings are essentially members of society, but not of any particular kind of society. On the other hand, although Hegel thinks that people are formed by the culture of the country in which they are born and can never fully appropriate the particularities of a foreign culture, he does not deny the obvious fact that people can emigrate without (literally) ceasing to be the persons they are or ceasing to be spiritual beings. Instead of thinking that modern people are essentially members of particular nations, Hegel thinks they are essentially members of a universal set of arrangements concretely actualized in a variety of particular nation-states: the universal set of arrangements that constitutes the modern social world.

In saying that modern people are essentially *members* of the modern social world, Hegel means that they participate in its central institutions and (at least tacitly) conceive of themselves as participants in these institutions. Hegel maintains that they participate in this world because they are born there. He recognizes that it is of course possible in principle for particular individuals to leave modern society by moving into a culture that is not organized around modern social institutions or to leave society altogether, say, by becoming hermits. But Hegel would say these are not real options for most people. Realistically speaking, people in the modern social world have little choice but to participate in one way or another in its institutions. They are born into the framework these institutions form and it is there they die.[12] Hegel maintains that the reason modern people conceive of themselves at least tacitly as family members, members of civil society, and citizens is that their self-conceptions are formed through their participation in the family, civil society, and state. In participating in these arrangements modern people come to conceive of themselves, if only implicitly, as members of the family, civil society, and state.

In saying that people are *essentially* members of the modern social world Hegel means that the roles of family member, member of civil society, and citizen (the central social roles) are 'essential' to who they are in both a nonmetaphysical and a metaphysical sense. The *nonmetaphysical* sense in which the central social roles are essential is that they are extremely important. Hegel contends that there are three main reasons why.

The first reason is that the roles of family member, member of civil society, and citizen figure centrally in the psychological makeup of modern people. Hegel maintains that the attitudes, habits, and ideals internal to these roles constitute core features of personality

12 This formulation derives from Rawls (1989, 242).

and character (PR, §§147, 153, 268). These roles are also intimately bound up with basic needs and desires. Thus, for example, Hegel claims that people in the modern social world need and desire the sort of intimacy that modern family life ideally provides. Although the obligations of family life, such as caring for one's children, may, on occasion, conflict with one's separate and particular interests, they do not constitute external demands disconnected from one's own feelings and values but instead reflect norms that are part of one's own basic values and desires (see PR, §147).

Hegel contends that this congruence between self and role is to be explained by reference to the institutional process through which needs and values are formed. His moral psychology is thus rooted in his sociology. He maintains that the most central and fundamental needs and values that people have are formed through a *Bildungsprozeß* (a process of socialization, acculturation, and education) (see PR, §187R). In the modern social world this process takes place within the family, civil society, and the state. These institutions channel and shape needs and desires in such a way that modern people come to need and value the forms of life that are internal to these institutions. In this way they "form the will" of people in the modern social world.[13]

In maintaining that the process of will formation is institutional, Hegel does not mean to deny that social institutions need raw, biological material on which to operate. He maintains that social institutions initially form the will by shaping and channeling a variety of drives, needs, and desires that are biologically given (PR, §§161, 194). *Bildung* consists largely in a process of giving determinate social and cultural shape to biological needs (PR, §§161, 163R). The family, for example, molds the natural desire for sex and offspring (which can be satisfied in any number of ways) into the socially specific desire for marital life and family (which can be satisfied only within a very specific institutional context). It makes these originally natural desires 'social' in that it provides them with social – institutionally defined – objects (marital life and family). This *social* desire for marital life and family, not its raw biological antecedents, leads people to marry. Thus, the institutional process of will formation plays a very strong role in shaping individual character and personality.

---

13 The term 'will formation' (*Willensbildung*) derives from Habermas (1973a, 148; 1975, 108).

Hegel does not, however, claim that a person's character and personality are wholly determined by this process. Nor does he hold that they are completely fixed by social roles. His contention is that the central social roles constitute core features of the psychological makeup of modern people, not that they exhaust personality and character. Put another way, he claims that the central social institutions shape the fundamental needs and values of modern people, not that they uniquely fix them.

It should also be stressed that Hegel does not think, as is sometimes suggested, that human beings are 'mere particularizations' of their roles. He recognizes that the particularities, eccentricities, and idiosyncrasies of individual people are myriad. Moreover, he thinks that civil society and the modern family each provide a sphere for the realization of different aspects of human particularity. He argues that modern people can express and develop their emotional and psychological needs within the family (PR, §§164R, 175) and that they can express and develop their interests, talents, and skills within civil society (PR, §§182–7).

The second reason the central social roles are extremely important is that these roles and the institutions of which they are a part provide the basic elements and constitute the basic framework of the lives modern people actually live (see VPRHO, 485). The particular person to whom one is married and the particular job one has constitute basic elements of the particular life one leads. Yet these elements depend on a social world organized around the family and civil society. Moreover, the choice of work and spouse constitutes part of the basic framework within which modern people live. In making these choices, one chooses the particular life that one will lead. These are, in Hegel's view, *the* basic life choices the modern social world offers. They represent the main arenas within which modern people exercise individual choice.[14] It is perhaps also worth pointing out that even if one chooses not to marry or not to work, or is unable to find work or to marry, one's basic life choices

14 One obvious difference between Hegel's social world and ours is that our social world provides a wider range of domestic options than Hegel's did. Not marrying is far more acceptable in our time than it was in Hegel's. And there now exist alternative forms of familial life and committed relationships that were not available in Hegel's social world. But the underlying point remains the same. If, for example, one of the basic personal choices people face today is between a married and an unmarried committed relationship, this is largely due to a change in the social world, a transformation of the possibilities it provides.

will still be framed by the social world and one's status will still be defined in institutional terms (e.g., unemployed, unmarried).[15]

Hegel contends that the third reason the central social roles are extremely important is that the personal cost of rejecting them will be extremely high. If one rejects these roles in *thought* – for example, by refusing to conceive of oneself in terms of them – one's self-understanding will become abstract and impoverished. If, for example, one refuses to conceive of oneself as a citizen or refuses to recognize that one conceives of oneself as a citizen, one will not be able to understand why one is so embarrassed or angered by one's country's foreign policy.[16] In a well-ordered social world, if one rejects these roles in *practice* (if, e.g., one resists participating in the family, civil society, or state), one's *life* will become abstract and impoverished. In addition to forgoing the good of participating in these institutions, one will fail to realize certain fundamental potentialities and meet certain deeply seated needs (e.g., the need for a maximally deep and stable personal relationship, the need to realize one's distinctive talents and abilities, and the need to pursue common ends in a self-conscious and rational way). Hegel argues that the explanation for the resultant abstraction and impoverishment is in both cases the same: to reject the central social roles is to reject core features of one's own personality and character. In rejecting them, one rejects much of what gives content and meaning to one's life.

It is crucial to note that Hegel recognizes that there may be historical circumstances in which it is reasonable to withdraw from the social world. Thus, for example, he says, "When the existing world of freedom has become unfaithful to the better will, this will no longer finds itself in the duties recognized in this world and must seek to recover in ideal inwardness alone that harmony which it has lost in actuality" (PR, §138R). He maintains that the social worlds in which Socrates and the Stoics lived provided a real example of

---

15 Compare: "Marriage is the destiny traditionally offered to women by society. It is still true that most women are married, or have been, or plan to be, or suffer from not being. The celibate [i.e., single] woman [*la célibataire*] is to be explained and defined with reference to marriage, whether she is frustrated, rebellious, or even indifferent in regard to that institution" (De Beauvoir 1949, 9; 1989, 425).

16 Note the following remark of Thomas Nagel: "Citizenship is a surprisingly strong bond, even for those of us whose patriotic feelings are weak. We read the newspaper every day with rage and horror, and it was different from reading about the crimes of another country" (1979, xii).

such circumstances. And so, it is not Hegel's view that there is a sort of transhistorical guarantee that people will always be able to find meaning in the existing social roles.

It is also essential to stress that Hegel does not maintain that modern people should accept the central social roles simply because these roles are deeply rooted in their personalities and characters and provide the basic elements and constitute the basic framework of the lives they live. Nor does he argue that they should accept them simply because the personal costs of rejecting them would be high. Although Hegel does think that these considerations do provide reasons for accepting these roles, he also thinks that it is crucial to show that the central social roles are reflectively acceptable. One of his central aims in the *Philosophy of Right* is to show that the roles of family member, member of civil society, and citizen are reflectively acceptable by showing that the arrangements of which they are a part – the family, civil society, and the state – are themselves reflectively acceptable. This aspect of Hegel's project will be taken up in Chapter 6.

In addition to maintaining that the modern social roles are essential in the nonmetaphysical sense we have just considered, Hegel also maintains that there is a specifically *metaphysical* sense in which these roles are essential. Because one of my aims in this reconstruction is to avoid going into the metaphysical aspect of Hegel's theory, I do not want to explore this point at length. But since there *is* a metaphysical sense in which Hegel takes the central social roles to be essential, we need to account for this fact. We need to have some basic understanding of what this metaphysical sense is.

The first thing to get clear about is what it is not. In claiming that there is a metaphysical sense in which the central social roles are essential Hegel is not addressing the issue central to analytical philosophers of mind: what is necessary for the persistence of the person? This is simply not a question that interests Hegel.

What interests Hegel is rather different. His philosophical concern is with the conditions that people must satisfy in order to realize themselves as the kind of beings they are. Hegel maintains that the kind of beings people most fundamentally are is *Geist*, and by this he means that they are most fundamentally social and cultural beings.[17] Accordingly, he maintains that the metaphysical sense in

---

17 The notion of *Geist* and the claim that people are *Geist* are discussed in the first part of Chapter 2.

which the central social roles are essential is that they are roles that modern people must exercise in order to realize themselves as *Geist*.

This claim is grounded in his view that in order fully to realize themselves as *Geist*, modern people must participate in that form of human social life that expresses the correct understanding of the human spirit. He contends that that form of human social life is to be found within the system of social arrangements constituted by civil society and the modern family and state: the modern social world. Thus, modern people participate in these arrangements, and thus realize themselves as *Geist*, precisely by exercising the roles of family member, member of civil society, and citizen.

Hegel does not think that exercising the central social roles is a sufficient condition for *fully* realizing oneself as *Geist*. It is also necessary to engage in art, religion, and philosophy. The point I have been urging here is that he does think that exercising the central social roles is a *necessary* condition for fully realizing oneself as *Geist*.

The preceding account of Hegel's understanding of the metaphysical and nonmetaphysical senses in which the central social roles are essential has, I trust, made it clear that his conception of modern social membership is strong. In his view, the roles of family member, member of civil society, and citizen are not merely 'external' roles, unconnected with the personality, character, or essence of the people who inhabit them. They instead constitute core features of people's personalities and characters, provide the basic elements and constitute the basic framework of their lives, and are indispensable for the realization of their essence as *Geist*. Thus, it is plausible to contend that, as Hegel conceives of them, modern people are full-fledged social members.

I close this preliminary discussion of Hegel's conception of modern social membership by contrasting it with two other conceptions: first, his own conception of ancient Greek social membership and, then, the communitarian conception of social membership.

Hegel's conception of the social membership of the ancient Greeks represents the flip-side of his view that they were not individuals in the strong sense of the term.[18] Because the ancient Greeks had no conception of themselves *as selves* apart from their social roles, their social membership was 'immediate' in that it was not mediated by a conception of the self as a self. This is what Hegel has in mind when he says that "the individual [in the Greek world]

18 See n. 9.

is therefore unconsciously united [*in unbefangener Einheit*] with the universal end [i.e., the maintenance of the community]" (VG, 249/ 202).

Two comments are in order. In claiming that the ancient Greeks had no conception of themselves as selves apart from their roles, Hegel does not mean to suggest that they failed to conceive of themselves as individuals in the minimal sense or that they were incapable of reflexive thought. He is simply saying that they did not conceive of themselves as having the capacity to abstract from any given social role. Nor does Hegel mean to suggest that the ancient Greeks *could not* abstract from their social roles because something was missing from their biological makeup. He contends, rather, that they lack this capacity because they were not brought up to do it. He assumes, quite plausibly, that the capacity to abstract from social roles is the result of education and upbringing, a product of *Bildung*. And he also assumes, still plausibly I think, that societies could exist in which people are not brought up to abstract from their social roles. Whether or not we decide to accept Hegel's view of the ancient Greeks, the conception of social membership it expresses – a conception of immediate social membership – is not impossible.

In the communitarian conception of social membership, people (including *modern* people) are essentially social in that they take their social roles and group memberships to be essential to who they are. The sense in which they take these roles and attachments to be essential to their 'identity' is that they *believe* that they could not possibly reject them.[19]

The intuition behind this conception is that people take their social roles and attachments to be so central to their self-understanding that they would not know how to begin to understand themselves apart from them. Communitarians note that many people believe that were they to abandon these roles and attachments, their lives would cease to have point or meaning. And they observe that some people believe that turning away from these roles and attachments would transform them to such a degree that they could be said to be different persons.[20]

On the face of things, the communitarian conception closely resembles Hegel's understanding of ancient Greek social membership. Both involve the idea of not being able to abstract from one's social roles. But the use these conceptions make of this idea is quite

19 Sandel 1982, 150.
20 Ibid., 62, 150, 179; cf. Rawls 1985, 241–2; and Frankfurt 1988, 80–94.

different. People are social members in the immediate sense if they *cannot* abstract from their social roles and attachments. People are social members in the communitarian sense if they *believe* they cannot reject their social roles and attachments. The communitarian conception, thus understood, is not committed to the thesis that modern people lack the capacity to abstract from their social roles.[21]

The communitarian conception of social membership differs from Hegel's conception of modern social membership in four important respects. The first is that, although it is meant to apply to modern people, it draws no distinction between ancient and modern social membership and speaks instead of social membership generally.[22] A second respect in which it differs is that it assumes that modern people explicitly conceive of themselves in terms of their social roles and attachments and that they take these roles and attachments to be central to their self-conception.[23] Although Hegel would agree that social roles and attachments figure centrally in the self-conception of modern people, he rejects the assumption that it is generally true that modern people *explicitly* conceive of themselves in these terms. He would say that some modern people explicitly conceive of themselves in this way, but not all. He recognizes that a significant number of people in the modern world conceive of themselves atomistically, as individuals in the strong sense rather than as social members. And it should be stressed that it is not his aim to convince them to abandon their understanding of themselves as individuals in the strong sense. His goal is, rather, to establish that this self-conception, properly understood, is compatible with thinking of oneself in terms of the central social roles and to show how it is possible to combine the conception of oneself as an individual in the strong sense with the conception of oneself as a social member. Unlike the communitarians, Hegel is clearly and unequivocally a friend of individuality in the strong sense.

Let us look more closely at Hegel's claim that the conception that modern people have of themselves as family members, members

---

21 One does sometimes find communitarians suggesting that modern people *cannot* abstract from their social roles (e.g., because there is no self apart from those roles that could assess them; see, e.g., Sandel 1982, 182). *Thus* understood, the communitarian conception of modern social membership is essentially the same as Hegel's conception of Greek social membership, or, more precisely, it extends the basic features of Hegel's conception of Greek social membership to modern social membership.

22 But cf. MacIntyre 1981.

23 Sandel 1982, 150, 179.

of civil society, and citizens is often tacit. He holds, more specifically, that modern people characteristically conceive of themselves *in the ways in which* family members, members of civil society, and citizens do. An example may help. The man who goes out to buy shoes for his daughter has a certain view of himself and his world. Even if he does not explicitly recognize that he conceives of himself as a father (in other words, even if he does not explicitly recognize that he identifies with the role of father), his ends, his sense of his obligations, and his understanding of his relations with the members of his family are those *of a father*. He has these ends, obligations, and understandings because he is a father, and these ends, obligations, and understandings are constitutive of what it is to regard oneself as a father. One can conceive of oneself *in the way in which* a member of the family, civil society, or state does without explicitly regarding oneself as a family member, member of civil society, or citizen; and, indeed, without even recognizing that one conceives of oneself in the way in which a family member, member of civil society, or citizen does.

One of Hegel's central aims in the *Philosophy of Right* is to help his readers recognize that they do in fact conceive of themselves as members of the family, civil society, and the state. His strategy is, first, to show them that they conceive of themselves *in the ways in which* family members, members of civil society, and citizens do. Once they grasp this fact, they will recognize that they *implicitly* regard themselves as family members, members of civil society, and citizens. And once they grasp *this* fact, they will come to view themselves *explicitly* in this way. Thus, from a Hegelian standpoint, the communitarian view that modern people start out explicitly conceiving of themselves in terms of their social roles gets things exactly backward. Modern people do not begin by explicitly thinking of themselves in this way; that is where they are supposed to end up.[24] Coming to explicitly think of oneself as a family member, member of civil society, and citizen is, in Hegel's view, one of the crucial steps in the subjective process of reconciliation.

The third respect in which the communitarian conception of

24 Hegel recognizes that the task of showing people that they (implicitly) regard themselves as *citizens* may be especially difficult. One reason is that their participation in the modern political state is strikingly limited. Moreover, the modern political state is itself especially hard to understand. Accordingly, one of the central tasks of the *Philosophy of Right* is to provide an account of the modern state and modern citizenship that will help people grasp that they are citizens and to come to explicitly conceive of themselves as such.

modern social membership differs from Hegel's is in its claim that people generally believe that they cannot reject their social roles.[25] Hegel would deny this. He maintains that modern people do generally recognize that they have the capacity to abstract from – and reject – their social roles and that this is an essential feature of modern social life (see VPG, 308/252). Hegel recognizes, of course, that there are people in the modern social world who believe that they cannot reject their social roles. But he would contend they are mistaken. He would say that although such people may, quite understandably, be *unwilling* to reject their social roles and may couch this unwillingness in the language of impossibility, they do in fact have the capacity to reject any given social role (see PR, §5).

As we have seen, Hegel recognizes that the cost of rejecting one or other of the central social roles may be extremely high.[26] But he thinks it is a cost human beings can bear. He claims that modern people can reject these roles because he maintains that the human capacity to negate its determinations extends to the deepest and most firmly entrenched characteristics of the self (PR, §5; EG, §382, Z). Thus, for example, "it is inherent in this element of the will [its ability to abstract] that I am able to free myself from everything, to renounce all ends, and to abstract from everything" (PR, §5, Z; VPRG, 111; VPRHO, 112). In saying that modern people can reject the central social roles, Hegel is not minimizing the depth or significance of these roles.[27] He is instead affirming the power of human freedom (PR, §5; EL, §382, Z).

The fourth and final contrast between the communitarian conception of modern social membership and Hegel's is the following. Whereas the communitarian conception tends to emphasize membership in smaller groups (e.g., families) and communities (e.g., neighborhoods), Hegel stresses membership in the larger structures constituted by the family, civil society, and the state.[28] To be sure, Hegel thinks that membership in these larger structures always takes

---

25 There is also a strand of communitarian thought that does not deny that people can reject their social roles but holds, in effect, that they *ought* not to do so (Sandel 1982, 62, 179, 182) or that they ought to have commitments that "run deep enough to be defining" (ibid., 182).

26 Cf. ibid., 179.   27 Cf. ibid., 62, 179, 182.

28 Admittedly, communitarians do also place emphasis on membership in the state, but it is, I think, true that there is a strong tendency in communitarian thought to stress the importance of membership in smaller groups and communities at the expense of membership in larger structures. An exception to this rule, which may mark a development in communitarian thinking, is Bellah et al. 1992.

the form of being a member of *a* family, *a* civil society, and *a* state, but from his point of view, the sheer particularity of the objects of these attachments is not what makes them important.[29] For Hegel, the important thing about my being a citizen of *this* state is that it is only in virtue of being a member of some particular state (*this* state, as the case may be) that I can be a member of *the* state. In this regard, Hegel's understanding of modern social membership is far more universalistic than that of the communitarians.

III. The compatibility of individuality and social membership

Having considered Hegel's conception of modern individuality and modern social membership, it is time to examine his understanding of their relation. To begin with, Hegel contends that modern individuality and modern social membership are compatible. This amounts to the claim that modern people can in principle be individuals in the strong sense as well as members of the modern family, civil society, and the modern state. The first thing to observe about this claim is that Hegel's conception of modern individuality and social membership makes it eminently plausible. Hegel seems to have found a way of conceiving things such that a full-fledged form of individuality and a full-fledged form of social membership *can* be combined. But before we conclude that he has succeeded in doing so, two worries need to be addressed.

The first worry flows out of Hegel's wish to maintain that modern people can reject the central social roles even though these roles are essential to who they are. On the face of things, this claim may seem incoherent. What could the essentiality of these roles come to if not that they cannot be rejected?

But recall what Hegel means in asserting that the central social roles are essential. Neither the metaphysical nor the nonmetaphysical sense in which he represents them as essential precludes their rejection. The nonmetaphysical sense is that they are extremely important. But, as we have just seen, Hegel maintains that modern people can reject their social roles no matter how important they are. The metaphysical sense is that they are roles modern people must exercise in order fully to realize themselves as *Geist*. But this does not mean that it is *inevitable* that people will exercise these roles.

---

29 Cf. Sandel 1982, 179.

It simply means that unless they exercise these roles, they will not fully realize their essence as *Geist*. And, again, Hegel thinks that modern people can reject *any* given social role, including those that are necessary for realization of their essence. Thus, Hegel's interpretation of the idea that the central social roles are essential makes it possible to conceive of these roles as being essential *and* as being such that they can be rejected.

The second worry is whether people can *conceive* of themselves both as individuals in the strong sense and as members of the central social institutions. Hegel argues that they can. He maintains that conceptions of the self as bearer of separate and particular interests (PR, §§189–207), possessor of individual rights (PR, §§209–28), and subject of conscience (PR, §§136, Z, 137, R, Z) are all internal to the role of member of civil society. To conceive of oneself along these lines is to conceive of oneself precisely in the way in which a member of civil society does. Hegel further contends that civil society provides the proper institutional sphere for the expression of these conceptions of the self. It is in civil society that one pursues one's separate and particular interests, insists on one's individual rights, and acts on the basis of conscience.[30] And so there is no incompatibility between conceiving of oneself as a bearer of separate and particular interests, possessor of individual rights, and subject of conscience on the one hand and conceiving of oneself as a member of civil society on the other. Moreover, Hegel argues that the modern social world is structured in such a way that one can be a member of civil society as well as a member of the family and the state (PR, §145). And so he contends there is no incompatibility between conceiving of oneself as a family member and citizen *and* conceiving of oneself as a bearer of separate and particular interests, possessor of individual rights, and subject of conscience.

One might wonder, however, whether conceiving of oneself as a member of the family, civil society, and state is compatible with regarding oneself *as a self*. The question arises because for Hegel conceiving of oneself as a self is a matter of regarding oneself as independent of and distinct from one's roles. How can one both

---

30 The point here is not that Hegel thinks that the family and state are not subject to the assessment of private conscience. On the contrary, one of his central aims in the *Philosophy of Right* is precisely to show that these institutions are reflectively acceptable. It is rather that he thinks that in a well-ordered social world, civil society – unlike the family and state – will constitute a sphere in which people will characteristically be called upon to make ethical decisions on the basis of conscience. I take up this point below.

conceive of oneself in this way and conceive of oneself in terms of one's roles?

Hegel's answer turns on his interpretation of the idea of independence and distinctness. As he interprets this idea, conceiving of oneself as independent of, and distinct from, one's roles requires only that one regard oneself as *having the capacity* to abstract from any given role. The salient feature of this interpretation is that it makes it possible to be independent and distinct from one's roles while conceiving of oneself in terms of them. I can, for example, conceive of myself as a citizen and regard myself as being able to abstract from this role (e.g., as being able to surrender my citizenship). There is no incompatibility between conceiving of oneself in terms of a given social role and conceiving of oneself as having the capacity to abstract from a given social role.

Now it is true that there is a sense in which, in abstracting from a social role, one conceives of oneself as 'external' to that role. One then takes oneself to be able to question and evaluate and accept or reject that role. It is equally true that there is a sense in which, in abstracting from a social role, one conceives of the role as external to oneself. One then takes it to be something one can question and evaluate and accept or reject. And so it turns out that the act of abstraction contains within itself a moment of reflective separation between self and role (see PR, §5). Indeed one might say: a moment of alienation. This, in turn, might lead one to wonder whether there is not some kind of fundamental incompatibility between actually exercising the capacity to abstract from one's social roles and conceiving of oneself in terms of them.

Hegel would reply by observing that although it is true that there is a moment of separation, and indeed alienation, that is internal to abstraction, this separation need not be permanent. The person who asks of a given role, "Is this role suitable for me?" or "Do I want to play this role?" may in principle answer these questions in the affirmative. In answering such questions in the affirmative, one 'identifies reflectively', as I shall say, with the role (see PR, §7).

Reflective identification, as Hegel conceives of it, is a form of *identification* because it involves conceiving of oneself in terms of one's role. One says to oneself, for example, "I am a sister and I affirm my role as a sister." Reflective identification is *reflective* in that it proceeds through the reflective act of stepping back from a social role and evaluating it. It thus differs dramatically from 'immediate identification', the form of identification Hegel takes to be exemplified by the ancient Greeks. Immediate identification is so called because it is a form of role identification that is not mediated by a conception of the self as a self. The crucial fact about *reflective* identification, by contrast, is that it *is* mediated by a conception of the self as a self. To identify *reflectively* with one's social roles is to identify with them *as a self*. Reflective identification thus provides a (Hegel would say *the*) reflective means of bridging the gap between the self and its roles that is opened by the reflective act of abstraction. Reflective identification makes it possible to overcome the moment of alienation internal to reflection *without* abandoning reflection (see PR, §147R).

That modern people have the capacity to identify reflectively with their social roles is a striking fact about them. It means that the alienation internal to reflection need not be final.[31] It means that people can both reflect on *and* identify with their social roles. Philosophers before Hegel had called attention to the fact that people can abstract from their social roles. (Kant's conception of the moral subject turns crucially on this fact.) But to my knowledge, no philosopher before Hegel had called attention, at least in this very clear and explicit way, to the fact that people – modern or otherwise – can identify reflectively with their social roles. Hegel's discovery of this capacity represents one of his greatest insights.

IV. Social membership as making individuality possible

In addition to arguing for the compatibility of modern individuality and social membership, Hegel also contends that modern social membership – or, better, the modern social world – makes modern individuality possible. The distinctively modern features of modern individuality are those that fall under the heading of strong individuality. Hegel maintains that the constituent understandings of strong individuality (conceiving of oneself as a self, bearer of separate and particular interests, possessor of individual rights, and subject of conscience) belong to the self-conception people have as members of civil society (PR, §§189–207, 209–28, 242). He holds that civil society provides the proper sphere for the exercise of these self-understandings; within this sphere as opposed to, say, that of

31 Cf. Sartre 1943.

the family, it is appropriate to pursue one's separate and particular interests and insist upon one's individual rights.

Hegel also holds that these self-understandings are *engendered* by the practices of civil society. It is precisely as a result of participating in civil society that modern people come to think of themselves as selves and as bearers of separate and particular interests (see PR, §§189–207).[32] Participating in civil society is a matter of abstracting oneself from one's role of family member and citizen (PR, §§182Z, 238; VPRG, 472) and pursuing one's separate and particular interests in the world of work (*die System der Bedurfnisse*) (PR, §§189–207). These interests are protected by the rights codified by the administration of justice (*die Rechtspflege*) (PR, §§209–29) and by the public authority (*die Polizei*) (PR, §§231–55). One comes to think of oneself as a possessor of rights by performing such acts as entering into formal legal relations (e.g., by making contracts) and making use of the legal system (e.g., by filing lawsuits). And, in Hegel's view, it is within civil society that one is most likely to be confronted with ethical situations that engage one's conscience (PR, §242), for within this sphere (in contrast, he thinks, to the family and the state)[33] one cannot rely on custom to determine what one ought to do. One is forced instead to appeal to private moral reflection. The upshot of this is that it is *through* participating in civil society, *through* actualizing oneself as a member of civil society, that one actualizes oneself as an individual in the strong sense.

Hegel does not, however, maintain that strong individuality is the provenance of civil society alone. An important function of the modern family is to raise children to be members of civil society (see PR, §§177, 180, 238), which is largely a matter of raising them to have the dispositions characteristic of individuals in the strong sense (e.g., to pursue their separate and particular interests, to insist upon their rights, and to consider things from the standpoint of their consciences) and to conceive of themselves as individuals in the strong sense. One basic function of the modern state is to maintain and support the framework of civil society within which modern people can actualize themselves as individuals in the strong sense (PR, §§260, Z, 287; VPRG, 635; VPRHO, 717).[34] Thus, as

32 It must be pointed out that, in Hegel's view, women do not participate in civil society. This point is taken up in the first section of Chapter 6 and again in the Conclusion.

33 It is clear and generally recognized that this aspect of Hegel's view of the state in particular is, to say the least, overly optimistic.

34 This point is taken up in Chapter 6.

Hegel conceives of them, both the modern family and the modern state cooperate with civil society in fostering and engendering individuality in the strong sense.

V. The social dimension of individuality

We have, in effect, already entered the topic of this section: the social dimension of modern individuality, for the account presented in the preceding section suggests that Hegel's understanding of strong individuality is radically social. Far from its being the case that modern people act as individuals *rather than* social members when acting as individuals in the strong sense, it is evident that they then act *as* members of civil society. Moreover, it is not merely true for Hegel that people need to live in *society* (some form of society or other) if they are to actualize themselves as strong individuals – a fact that even the defenders of atomistic conceptions of individualism would concede. Hegel also contends that modern people need to live in a highly determinate *kind* of society: a social world containing a civil society. Furthermore, Hegel argues that the modern family and the modern state are both preconditions of strong individuality. In order to become individuals in the strong sense, people must be raised within modern families, because, Hegel contends, the modern family is uniquely suited to provide the sort of *education sentimentale* people must have in order to become individuals in the strong sense. And he holds that the modern political state provides the institutional maintenance and support necessary for the preservation of the existence of civil society (PR, §§260, Z, 287; VPRG, 635; VPRHO, 717). Without the support of the political state, the institutional sphere within which alone people can actualize themselves as individuals in the strong sense – civil society – could not maintain and reproduce itself.

What needs to be added here is that Hegel maintains that individuality in the strong sense is *only one component* of the full structure of modern individuality. Individuality in 'the complete sense', as Hegel conceives of it, also includes membership in the modern family and state. For Hegel, to be an individual in the complete sense is, inter alia, to be a member of the modern family, civil society, and the state. It is *through* one's participation in these arrangements that one actualizes oneself as an individual in the complete sense.

As we have seen, Hegel contends that the attitudes, habits, and ideals internal to the role of family member are rooted in the personality and character of modern people. And we know that he also maintains that modern people characteristically conceive of themselves *in the way in which* family members do even if they do not explicitly conceive of themselves *as* family members. They attach a certain weight to their familial obligations, regard the maintenance of their families as an important final end, are willing to make certain personal sacrifices for the sake of their families, and so forth. Considerations such as these lead Hegel to maintain that family membership figures crucially in modern individuality. He maintains that if we want to understand who modern people are, we must understand the role that family membership plays in their lives.

Hegel would also make the parallel argument with respect to membership in the state. He maintains that the attitudes, habits, and ideals internal to the role of citizen are also rooted in the personality and character of modern people (see VG, 52–3/46, 111/94). And he holds that modern people characteristically conceive of themselves in the way in which citizens do. They attach a certain weight to their obligations to the state, regard the maintenance of their country as an important end, and are willing to make certain personal sacrifices – even, in wartime, the sacrifice of their own lives – for the sake of their country (PR, §324). Hegel contends that if we want to understand who modern people are, we must understand the role that membership in the state plays in their lives.

It should also be added that Hegel maintains that the personality and character of modern people will generally be shaped by the *Geist* – the customs, practices, and ideals – of the particular nation in which they are raised. Thus, for example, the habits, values, and ideals of people raised in the United States will typically be American. For quite understandable reasons, many Americans reject certain central features of the American way of life. But the way in which they reject these features will typically fall into characteristically American patterns. And the standard experience of Americans who go to Africa or Europe seeking their roots is that they discover, for better or worse, that they are Americans, not Africans or Europeans (see PR, §195Z; VPRHO, 598).

Although Hegel himself does not stress the point, the analogous claim could be made about the relation between the personality and character of modern people and the particular families in which they are raised. Each particular family has its own particular *Geist*, its own particular customs, values, and ideals. Part of what it is to grow up in a particular family is to be shaped by *its* particular *Geist*.

Many people do, it is true, reject the spirit of their families, but this rejection can never be complete, and the trajectory of their rejection will characteristically be shaped by the very customs, values, and ideals they seek to reject. From Hegel's point of view, people are no less ineluctably the products of their particular families than they are the products of the particular countries in which they were born. The paradigmatic occasion upon which they come to recognize that they share the *Geist* of the family in which they were raised is when they marry. To marry is to encounter the *Geist* of another family in the most intimate and intense way possible. Each particular marriage is the marriage not only of two particular individuals but also of the customs, values, and ideals of two particular families.

One might, of course, take issue with Hegel's contention that family membership and membership in the state constitute components of the *individuality* of modern people. After all, these roles are roles that people *share.* But here it should be pointed out that Hegel rejects the commonsense identification of individuality with eccentricity and idiosyncrasy. He maintains that roles – like projects, character traits, and physical features – can be part of a person's individuality despite the fact that they are shared. This is, I think, an extremely plausible view.

Consider the man who self-consciously identifies with the role of father. This role is occupied by many men. But if we want to understand who *this* man is *in his individuality*, we must recognize that he is a father and conceives of himself as such. Not the least reason why these are facts about him as an individual is that they are facts about the particular human being he is. They are also facts that figure centrally in his sentiments, self-conception, and personal view of the world – in other words, his subjectivity. To be sure, there will be ways in which his way of being a father will be unique and original; part of what it is to become a father is to tailor the role to one's own temperament and circumstances. But the central fact about him is not that his way of being a father is unique but rather that he, like many other fathers, is *a* father and conceives of himself as such.

The general philosophical point behind this example is Hegel's view that individuality (*Einzelheit*) consists in the unity of particularity (*Besonderheit*) and universality (*Allgemeinheit*) (PR, §7R; EL, §§163–5; cf. PR, §258R). From a Hegelian standpoint, the man's 'universality' consists (in part) in his role as a father (see PR, §303R).

His 'particularity' consists (in part) in the specific way in which he inhabits this role, his being the father of this child, his being this specific kind of a father, and so forth. We cannot understand who this man is 'in his universality', unless we consider the fact that he occupies this 'universal' role. Nor can we understand who he is 'in his particularity' (a man who inhabits the role of father in this particular way) unless we consider how he occupies this role, *his* way of being a father. And so Hegel would insist that his individuality is to be understood in terms of both his particularity and his universality. It is perhaps worth pointing out that Hegel maintains that individuality, thus understood, exhibits the structure of what he calls the *Begriff* (concept) (EL, §§163–5; WL, 2:273–301/600–22), which Hegel regards as the basic structure of reason (see PR, §258R).

VI. The individual dimension of social membership

Let us turn, finally, to the individualistic dimension of modern social membership. The most obvious component of this dimension is the role of member of civil society. As we have seen, it is in their capacity as members of civil society that modern people are able to actualize themselves as individuals in the strong sense. Perhaps the most striking difference between the ancient and modern social worlds, as Hegel conceives of them, is the fact that the latter, unlike the former, contains a sphere within which people not only *can* but *ought* to pursue their separate and particular interests (PR, §§185R, 260Z; VPRG, 635; VPRHO, 718). It is precisely by pursuing their separate and particular interests within civil society that modern people actualize themselves as members of civil society and satisfy the separate and particular interests of one another (PR, §§184, Z, 199; VPRHO, 571). Individuality in the strong sense is thus the lifeblood of civil society (PR, §§185–6).

But the role of member of civil society is not the only component of the individual dimension of modern social membership. For Hegel, the modern roles of family member and citizen each contain an individualistic aspect as well. Consider the modern family. In his view, parents have the aim of raising their children to be individuals in the strong sense (PR, §§177, 238) and children have the aim of leaving the family and becoming individuals in the strong sense (PR, §§175, 238). An important component of the self-conception of a modern citizen is the understanding that one end of the state is the individuality of its members (PR, §261, Z; VPRHO,

719). And although Hegel thinks one can be a perfectly good family member or citizen without reflectively identifying with these roles, he maintains that reflective identification represents something like the highest stage of social membership (see PR, §147, R). It is his view that in order fully to actualize oneself as a social member, one must reflectively identify with the roles of family member, member of civil society, and citizen. In reflectively identifying with these roles, one absorbs these roles into one's subjectivity, thereby actualizing one's social membership *through* one's individuality. People who actualize their individuality through their social membership and their social membership through their individuality in the ways just described could be said to actualize themselves as individual social members. Hegel's conception of individuality and social membership can be thought of as a conception of individual social membership.

6

THE FAMILY, CIVIL SOCIETY, AND THE STATE

Hegel's account of the modern social world represents the culmination of his project of reconciliation. It is here that he seeks to show that the modern social world is in fact a home. My purpose in this chapter and the next is to provide a reconstruction of this final stage of his argument. In this chapter, I present Hegel's account of the structure of the modern family, civil society, and the modern state. I explain how, according to Hegel, these institutions make it possible for modern people to actualize themselves as individuals and as social members.

Throughout the discussion that follows it will be crucial to bear in mind that Hegel presents his treatment of the modern social world neither as a purely descriptive account of the de facto features of existing modern institutions nor as a purely normative account of how these institutions ought to be. As we saw in Chapters 2 and 4, Hegel instead presents his theory of the modern social world as an account of the 'actuality' (*Wirklichkeit*) of the family, civil society, and the state in his technical sense of the term. That is, he presents it, on the one hand, as an account of the underlying essences of these institutions, insofar as their essences are realized in existing institutions and groups, and, on the other hand, as an account of existing institutions and groups, insofar as they realize their essences.

In discussing Hegel's conception of the modern family, civil society, and the modern state, I examine each of these institutions in turn.

I. The family

1. Hegel's conception of the modern family is familiar in many respects. It is a conception of the modern family as nuclear, bourgeois, and patriarchal. The modern family is *nuclear* in that the basic family unit is composed of the father, the mother, and their biological children. This unit is basic in that it constitutes a complete and self-sufficient family in its own right. The modern family is thus separate from the wider kinship group (*Stamm*) (PR, §§168, 172). It differs in this respect from the traditional family (e.g., the family of the medieval world), in which the basic family unit is composed of the larger grouping that would nowadays be called 'extended'. And, in contrast to the family in ancient Greece (the *oikos*), the modern family does not extend across generations.[1] When children come of age in the modern world, they leave their family of origin and form families of their own (PR, §177). "Every marriage leads to the renunciation of previous family relationships and the establishment of a new and self-sufficient family" (PR, §178).

Hegel maintains that the modern family is *bourgeois* in that, unlike the traditional family, it is not an independent unit of economic production but is instead a unit of consumption. Its internal economic life is characterized by the purchase and enjoyment of commodities rather than by productive activities such as farming. In the modern social world, civil society, not the family, is the locus of productive economic activities, and modern families depend on this sphere to satisfy the material needs of their members (PR, §238). The modern family is thus essentially a part of the bourgeois world of civil society (see EG, §523). It is also essential to this world. If modern families need civil society to provide the material goods their members consume, civil society needs modern families to purchase the products its members produce. Civil society also depends upon the modern family to supply its members. Human reproduction takes place within the family, not the marketplace, and modern families have the task of raising the children to have the abilities, dispositions, and attitudes they will need to participate in civil society.

---

1 For a discussion of the Greek family, see Lacey 1968.

A further respect in which the modern family is bourgeois is that it provides the institutional setting for the form of sentimental personal relations characteristic of bourgeois life. Hegel maintains that modern families are characteristically private, self-contained, emotional units whose members provide one another with emotional support and recognition (PR, §§158, Z, 164; VPRG, 420). Hegel suggests that the modern family came to acquire this character as the result of undergoing a structural transformation corresponding to the emergence of civil society (PR, §§180, R, 238). With the birth of civil society, the family withdrew from the wider kinship group and relinquished its productive activities. It became a smaller, closer, and more private unit within which affective relationships were especially intense.[2] Hegel does not, however, hold that love is somehow unique to the modern family. It is clear, for example, that he thinks that Antigone loved Polyneices. But Hegel does think the emphasis placed within the family on personal feeling is specifically modern. Indeed, he contends that one of the most striking and attractive features of the modern family is that it provides the framework within which alone people can find affective recognition of the psychological dimension of their particularity.

Thus, it is clear that Hegel would reject the view that has become popular in recent times that the structural transformation of the family represents a lamentable defensive retreat.[3] He holds, on the contrary, that this transformation constitutes the very development through which the family finally attained its mature form. Hegel would concede that the modern family *is* more specialized than its traditional predecessor but would argue that it is precisely this specialization that allows it to meet the need for emotional recognition of particularity that modern people characteristically have. Furthermore, Hegel thinks that civil society is, on the whole, far more effective at meeting human material needs than the traditional family was. His view is that the separation of the affective and economic spheres corresponding to the emergence of civil society and the structural transformation of the family allowed for the optimal satisfaction of both affective and material needs and, as such, is something to be affirmed.

The modern family is *patriarchal* in that the father is the head of the household, the legal representative of the family, and the figure responsible for controlling and administering the family's re-

2   Cf. for similarities Stone 1979.   3   Cf. Lasch 1977.

sources, as well as caring for the family generally (PR, §171). It is also patriarchal in virtue of the fact that the wife is in charge of the domestic life of the household and bears chief responsibility for child rearing (PR, §166). Hegel does not, of course, think that patriarchy is somehow unique to the modern family, but he does think that there is a specifically modern form of patriarchy that is different from that characteristic of traditional families.

Modern patriarchy, as Hegel understands it, is essentially restricted. Thus, for example, although he maintains that the father's role as head of the household includes the administration of the family's resources, Hegel emphatically rejects the idea that these resources belong to the father. For reasons we shall consider below, he holds that all property within the family is held in common. Moreover, it is quite clear that Hegel rejects the idea that the wife is the property of the husband. Hegel recognizes that women are persons (*Personen*) – bearers of individual rights – and consequently not the kind of beings that can be taken as property (see PR, §§42, 44). In his view, a husband who treated his wife as if she were his property would be acting unethically (*unsittlich*), and such a family would be defective. Hegel is at pains to point out that in contrast to Roman families, in which the position of children was virtually that of slaves (PR, §173), there is no sense in which modern fathers own their children (PR, §§40R, 175, R, 180R). He says explicitly and repeatedly that Roman law was defective because it assigned fathers too much authority over their children, including the right of life and death. But, of course, none of this is to suggest that Hegel rejects the core features of patriarchy. As we have seen, Hegel affirms a traditional version of the sexual division of labor. Why he does so is something we will consider shortly.

2. Let us turn now to an aspect of Hegel's conception of the modern family that may be somewhat less familiar: its radical communalism. This aspect is best approached by considering his understanding of the status of the marital contract. Hegel rejects the view, which he associates with Kant, that marriage is "merely . . . a civil contract" (PR, §161Z; VPRG, 425). He does not, however, deny that marriage is contractual. Nor does he regard the marital contract as an inessential formality. He contends, rather, that this contract, being the legal and formal expression of the free consent (*freie Einwillung*) that constitutes the "objectives origin" (*objective Ausgangspunkt*) of marriage, is indispensable (PR, §162). Precisely by contracting (as bearers of individual rights) to become "man and wife,"

men and women enter freely into marriage (PR, §§75, R, 163, R, 164). Hegel also maintains that the marital contract is unique. It is, in his view, "a contract to transcend [*aufheben*] the standpoint of contract" (PR, §163R [Knox]). This is the point at which we encounter the communalistic aspect of Hegel's conception of the family. The "standpoint of contract" is the standpoint from which people are viewed as bearers of individual rights. The sense in which men and women "transcend" this standpoint when they contract to marry is that they agree to enter a relationship in which neither relates to the other as a bearer of individual rights. According to Hegel, this is a crucial part of what agreeing to marry involves. In his view, the internal life of the family (modern as well as traditional) falls outside the realm of individual rights.

Hegel gives two main reasons for thinking this is so. The first has to do with the self-conception appropriate to the family: that of family member. "The disposition [appropriate to the family] is to have self-consciousness of one's individuality *within this unity* . . . so that one is present in it not as an independent person [*eine Person für sich*] but as a *member*" (PR, §158). Conceiving of oneself as a family member is a matter of regarding oneself as a member of one's family rather than as a separate and particular individual. It also involves regarding one's family as a good in itself and a final end. Hegel further contends that the normative structure of the relations of family members is determined by the obligations and ideals of the familial roles, not by the rights they have as individuals. My brother does not drive me to the emergency room because I have some individual right against him that he should do so. He drives me there because he is my brother. Hegel would say that it is inappropriate to treat a member of one's family as a bearer of individual rights. To do so is, in effect, to treat him or her as a member of civil society. And Hegel would argue that *that* way of treating someone is not appropriate to the family. It is civil rather than familial, the way the shopkeeper relates to his customers, not the way in which a husband relates to a wife, parents relate to their children, or siblings relate to one another. This is not, however, to say that Hegel holds that people have no rights whatsoever within the family. He maintains that they do have what might be called 'familial rights', which derive from their position in the family. Thus, for example, "children have a right to be *brought up* and *supported* at the expense of the family" (PR, §174; see also VPRG, 424).

The second reason Hegel gives for holding that the internal life of the family falls outside the realm of individual rights is one we have already encountered. "No member of the family has particular property although each has a right to what is held in common" (PR, §171). This idea flows naturally out of Hegel's view that family members do not relate to one another as bearers of individual rights. To regard oneself as an individual property owner is, in effect, to regard oneself as a bearer of individual rights and, hence, not as a family member. Thus, as Hegel conceives of it, the normative structure of the family is incompatible with private property, and he concludes that all property within the family must, therefore, be communally owned. The family's resources are "common property" (PR, §171). Presumably, this does not mean that no item of family property is separately possessed (e.g., that all clothing is shared), but only that when family members do possess items of the family property separately (e.g., clothing), they do so in their capacity as family members. If I view myself as a family member in Hegel's sense of the term, I will not regard the things I possess as my private property. I will view them instead as things *we* own that *I* make use of. Thus, in claiming that all property within the family is communally owned, Hegel is not, as it might appear, proposing a radically communalistic alternative to the modern family. He is instead proposing a radically communalistic reconceptualization of modern family life, one that he takes to be truer to the deeper self-understanding of his contemporaries than that which assigns them individual property rights.

But to say that the *internal* life of the modern family falls outside the realm of individual rights is not to say that the modern family falls outside this realm altogether. As we have seen, the modern family is a part of the world of civil society, which is the realm of individual rights. Hegel contends that, from a civil standpoint, the modern family represents one single legal person (PR, §162). When a man and a woman agree to marry, they agree to become one legal person, and their offspring will remain part of this legal person until they come of age. Civil society accommodates the radically nonindividualistic union of marriage and family within its individualistic framework precisely by treating families and married couples as individuals.

Hegel does not, however, regard the single person the married couple becomes as a legal fiction. Hegel holds that, in marrying, husband and wife "consent to *constitute a single person* and to give up their natural and individual personalities within this union" (PR, §162). Taken by itself, the first half of this remark might of course be read as simply saying that when people marry, they agree to accept a particular external legal status. But the second half makes it clear that Hegel thinks that marriage involves a transformation not only of one's public status but also of one's private self-conception. In his view, marriage is not, strictly speaking, a partnership – a union in which the separateness of the parties is preserved – but, instead, a deeper and more thoroughgoing union in which the separateness of the parties is overcome. We might take exception to this view, but it is crucial to recognize that it *is* the view that Hegel holds. Marriage, he claims, "arises out of the *free surrender* by both sexes of their personalities" (PR, §168). It is important not to be misled here by Hegel's talk of the surrender of personality. His idea is not that one party abandons his or her own opinions, desires, and interests, simply taking over those of the other. Hegel says explicitly that the "surrender of personality" must be mutual: marriage "arises out of the free surrender by *both sexes* of their personalities" (PR, §167; my emphasis). He does not, on the other hand, hold that husbands and wives should adopt a new, third constellation of opinions, desires, and interests. His idea is rather that they should come to see themselves as pursuing *one* shared life plan and come to regard their own individual projects as having standing only as a part of the larger life they share. The 'single person' they constitute is the 'person' that pursues this shared life.

Hegel's conception of marriage and family life is, doubtless, far more communalistic than most people nowadays would be willing to accept. Even those of us who share his sense that marriage cannot be reduced to a civil contract and that familial relations are importantly different from civil relations are apt to be reluctant to accept a conception of the family that is as communalistic as Hegel's. But his conception is I think intelligible and one whose appeal can be understood. To fully understand its appeal, however, we have to consider how in Hegel's view the modern family reconciles individuality and social membership.

3. The first thing that needs to be emphasized is that Hegel's conception of the modern family does contain an individualistic dimension. Once one comes to appreciate just how radically communalistic his conception is, one might doubt that it provides any room for individuality at all. As we have seen, Hegel maintains that

men and women enter marriage through a free act of individual choice (PR, §162). Although Hegel approves of arranged marriages (PR, §162R), he insists that no one should be coerced into marriage (PR, §176). And if marriage is not a contractual relationship "as far as its essential basis is concerned" (PR, §163R), it contains what might be regarded as an essential contractual "moment." Marriage, furthermore, provides the institutional context within which men and women can in principle satisfy their individual need for sex and romantic love and realize what Hegel calls "the right of the subject's *particularity* to find satisfaction" (PR, §124R).

But the main way in which the modern family reconciles individuality and social membership, in Hegel's view, is by providing the institutional context within which people can develop and find recognition of the psychological dimension of their particularity: their emotional needs and traits. The modern family is the institutional setting within which personal feelings count and the institutional setting within which it is appropriate to relate to other people in an emotional way. It is there that one can reasonably expect that others will understand and care about one's psychology and respond emotionally to one's practical concerns. It is there that one can hope to be loved as the particular person one is. And it is there that one can hope to find immediate and unconditional love.

It is worth pointing out that Hegel maintains that the emotional acceptance people find within the family is not something different from the acceptance they find as family members. In the modern family, the way in which one accepts family members as family members is by accepting their emotional idiosyncrasies and psychological needs. Thus, within the modern family, being accepted in one's emotional particularity and being accepted as a family member coalesce. In this coalescence, individuality (understood as emotional particularity) and social membership (understood as family membership) are reconciled.

Stepping back, we can see that, for Hegel, the reconciliation of individuality and social membership the modern family provides is absolutely essential to the reconciliation of individuality and social membership the modern social world brings about. In his view, there is no other institutional sphere that allows people to realize and find acceptance of the emotional aspects of their particularity. It is evident that the modern political state does not provide a setting within which this can occur. And civil society is no more suited to fulfilling this function than the state. Within civil society it is not personal feelings that count but rather talent, skill, and achievement. And precisely for this reason, it would be unreasonable to hope to find immediate and unconditional emotional acceptance within this sphere. What one can hope to find there is acceptance based on the objective assessment of one's talents, skills, and achievements, a form of acceptance that, it might be added, is generally unavailable within the family.

The modern family is also essential because there is no other sphere in the modern social world whose central function is to reconcile individuality and social membership at an emotional level. Hegel does, it is true, think that the reconciliation the state provides includes an emotional component, patriotism (*Patriotismus*),[4] which he characterizes as the outlook (*Gesinnung*) of trust "or the consciousness that my substantial and particular interest is preserved in the interest and end of an other (in this case, the state), and in the latter's relation to me as an individual" (PR, §268).[5] But reconciling individuality and social membership at an emotional level is not, in Hegel's view, the central function of the state (PR, §257R). Reconciliation at the emotional level, Hegel insists, is the central task of the family (PR, §158). Thus, from a Hegelian point of view, were the modern family to be absorbed into civil society – were familial relations to become indistinguishable from civil relations – an absolutely crucial respect in which individuality and social membership are reconciled would be lost, and the modern social world would cease to be a home.

On the other hand, although Hegel regards the reconciliation provided by the modern family as essential, he also takes it to be limited. It is limited with respect to form because it is purely emotional. Although the modern family makes it possible for people to *feel* that they are both individuals and family members, it does not make it possible for them to grasp this at a cognitive level. People can of course reflect upon the nature of the family, but reflection is not an internal feature of modern family life, as Hegel understands it. By contrast, reflection *is* an internal part of Hegel's conception of modern political life. He thinks that the modern state aspires to

---

4 Cf. Westphal 1984, 88.
5 It is important to bear in mind that Hegel rejects the view that patriotism, properly understood, consists essentially in a "willingness to perform *extraordinary* sacrifices and actions," holding that "in essence, it is that disposition which, in the normal conditions and circumstances of life, habitually knows that the community is the substantial basis and end" (PR, §268R).

make it possible for people to cognitively grasp that its structures enable them to actualize themselves both as individuals and as social members. He contends that in its rational form, the modern state includes a representative body – the assembly of estates – whose function is to bring them to awareness of this fact (PR, §§301–15).

Hegel contends that the reconciliation provided by the modern family is also limited with respect to content. Although people can actualize the psychological aspects of their particularity within its structures, they cannot actualize themselves there as bearers of individual rights nor can they pursue their separate and particular interests. Moreover, modern people need a social sphere within which they can obtain recognition for their objective talents, skills, and achievements, and this is something the family cannot provide. From Hegel's point of view, a social world that contained the communalism of the family but lacked the individualism of civil society could not be a home for modern people. Hegel contends that the modern family, together with the modern state, provides an essential counterbalance to the individualism of civil society. And, he suggests, one of the most important things that modern people need to understand about their social world is the complementary nature of the relation between civil society, the family, and the state (PR, §145).

Finally, Hegel contends, the reconciliation the modern family provides is limited with respect to scope. It is limited in this respect because the form of social membership it provides is limited. As a family member, one belongs to one particular group within the community, not the community as a whole. In order to find reconciliation with the community as a whole, one must turn to the institutional spheres that lie outside the family: civil society and the political state. Hegel thinks that the reconciliation the family provides is only one part of the larger process of reconciliation that takes place within the modern social world. His general view is that each of the three central social institutions – the family, civil society, and the state – performs part of the task of reconciling individuality and social membership and that the complete social process of reconciliation requires the cooperation of all three institutional spheres.

4. I conclude this discussion of Hegel's conception of the modern family by addressing the issue of his conception of gender roles within the family and society at large. As we have seen, Hegel's conception of the domestic division of labor is very traditional. The

husband is the head of the household and the breadwinner, and the wife is the homemaker and primary caretaker of the children. This division of gender within the family reflects the broader division of gender in the modern social world. Hegel maintains that the private life of the family constitutes the social sphere of women and that the public life of civil society and the state constitutes the social sphere of men (PR, §166). Women lead their lives within the family. Men pursue their lives within civil society and the state. However unattractive we may find this view, we should remember that it is in no way idiosyncratic. It is precisely the sort of view held by most theorists in Hegel's time.

Hegel's justification of the traditional division of gender derives from his rather traditional conception of the differences between men and women. Men, he contends, are characterized by "personal self-sufficiency" (*personliche Selbständigkeit*; PR, §166). They are "powerful" and "active" by nature, capable of conceptual thought (*begreifender Gedanken*, e.g., grasping abstract relationships and matters of principle), and essentially oriented toward "the objective" and "the universal" (e.g., objective inquiry in science and the sort of impersonal relations characteristic of civil society and the state) (PR, §166). Women, by contrast, are oriented toward "the concrete" (e.g., particular personal relationships). Their dominant cognitive faculty is that of feeling (*Empfindung*): they are especially good at understanding the psychological aspects of personal relationships and responding to them in an emotionally appropriate way. And they are by nature "passive" and "subjective" (PR, §166). Hegel writes:

> Man therefore has his actual substantial life in the state, in learning, etc., and otherwise in work and struggle with the external world and with himself, so that it is only through his division that he fights his way to self-sufficient unity with himself. In the family, he has a peaceful intuition of this unity, and an emotive and subjective ethical life. Woman, however, has her substantial vocation in the family, and her ethical disposition consists in this [family] *piety*. (PR, §166)

Hegel even goes so far as to say that "when women are in charge of government, the state is in danger, for their actions are based, not on the demands of universality, but on contingent inclination and opinion" (PR, §166Z; VPRHO, 525).

Hegel's view of women is not, however, wholly disparaging. He regards their ability to respond emotionally to the particularities of personal relationships as a specifically ethical capacity, one with respect to which they are generally superior to men. His general view is that the ethical capacities of men and women are complementary, and hence that men and women need one another to be ethically complete. He contends that one of the advantages of marriage is precisely that it enables men and women to overcome the ethical one-sidedness that is intrinsic to each sex. It is also worth remembering that one of Hegel's greatest heroes – Antigone – is a woman and that what he admires in her is precisely her courageous affirmation of the claim of family piety against the male claims of the state.[6] Hegel's respect for women is, I believe, genuine and deep. Nonetheless it is plain that his view of women is fundamentally inegalitarian. However high and however genuine his regard for women may be, it is absolutely clear that Hegel regards them as the intellectual inferiors of men, as beings who are incapable of participating in public life. And there is no question but that he thinks that it is appropriate for them to be excluded from the public sphere and assigned a subordinate position within the family (PR, §166Z; VPRG, 444).

I assume that most readers will of course reject this view of women. That women are free and equal beings, fully capable of participating in public life, is, I take it, a fixed point of both feminism and enlightened common sense. And, obviously enough, once this traditional view of women is rejected, Hegel's justification of the traditional sexual division of labor within the family and society as a whole loses its force. It will be natural to conclude that the social world Hegel describes in the *Philosophy of Right* is not a place where women can be at home. This problem is not of course unique to Hegel. One of the most pressing political questions facing us today concerns how our social world must be transformed in order to make it a place in which women can be at home. But the point I want to urge here is a historical one: that Hegel's traditional conception of the capacity and vocation of men and women, objectionable though it may be, makes it possible to understand his view of the sexual division of labor. It follows from this conception that men are naturally suited to the public world of work and politics; women to the private life of family. Men will generally want to enter the life of civil society and the state and will generally have the aptitudes and abilities these spheres require. By the same token, women will generally want to marry and have children and will have the abili-

6 See Wood 1990, 244–5.

ties and aptitudes these activities require. Hegel's view also allows us to regard the stratification internal to his conception of the modern family not as arbitrary but rather as a reflection of the natural differences characteristic of men and women.

It should be clear that Hegel would reject the idea of what the political theorist Susan Okin has called a "genderless society" – a society in which, as she puts it, "one's sex would have no more relevance than one's eye color or the length of one's toes."[7] He maintains that one of the things that makes the modern social world a home is precisely the fact that its central social institutions articulate and express the differences of gender. These differences must, Hegel thinks, be institutionally expressed in order for it to be possible for men to be at home in the social world *as men* and women to be at home in the social world *as women*. The institutional articulation of gender differences is a condition of the social world's being a home: a social world that failed to satisfy this condition would be alienating along the dimension of gender.

But even if we grant that Hegel's conception of the differences between the sexes makes his view of the sexual division of labor intelligible, it remains true that he excludes women from civil society. This is important because, as we have learned, it means that women cannot realize themselves as individuals in the strong sense. In Hegel's view, civil society is that sphere within which alone it is possible for people to realize themselves as individuals in the strong sense.

Hegel could reply that women can enjoy the reconciliation of individuality and social membership the family provides. He could say that as daughters, sisters, wives, and mothers women can find emotional recognition of their particularity there. He could also argue that the family provides women with what is in effect their own counterpart of civil society, a field within which they can develop and exercise their specifically female abilities, talents, and skills (e.g., homemaking, reproduction, and childcare) (see PR, §166). But none of this would change the fact that in the social world Hegel endorses, women are excluded from the sphere within which alone they could actualize themselves as individuals in the strong sense. And so the question arises: If women cannot actualize themselves as individuals in the strong sense in the modern social world, how *from a Hegelian point of view* can they possibly be at home there?

7 Okin 1989, 184, 171.

It is worth observing that the problem generalizes. Women are not the only group whose members cannot actualize themselves as individuals in the strong sense in the modern social world as Hegel represents it. The same is true of peasants. They, too, are excluded from the commercial world of civil society. They live in the country, not the city. Their lives are shaped by the material requirements of caring for the land and the patriarchal traditions of rural life. Hegel says that their "substantial disposition" is in general one of an "immediate ethical life based on family relationship and trust" (PR, §203). And so the question we must address can be put this way: How for Hegel can the modern social world be a home, if the members of two of its most important social groups cannot actualize themselves as individuals in the strong sense? Why doesn't the fact that the members of these groups cannot actualize themselves as individuals in the strong sense show that the modern social world is not a home?

The reason is that Hegel's conception of what it is for the modern social world to be a home is rather less individualistic than it might first appear to be. Before going on I should say that the discussion that follows will necessarily be rather speculative. My concern here is *not* to defend Hegel's view of the social position of women or peasants but simply to deepen our understanding of the basic character of his social philosophy. The crucial point is this: Hegel does not think that the modern social world must make it possible for *each member* of the community to realize himself or herself as an individual in the strong sense. What he thinks is that this must be a possibility *within the community* – a possibility for at least some of its members. We need to consider what this means.

The first thing to be said is that the fact that strong individuality is not a possibility for a given individual or group of individuals is far less distressing from a Hegelian point of view than it may be from ours. Hegel, unlike Mill, does not regard strong individuality as a universal human vocation, as the end of each individual human being.[8] Nor does he think that actualizing oneself as an individual in the strong sense is a precondition of leading a full human life. Hegel instead views strong individuality as representing one important but restricted human possibility among others. He would say that both the peasant and the homemaker realize significant human possibilities that the burgher does not. In this respect, his

8 Mill 1859, 53–71.

life is no less one-sided than theirs. No individual human life is complete in itself.[9] A full *human* life is necessarily a limited one. Hegel thus accepts Humboldt's view that "man is inevitably destined to partial cultivation, since he only enfeebles his energies by directing them to a multiplicity of objects."[10] Hegel maintains that the way in which human individuals can lead full human lives is by adopting meaningful determinate positions within society and pursuing the possibilities these positions provide (see PR, §207, R, Z; VPRHO, 636). And part of the point of his account of the roles of women and the peasantry is to show that these roles are meaningful, and that women and peasants can lead full human lives in exercising them, despite the fact that the very exercise of these roles precludes them from actualizing themselves as individuals in the strong sense.

Looking more deeply into Hegel's view, we can see that there is an important sense in which the most basic ideal of self-actualization underlying his conception of what it is for the social world to be a home is communitarian – for the ideal is one of actualizing oneself *as a member of the community*. Hegel's identification of the actualization of strong individuality with the form of life that is lived within civil society is meant to allow us to see that actualizing oneself as an individual in the strong sense is not an alternative to actualizing oneself as a social member but instead one way of actualizing oneself *as a member* of the community. For Hegel, the ultimate significance of the fact that people within civil society are able to actualize themselves as individuals in the strong sense is not that these particular individuals enjoy the good of strong individuality but rather that through them the *community* is able to actualize the possibility of strong individuality. According to Hegel, the final philosophical way of understanding the social position of burghers is to see them as representatives of the community whose task it is to realize one of its constituent forms of life.

If we look still more deeply into Hegel's view, we can say that the crucial thing for him is not the actualization of any given single human being but rather the actualization of the community. Now in order for a modern community fully to actualize itself, it *must* respect the rights of individuals and promote the actualization of strong individuality (PR, §§209R, 260, Z; VPRHO, 717). There is

9 Cf. for similarities Rawls 1971, 520–9.
10 Humboldt 1862, 16; cited in Rawls 1971, 523–4, n. 4.

thus a sense in which Hegel's communitarianism is remarkably individualistic. But from a Hegelian standpoint, the most important need that is met in providing a social sector within which people can actualize themselves as individuals in the strong sense is not the need of the individuals who are members of the community but rather the need of the community itself.

Hegel thinks that a fully actualized modern community is one in which the different principles of modern social life (e.g., the principles of masculinity and femininity, town and country, substantiality and reflection) are each given separate institutional articulation. Only in this way, he thinks, can each principle be fully realized. And only in this way can the community's self-actualization be complete.[11] Hegel rejects the idea that the different principles of modern social life can be harmoniously integrated within each personality. Thus, in addition to being deeply sensitive to the unavoidable limits of individual human self-realization, Hegel believes that the full development of these principles requires a high degree of institutional specialization. This, then, is why he endorses the social division of gender and the division of modern society into different estates. Finally, it should be mentioned that Hegel maintains that it is specifically in the *shared life of the community* that these principles are reconciled. Individuals are able to enjoy this reconciliation by participating in the shared life of their community as determinate social members.

II. Civil society

1. Civil society (*bürgerliche Gesellschaft*), as Hegel understands it, can be initially characterized as the social sphere, distinct from family and state (PR, §182Z; VPRHO, 565), in which agents – more specifically, men – pursue their separate and particular interests (PR, §§182–3).[12] It is the specifically modern sphere of nondomestic private interactions, whose emergence corresponds to the development of capitalism, the beginnings of industrialism, and the rise of the bourgeoisie. Owing to the work of Manfred Riedel, it is now generally recognized that Hegel's use of the term *bürgerliche Gesellschaft* to refer to this sphere represents a dramatic conceptual innova-

---

11 Cf. for similarities Rawls 1971, 520–9.
12 See the discussion of the exclusion of women from civil society in the preceding section. This point is also taken up in the Conclusion.

tion.[13] Philosophers before Hegel, from Aristotle to Kant, including Locke, used the term 'civil society' and its cognates (*koinonia politiké, societas civilis*) interchangeably with 'political society'. For them, civil society *was* political society. In distinguishing *civil* from *political* society, Hegel recognized the emergence of a new social configuration: a separate, private social sphere, within which agents lived for themselves, without participating in political affairs. The heart of this new sphere was the modern market economy. Its form of life – the life of the *bourgeois* as opposed to the life of the *citoyen* – was crucially shaped by the nature of capitalist economic relations (PR, §190; VPRW, 108).[14] Hegel's understanding of civil society was strongly influenced by his intimate knowledge of the classical theorists of political economy: Ricardo, Say, Smith, and Steuart.

Marx, who borrowed the term *bürgerliche Gesellschaft* from Hegel, restricted its application to the economy, and, because of this, it can be extremely tempting to think that 'civil society' simply refers to the market system. But it is crucial that we appreciate that Hegel's conception of civil society is richer than this. In his view, civil society has a distinctive social, cultural, and ethical character that cannot be wholly understood in terms of economic relations. Moreover, civil society is not only the sphere within which people pursue their separate and particular interests but also the sphere within which people can form voluntary associations and enjoy the free life of civic association.

It is this wider understanding of 'civil society' that Central and Eastern European intellectuals fastened onto in their much celebrated recent revival of the idea.[15] They took civil society to consist in the network of associations that includes unions, professional associations, social movements, churches, and neighborhoods. This was the sphere within which dissidence flourished and a sphere whose associational form of life, restricted though it was, was desirable in itself. And it is civil society, understood in this wider sense,

13 Riedel 1974, 1984.
14 Hegel generally uses the French terms *citoyen* and *bourgeois* to distinguish between two senses of the German word *Bürger: Bürger*-as-citizen and *Bürger*-as-member-of-civil-society (VPRW, 93–4, 108; but cf. PR, §§187, 190). The basic idea is that the *bourgeois* views himself as a private person (*private Person*) and is primarily concerned with his own welfare (PR, §187), whereas the *citoyen* views himself as a member of the state and regards the continued existence of the state as a final end (PR, §§258, 260, 261R). The force of this distinction will be explored in the discussion of the state in section III.
15 For useful contemporary discussions of the idea of civil society see Walzer 1991 and Cohen and Arato 1992.

that people within the new European democracies are now hoping to rebuild within the framework of a democratic social order. Although civil society, as Hegel represents it, does not include the sort of social movements that have been so important in Central and Eastern Europe during the last two decades of the twentieth century, its institutional scope is, nonetheless, surprisingly broad.[16] It includes not only the modern market system but also the legal and judicial system, a public authority responsible for social and economic regulation and the provision of welfare, and a system of voluntary associations. Let us examine these component institutions in turn.

a. What Hegel calls 'the system of needs' (*das System der Bedürfnisse*) is a modern market economy of labor, production, and exchange.[17] Individuals within this system are subjects of need who, qua participants in this system (i.e., economic agents), are solely concerned with the satisfaction of their own separate and particular needs. It is civil society, considered as this system, that Hegel has in mind when he says "in civil society, each individual is his own end, and all else means nothing to him" (PR, §182Z; VPRHO, 567).[18] Nonetheless, the very separate and particular needs that individuals have within the system of needs drive them to enter into economic relations with one another (PR, §§182, Z, 183, 185). They must go into the marketplace to buy commodities and into the workplace to earn a living. This is what Hegel has in mind when he says that "the selfish end in its actualization . . . establishes a system of all-round interdependence" (PR, §183).

Hegel contends that, in pursuing the satisfaction of their own private ends within the system of needs, individuals inevitably satisfy the needs of one another. "In furthering my end," he maintains, "I further the universal [i.e., the economy], and this in turn

---

16 There is, however, an analogy between the economic and political roles of the Polish labor union Solidarity and the economic and political functions of the Hegelian corporation.

17 The phrase "labor, production, and exchange" belongs to Pelczynski (1984a).

18 My reason for emphasizing that it is qua participants in the system of needs and that it is within civil society *considered as* the system of needs that individuals are solely concerned with their own ends is that Hegel does *not* think that individuals within civil society are solely concerned with their own needs (cf. Rawls 1971, 521). One crucial feature of his conception of civil society is that it contains a form of association – the corporation – that cultivates civic-mindedness and concern for others. In focusing on the system of needs, we are simply focusing on one aspect of civil society (the economy) and the conception of the self (*homo oeconomicus*).

furthers my end" (PR, §184, Z). Thus *"subjective selfishness* turns into *a contribution towards the satisfaction of the needs of everyone else"* (PR, §199). As workers, individuals produce goods and services others consume; as consumers, they purchase goods and services others produce (PR, §184Z; VPRHO, 572). In each case, they promote the common good. Thus, the system of needs exhibits a Smithian 'invisible hand' that leads selfishly motivated individuals toward the common good.[19] The fact that individuals within the system of needs promote the common good is no accident. It is, instead, the result of the structure of the system. Hegel recognizes that the system of needs can *appear* to be anarchic and incomprehensible (and hence *appear* to be objectively alienating), but he holds that it is actually structured in accordance with the laws of classical economics, whose development makes it possible to see the hidden rationality of modern economic life (PR, §189, R).

Hegel maintains that this modern system of needs gives rise to the highly developed division of labor characteristic of modern society. As he represents it, this system is, inter alia, a system of need formation (PR, §§189-95), which leads to the infinite multiplication and differentiation of human needs (PR, §190-1), which in turn leads to the ever increasing interdependence of individual agents and specialization of economic tasks (PR, §198). Hegel recognizes that the modern division of labor may, as Schiller thought, appear to result in the "severing" (*zeriss*) of the "inner unity of human nature" (and hence appear to be objectively alienating). But he argues that the many occupations provided by the modern social world allow for the unfolding of human particularity and fall into groupings that are natural and cohesive: agriculture, business, and public service (PR, §§202-5). Thus, in his view, the modern division of labor is coherent.

Hegel further maintains that the modern division of labor is reflected in the modern world's articulation into different social groups, which he calls "estates" (*Stände*). These social groups, or orders, give the modern social world a determinate and organized structure, which in turn helps to make it a home. As he represents

---

19 Hegel, however, breaks with Smith (or the laissez-faire liberal) in maintaining (i) that the market requires government regulation (by the public authority) (PR, §236) and (ii) that the normal operation of the market necessarily leads to the impoverishment of a large number of people (PR, §243). This latter point is discussed in section III of Chapter 7.

them, the central social estates are three in number.[20] The estate he calls "substantial" (*der substantielle Stand*) is the agricultural estate (PR, §203).[21] The estate of "trade and industry" (*Stand des Gewerbes*) consists of what he calls the estate of craftsmanship (*Handwerkstand*), the estate of manufacturers (*Fabrikantenstand*), and the estate of commerce (*Handelstand*) (PR, §204). And, finally, there is the administrative "universal estate" (*der allgemeine Stand*), whose members belong to the civil service (PR, §205).

Each of these estates, Hegel suggests, has its own determinate way of life, its own set of practices, values, and ways of looking at the world. Thus, although the articulation of society into estates grows out of the division of labor and hence has a material base, this articulation is by no means purely materialistic. Hegel's estates are not Marx's classes. His substantial estate includes *both* landowners and peasants (PR, §203), and his estate of trade and industry includes *both* employers and employees (PR, §204). The members of a given estate are not united by a shared relation to the means of production but rather by their common form of social life.

Let us consider these three forms of social life. According to Hegel, the way of life shared by the members of the substantial estate is unreflective, rural, and patriarchal. "This first estate," Hegel says in a passage marked by nostalgia,

> will always retain the patriarchal way of life and the substantial disposition associated with it. The human being reacts here with immediate feeling as he accepts what he receives; he thanks God for it and lives in faith and confidence that this goodness will continue. What he receives is enough for him; he uses it up, for it will be replenished. This is a simple disposition which is not concerned with the acquisi-

---

20 Strictly speaking, there are *four* central social estates in Hegel's view, since he maintains that a well-ordered state will also contain a military estate (*Militärstand*), the "estate of valor" (*Stand der Tapferkeit*), consisting of professional soldiers (PR, §§325–8). Hegel ignores this fourth estate in his initial characterization of the estates (PR, §§201–7) because he holds that normally (i.e., in times of peace) the military will play no central role in the internal life of the state. Hegel's discussion of the military estate falls under the heading of "external sovereignty."

21 Hegel speaks of civil society in a broader and a narrower sense. In the broader sense (and strict sense) of the term, 'civil society' includes the agricultural life of the "substantial estate" (and hence peasants as well as burghers). In the narrow and more common use of the term 'civil society' refers to the life of trade and industry found in cities. Neither the substantial nor the universal estate is part of civil society thus understood. I shall generally use 'civil society' in this more restricted sense.

tion of wealth; it may also be described as that of the *old nobility*, which consumed whatever it had. (PR, §203Z; VPRHO, 625-6)

The way of life of the members of the estate of trade and industry is, by contrast, urban and reflective. It is the way of life of the modern burgher, who pursues his own separate and particular interests in the modern city. This estate "relies for its livelihood on its *work*, on *reflection* and the understanding, and essentially on its mediation of the needs and work of others" (PR, §204). In this estate "the individual has to rely on himself, and this feeling of self-hood is intimately connected with the demand for a condition in which right is upheld" (PR, §204Z; VPRHO, 629).

Like the estate of trade and industry, the way of life of the universal estate is, broadly speaking, reflective.[22] But unlike modern burghers, civil servants, as Hegel represents them, are dedicated to public service. This estate "has *the universal interests* of society as its business" (PR, §205). Its members are characterized by their concern for the common good, their high level of education, and their legal and political consciousness (PR, §297, Z; VPRHO, 787).

It is worth emphasizing that although Hegel regards this division of estates as fixed, and although he maintains that modern individuals actualize themselves as individuals through their membership in a particular estate, he also contends that modern individuals must have the right to choose their occupation and estate (PR, §§206, 308R). He suggests that this moment of free choice is one of the features that makes possible the reconciliation (*Versöhnung*) of "subjective particularity" with "the organization of the whole," that is, the articulation of society into estates (PR, §206R).

b. Hegel maintains that the administration of justice (*die Rechtspflege*) provides the legal structure necessary for the regulation of the system of needs. This structure consists of a public legal code (PR, §§211, 215) and a judicial system (PR, §219). The legal code

22   In the version of the philosophy of right contained in the *Philosophy of Mind* (EG, §§253-91) Hegel makes explicit a distinction that is present but less clear in the 1821 *Philosophy of Right*. In the later work he characterizes the estate of trade and industry as the "reflected" (*reflektiert*) estate, and the universal estate as the "thinking" (*denkend*) estate. He thinks the estate of trade and industry characteristically displays the kind of reflection he associates with "the understanding" (*der Verstand*; roughly, the faculty of making abstract distinctions) and that the universal estate characteristically exercises the form of thought he associates with reason (*die Vernunft*; roughly, the faculty of grasping the unity of the determinations that the understanding separates and holds apart). See EL, §§79-82.

specifies the rights individuals have under the law (PR, §213), and the judicial system – characterized by impartial judges (PR, §§219, 220), public proceedings (PR, §224), and jury trials (PR, §§228, R, Z) – enforces these rights (PR, §208).

More generally, Hegel holds that the administration of justice has as its central aim the protection of property and the contract (PR, §208). It constitutes the basic normative framework of the system of needs. This framework confers the status of legal persons on the participants in the system of needs and confers the status of property on the objects they produce, exchange, and consume (PR, §218). Within the system of needs the relations of individuals are legal as well as economic. They are bound together by contract no less than need. In making and honoring contracts, individuals respect one another as persons (*Personen*). And they are regulated in the pursuit of their needs by a scheme of individual rights specified by law, the very law that is codified, promulgated, and enforced by the administration of justice.

c. The public authority (*die Polizei*) is the system of public administration concerned with the regulation and control of civil society.[23] Its functions include those of the police in our contemporary sense of the term: the prevention and detection of crime, the apprehension of suspected criminals, and the maintenance of public order (PR, §§232–3). They also include a wide range of public services that fall outside the responsibilities of what we would call the police but are characteristically provided by public institutions in the modern social world. These services include the provision and operation of public utilities and works (PR, §235) (e.g., streets and bridge building; PR, §236Z; VPRHO, 695), the regulation of the market (e.g., through price controls) (PR, §236), consumer protection (PR, §236), public health (PR, §236Z; VPRHO, 695), public education (PR, §239), welfare, and prevention of unemployment (PR, §242, R).

Not the least task of the public authority is to correct the predictable contingencies arising within the system of needs that cannot be prevented by the administration of justice, such as crime, unemployment, and poverty (PR, §231). As Hegel conceives of it, the public authority is, inter alia, an all-purpose corrective mechanism.

---

23 Hegel's broad use of the word *Polizei* reflects the normal German usage of his day. It was not until the mid-nineteenth century that the word took on the more restricted meaning it shares with its English cognate 'police.' See Wood 1990, 283.

It also provides a range of public goods (e.g., crime protection, street maintenance, education) that individuals need as members of civil society. The most important thing that unifies the rather diverse assortment of services the public authority provides is that they are all services that people need in their capacity as members of civil society. This is what Hegel has in mind when he says that the public authority (and the corporations) "care for the particular interest as a *common* interest" (PR, §188). Each individual has a *particular* interest in having well-maintained streets, but the public authority (unlike, say, a private road-repair company) does not care for this particular interest as a private interest (as the sort of interests people have as consumers). It instead cares for this interest as an interest that people have as members of civil society. In providing these services, the public authority gives birth to a common civic sphere within the private realm of civil society, one that grows out of its private concerns.

Perhaps the most distinctive feature of Hegel's understanding of the public authority is his view that this body expands the sort of recognition that society gives to its members. He contends that the administration of justice provides people with one sort of recognition – legal recognition – by protecting their legal rights. The fact that it does so is important, since it means that there is an official body that provides formal recognition of the individuality of society's members (of their status as bearers of individual rights). But precisely because the recognition the administration of justice provides is individualistic, it is also limited. The administration of justice does not recognize members of society as members of civil society (*Mitglieder im System der bürgerliche Gesellschaft*) in any but the most formal sense.[24] But the public authority, as Hegel represents it, recognizes members of civil society *as* members of civil society (PR, §§238, 240) and thus overcomes this limitation.

Hegel contends that the public authority recognizes members of civil society as such by expanding the class of socially recognized

---

24 There is a rather striking asymmetry here. If a society fails to protect the legal rights of the members of some group, as, for example, American society failed to protect the legal rights of African Americans before the civil rights movement, there is a *very* significant sense in which it fails to recognize those individuals as social members, for it then fails to provide the minimal form of recognition a society can confer. On the other hand, the mere fact that a society provides this minimal form of recognition does not entail that it fully recognizes its members as social members. One thing we can learn from Hegel is that in order to do this, it must also protect their welfare.

rights to include what might be called 'positive social rights' – rights that members of civil society hold *as* members of civil society *against* civil society (see VPRG, 604). Hegel argues that "if a human being is to be a member of civil society, he has rights and claims in relation to it, just as he had in relation to his family. Civil society must protect its members and defend their rights, just as the individual owes a duty to the rights of civil society" (PR, §238, Z; VPRHO, 700). And he maintains, more specifically, that individuals, as members of civil society, have a positive right to the basic prerequisites of full social participation: work and a livelihood (PR, §238; VPRW, 138). Indeed, from a Hegelian point of view the most important thing about the welfare provision of the public authority is not that it is designed to protect the welfare of the members of society, although this too is important.[25] It is rather that it is designed to guarantee each member of society the material prerequisites of full participation in society.

d. The corporations (*die Korporationen*) as Hegel understands them are societies or associations recognized by the state as corporate bodies (PR, §§252, 255Z, 288; VPRHO, 711).[26] In the broadest sense of the term, corporations include churches (PR, §270) and municipal governments (PR, §288). The corporations that Hegel focuses on, however, are professional and trade associations, which in some respects resemble modern trade unions. One important respect in which corporations differ from trade unions is that they include both employers and employees. Hegel represents these corporations as the modern successors to the medieval guilds. They promote the professional interests of their members, whom they recruit, educate, train, and certify (PR, §252).[27] Drawing their members from the estate of trade and industry and organized around the major branches of this estate (e.g., commerce, manufacturing

---

25 Hegel maintains that a modern society that lacked an institutionalized form of public welfare provision would be hostile or indifferent to the needs of its members and hence objectively alienating.

26 Knox says that this now archaic use of the term *Korporation* derives from the workingmen's fellowships in ancient Rome (Knox 1952, 360). Heiman describes the original Roman corporations as "groups of like-minded individuals who had banded together for the furtherance, protection and administration of certain common, limited interests" (Heiman 1971, 115). Interestingly, the *Oxford English Dictionary* tells us the English word 'corporation', which, like *Korporation*, derives from the Latin *corporātiōn*, once was used to refer to "an incorporated company of traders having (originally) the monopoly and control of their particular trade in a borough or other place; a trade guild, a city company."

27 The expression "recruit, educate, train, and certify" belongs to Wood (1990, 241).

industries, etc.), these modern corporations reflect the division of labor and thus the social articulation of civil society (PR, §§250, 311). It should be clear then that by 'corporation', Hegel does not mean 'business corporation' in our sense of the term. The corporations he has in mind are not limited liability companies.

Hegel maintains that the corporations "come on the scene" in civil society "like a second family" (PR, §252 [Knox]). Unlike the 'first family' (the family into which one is born) the corporation is an association one enters through a free act of choice. They are voluntary associations par excellence.[28] In contrast to marrying, becoming a member of a corporation does not involve surrender of one's individual rights. Corporations are associations of separate individuals who relate to one another as separate persons with a shared set of interests and concerns. The form of social life they offer is not the familial life of intimacy and love but rather the specifically associational life of friendship, collegiality, and solidarity. Corporations also differ from "natural families" in that they offer their members objective recognition of their skills, abilities, and achievements (PR, §253). Corporations resemble natural families in that their members share a common outlook and way of viewing themselves and the world, in a word, a common *Geist* (a spirit that, however, arises from the shared form of associational life rather than the ties of blood and shared domestic life). Corporations also resemble natural families in that they are structured to care for their members, to look out for their own. Should members of a corporation become ill or lose their jobs as the result of economic downturns, they can turn to their corporation, their "second family," for assistance (PR, §252).

In providing assistance of this kind, the corporations also resemble the public authority, the public body responsible for welfare provision. The corporations, however, are private, rather than public, bodies, and the assistance they provide differs from that provided by the public authority in a number of important respects. It comes from an association that its members can regard as their own rather than from the *external* agency of the state (PR, §183). The people who administer this assistance are not officials in the civil service (and hence members of an entirely different estate) but

---

28 Hegel does, it is true, think that from the standpoint of entrance marriage is a voluntary association, but he also insists that at the most fundamental level marriage is not a voluntary association. Unlike the corporation, marriage is not an association from which one can exit at will.

fellow members of the corporation, who, at least ideally, are able to understand the details of the objective circumstances of their fellows and appreciate what it means subjectively for someone in that profession or trade to need assistance.[29]

None of this is to say that Hegel thinks that the relations between the public authority and the members of civil society are intrinsically defective. He maintains, on the contrary, that the sort of institutionalized impersonal concern for welfare the public authority provides is an essential feature of a well-ordered modern society. A society that failed to exhibit such concern would, in his view, be hostile and indifferent to the needs of its members and, as such, objectively alienating. But Hegel holds that the impersonal concern a well-ordered society provides must be supplemented by the more particularized and personal assistance offered by the corporations.

One of the crucial social tasks the corporations perform is that of providing their members with a determinate socially recognized identity. Corporation members, he maintains, have the standing of trained, competent, and professional practitioners of a particular socially useful profession or trade, and are recognized as such (PR, §253). A member of a corporation "has no need to demonstrate his competence and his regular income and means of support – i.e., the fact that he is *somebody* – by any further *external evidence*" (PR, §253). Membership in a corporation should not, however, be understood simply as a social status. There is more to entering a corporation than learning the skills of one's trade and acquiring a position in society. As Hegel represents it, this process involves internalizing the ends and values of the corporation, coming to regard its interests as one's own, and coming to adopt the form of private life that corresponds to one's profession or trade (a way of life that is, as people used to say, 'appropriate to one's station'), and coming to have what Hegel calls the "honor belonging to an estate" (*Standesehre*) (PR, §§252, 253R). It also involves coming explicitly to conceive of oneself as a member of the corporation. Thus, becoming a member of a corporation is also a matter of making one's membership central to one's *personal* self-conception, central to one's *private* sense of who one is.

---

29 One might of course worry that the officials within the corporations might lose touch with their members, a phenomenon common in modern trade unions. One of the reasons that Hegel insists that these officials be supervised by the state is precisely to prevent this from happening (PR, §§255Z, 288, 289R). Cf. for similarities Walzer 1991, 302.

In providing their members with the status of corporation members, the corporations expand the range of recognition society gives to its members, because they recognize and make it possible for others to recognize their members as social members with a determinate social identity. The public authority also performs the crucial function of recognizing people as members of civil society, but, Hegel contends, there is an important sense in which the recognition this body provides is abstract, for the public authority does not recognize people in what might be called their 'social particularity'. This is to say, it does not recognize them as occupants of a determinate social position, as bearers of a determinate social identity (PR, §253; cf. §308). Hegel does not regard this as a defect, since, as we have seen, he thinks that it is crucial that there be an official body that recognizes people generically as members of civil society. But he does regard it as a limitation. In his view, people in civil society are not simply members of civil society in general; because they also occupy a determinate place within this sphere, they have a determinate social identity. This is part of what makes them members of civil society in the strong sense of the term. And if civil society is to fully recognize its members *as members* of civil society (something it must do if it is to be a home), it must recognize this more particular side of their social membership as well. And this, Hegel contends, is precisely what the corporations do when they recognize their members as members of the corporation. They do so in a formal way when they confer the rights and privileges of membership in the corporation, thereby giving their members a determinate place within the social world, and they do so more concretely when they provide their members with assistance in times of need.

The corporations also have another crucial function: that of expanding the ability of members of society to identify with others. In becoming a member of a corporation, one comes to see one's fellow members as sharing one's trade, outlook, and way of life. And one's sense of connection, loyalty, and camaraderie is enhanced when one carries out activities on behalf of the corporation, something that belongs to the normal responsibility of a member of a corporation (PR, §255Z). Indeed, in Hegel's view, one of the reasons that corporations assign this task to their members is precisely to help them recognize that they are pursuing a common end and share a common project. When members of a corporation come to recognize the commonality of their aims and projects, they will begin to act not just for their own sakes (or for the good of their families) but also for the sake of their fellow corporate members and for the corporation itself.

Corporations also serve a crucial political function. They mediate between individual members of society and the political apparatus of the state.[30] Hegel maintains that in a well-ordered society individuals do not vote for their political representatives – their deputies (*Abgeordneten*) – directly. Members of civil society, or, more precisely, members of the estate of trade and industry, vote through their corporations. Each corporation elects its own deputy, whose task is to represent the shared interests of the members of his corporation in the assembly of estates, the government's representative body. One of the main reasons why Hegel advocates this form of corporately mediated representation is that he thinks it necessary for people to be represented in their social particularity (their identification with the ends and attitudes of the corporation), which he maintains gives their individuality its content (PR, §308R). Corporate representation is designed to guarantee that the corporation members' basic interests, values, and attitudes will be represented in the state in a systematic and explicit way (PR, §§308, 309, Z; VPRG, 718).

Finally, in addition to this direct political function, the corporations also play an important quasi-political role. As we shall see, Hegel thinks that modern political conditions are such that ordinary citizens can at best play only a very restricted role in the public business of the state (PR, §255Z; VPRHO, 709). The real work of running the machinery of government devolves upon a group of highly trained experts drawn from the universal class of civil servants (PR, §§287–97). One consequence of this is that the political state does not provide a context within which ordinary citizens can work actively for public ends. The ordinary Athenian citizen could participate actively and directly in the public life of his community by taking part in its political institutions; the ordinary citizen of the modern social world cannot. This circumstance creates a kind of institutional gap. Modern citizens both need and want to participate actively and directly in the public life of their community. But they cannot do so within the state. Nor can they do so within the system of needs. Hegel thinks that this gap can be at least partially bridged by participating in the corporation. The corpora-

---

30 For an illuminating discussion of the political role of secondary associations in present-day democratic societies, see Cohen and Rogers 1992, 393–472.

tions provide an institutional context within which people can pursue public ends (PR, §255Z; VPRHO, 713). Service for the corporation provides the corporation member with "a universal activity in addition to his own private end" (PR, §255Z; VPRHO, 713). Although this activity is not political in one respect, since it does not involve direct participation in the machinery of government, it is political in another sense: It consists in public action directed at public ends. Thus the corporations open up a kind of quasi-political space within the social sphere of civil society. They transform civil society into the central locus for public participation.[31]

2. We can think of the institutions of civil society as falling into two groups: first, a 'sphere of private activity' constituted by the system of needs and the administration of justice; second, a 'civic community' constituted by the components of the private society plus the public authority and the corporations. And we can think of Hegel's account of civil society as consisting of two main stages: first, an account of civil society as a sphere of private activity; second, an account of civil society as a civil community. By a 'sphere of private activity' I mean a form of social life in which agents conceive of themselves as private persons rather than as social members, and are motivated by private rather than social concerns.[32] In a sphere of private activity, individuals relate to one another and their social institutions in a purely instrumental way, regarding them as means to their own private ends rather than as final ends to be supported or pursued for their own sake. By a 'civic community' I mean a form of social life in which agents think of themselves as members of society, are motivated by social concerns, and regard society as a union containing forms of association that represent final ends.

It is clear that the system of needs, considered by itself, constitutes a sphere of private activity, for, as we have seen, qua participants in this system, individuals do not view themselves as members of civil society. They regard themselves instead as "private

31 Cf. Walzer's discussion of the sort of public activity that can ideally be pursued within civil society: "The kinds of 'action' discussed by theorists of the state need to be supplemented (not, however, replaced) by something radically different: more like union organizing than political mobilization, more like teaching in a school than arguing in the assembly, more like volunteering in a hospital than joining a political party, more like working in an ethnic alliance or a feminist support group than canvassing in an election, more like shaping a co-op budget than deciding on national fiscal policy" (1991, 303).

32 Cf. Rawls 1971, 521. My term 'sphere of private activity' corresponds to his term 'private society'.

persons" (*private Personen*), as self-standing individuals with their own private ends and concerns (PR, §187). Their relation to other individuals and to the economic structure is purely instrumental. They do not participate in the economy in order to promote the general good but simply to satisfy their own private ends.

The administration of justice can also be regarded as a part of the sphere of private activity: as the legal structure necessary for the regulation of the economy. Individuals under its administration may think of themselves simply as private persons with legal rights entitling them to pursue their own private ends. Individuals with this outlook obey the law simply in order to avoid legal sanctions and use the courts merely as a vehicle for the advancement of their own private interests (e.g., to settle a contractual dispute in their favor). But the administration of justice can also be thought of as a transitional structure, and Hegel's account of this institution can be thought of as representing a step toward an account of civil society as a civic community. The administration of justice serves an important pedagogical role by encouraging participants in the system of needs to adopt a subjective attitude of mutual respect, so that they refrain from violating one another's legal rights not simply out of fear of legal sanctions but also out of respect for one another as persons. Even if respect for others and the law falls short of civility, it represents an important step toward this end.

Hegel maintains that it is the public authority that first makes it possible to regard civil society as a civic community. The public goods it provides (e.g., public order, well-maintained roads, good public education) are all services a society must have if it is to be a civil place in which to live. The public authority also plays a crucial pedagogical role in making it possible for people to think of themselves as members of civil society. In demanding that the streets be well paved and well lighted or that their neighborhood schools be improved, individuals begin to think of themselves, if only implicitly, as *members* of civil society. Hegel also maintains that individuals who make claims upon the welfare functions of the public authority do not or should not think of themselves as private individuals asking for charity but rather as members of civil society who have a right to its support (PR, §238).

But in Hegel's view, it is the corporations that play the decisive role in making civil society a civic community. They provide a social sphere outside the family within which individuals not only respect one another's rights but care for one another's needs. They constitute a form of association that their members can regard as a final end. And they engender a concrete sense of social membership by leading their members to conceive of themselves as members of a corporation. In so doing, the corporations also deepen their members' sense of connection to civil society as a whole, for in coming to see themselves as members of a particular corporation that fulfills a specific social function and occupies a specific place in society, corporation members come to see that *they* serve a specific function and occupy a determinate place in the social world (PR, §253).

3. I close this discussion of civil society by reviewing some of the main ways in which civil society reconciles individuality and social membership. Let us first consider the way in which it does this as a sphere of private activity and then examine the way in which it does this as a civic community.

Hegel maintains that, considered as a sphere of private activity, civil society offers a domain within which people can actualize themselves as individuals in the strong sense. They do so within the system of needs by pursuing their own separate and particular needs, and they do so under the administration of justice by exercising their individual rights. In the course of working, exchanging, and consuming within the system of needs, they come to conceive of themselves as subjects of separate and particular needs (PR, §187). And in the course of acquiring property and making contracts under the administration of justice, they come to conceive of themselves as bearers of individual rights (PR, §§209, 217).

It is also Hegel's view that individuals develop the specific needs they have – the content of their separate and particular interests – through their participation in the system of needs (PR, §§189–98). Similarly, the administration of justice protects the legal rights that individuals have, thereby making actual (effective and recognized) the 'abstract' rights they have simply by virtue of being persons (PR, §§210–12). Hegel not only holds that people actualize themselves as strong individuals by participating in the sphere of private activity but also thinks that people come to *be* individuals in the strong sense as the result of participating within this sphere. Thus, it is precisely the *social* sphere of private activity – the system of needs and the administration of justice – that makes strong individuality possible. In this way civil society, considered as a sphere of private association, reconciles individuality and social membership. A modern social world that lacked a sphere of this sort would not make it possible for people to actualize themselves as individuals in the strong sense and hence would not be a home.

The sphere of private activity does not, however, enable people to actualize themselves as social members in any but the weakest sense. As participants within this sphere, individuals are merely private persons, concerned with their own ends and projects. They do not regard the institutions of which they are a part as final ends. Nor does this sphere provide mechanisms that make it possible for people to see that their participation in the social world makes their strong individuality possible. Thus, the reconciliation that occurs within the sphere of private activity takes place behind the backs of the participants. In this respect, it is fundamentally limited.

As a civic community, civil society provides a form of social membership that allows individuals to actualize a strong form of social membership. The public authority makes it possible for individuals to actualize themselves as members of civil society by providing them with a public sphere within which they can self-consciously act as members of civil society.

As we have seen, the corporations provide individuals with a form of social membership that is both concrete and expressive of individuality. Corporation members conceive of themselves as members of *their* particular corporation, identifying with *its* aims and values and regarding the way of life customarily thought to be appropriate to its members as being suitable for themselves. In joining a corporation, individuals transcend their status as private persons and acquire a determinate, socially recognized social identity.

III. The state

1. The state, or more precisely, the strictly political state (*der eigentlich politische Staat*), as Hegel understands it, can initially be identified with the government. The specifically modern form of government, Hegel maintains, consists of a constitutional monarchy (PR, §273, R), which in its rational form contains three branches (PR, §273): (i) the crown, or princely power (PR, §§275–86); (ii) the executive (PR, §§287–97), run by professionally trained bureaucrats, who are members of the universal estate; and (iii) the legislature (PR, §§298–319), which includes a two-chamber legislative assembly in which the members of the upper house belong to the substantial estate (PR, §§305–7) and the members of the lower house are deputies of the corporations and belong to the estate of trade

and industry (PR, §§308-11). This identification of the political state with the government immediately raises a problem concerning Hegel's understanding of the relation between civil society and the political state.

The problem is that Hegel places enormous weight on the distinction between civil society and the political state (PR, §§182Z, 258R; VPRHO, 565). Indeed, he regards his discovery of this distinction as one of his crowning philosophical achievements (see PR, §260). But civil society, as he represents it, includes two public institutions, the administration of justice and the public authority, that would ordinarily be thought of as belonging to the government. In fact, Hegel himself holds that these institutions do belong to the political state (as well as civil society). "The executive *power*," he says, ". . . also includes the powers of the judiciary and the police" (PR, §287). But if civil society includes two state, or governmental, institutions, how can it be distinct from the political state? Alternatively, if civil society and the state are truly distinct, how can the administration of justice and the public authority belong to both spheres?[33]

33 Matters are further complicated by the fact that Hegel says of civil society: "One may regard this system in the first instance as the *external state*, the *state of necessity, of the understanding*" (PR, §183; EL, §25). For our purposes the most important thing to appreciate about this passage is that it does not identify civil society (discussed in PR, §§182-255) with the political state (discussed in PR, §§257-339). Rather Hegel is speaking from (or acknowledging the existence of) a standpoint from which the distinction between civil society and the state has not been made and from which the true character of civil society has not been understood. He is saying that, from *that* standpoint, the system of needs, administration of justice, and public authority will appear to be purely external powers. The system of needs will seem to be external since its members relate to it in a purely instrumental way (PR, §§182, Z, 183, 187; VPRG, 472), driven by material necessity to enter the world of work. The system of needs will also seem to be external since it operates behind the backs of the people who participate in it (PR, §187). The participants within this system do not recognize that, in pursuing their own separate and particular needs, they also promote the common good. And if people are solely concerned with their own needs, it is inevitable that they will regard the administration of justice as an external authority. Moreover, it is only as citizens that people can participate in the process of legislation that generates the laws that the administration of justice enforces (PR, §§310-11) and only from the standpoint of the political state that they can gain insight into the working of the government, of which the administration of justice is a part (PR, §§301, 314-15). Similarly, so long as people view themselves exclusively as private persons, the public authority will also appear to be a purely external body. In order to see it as an expression of their will, they must regard themselves as members of civil society and as citizens. Hegel's point in speaking of civil society as the state "of the understanding" is that the understanding cannot grasp the true nature of the political state. The understanding, Hegel con-

One possible solution would be to maintain that, despite the fact that the administration of justice and the public authority occupy a place within civil society, they do not actually belong to it. This proposal fits well with one extremely familiar way of drawing the distinction between civil society and the state. Civil society is often identified with the 'private sphere' (i.e., as the market or the market plus the network of private voluntary associations outside the market) and opposed to the 'public sphere' (which is identified with the government, or state). Private institutions (apart from the family) belong to civil society, and public institutions (such as the administration of justice and the public authority) belong to the state.

It is perhaps worth observing that this way of drawing the civil society/state distinction is shared by both libertarians and welfare liberals. Their disagreement has to do with the scope and kind of state intervention that are legitimate, not the distinction between civil society and state. Both would regard the administration of justice and the public authority as belonging to the state rather than to civil society.[34] Libertarians hold, in effect, that the administration of justice and the law enforcement functions of the public authority provide an indispensable external framework for the protection of property and contract. But they reject the public authority's welfare functions, which they regard as representing the unwarranted intrusion of the state. Welfare liberals, on the other hand, hold that the provision of welfare is no less a proper task of the state than the protection of property and contract. And, accordingly, they take the welfare functions of the public authority to represent a legitimate, and indeed necessary, function of the state.

It is not surprising, then, that Hegel's advocacy of the welfare function of the public authority is often thought to resemble welfare liberalism in being a defense of an institution that is external to civil society. But the fact that Hegel holds that the public authority belongs to civil society no less than to the political state makes it clear that this interpretation runs counter to his own understand-

tends, confuses the state with civil society, taking its ends to be "the security and protection of property and personal freedom, *the interests of individuals as such*" (PR, §258R). But since "the security and protection of property and personal freedom, the interests of individuals as such," *are* the proper ends of civil society, civil society can be thought of as the state *as the understanding* takes it to be (see PR, §183).

34 Presumably, libertarians and welfare liberals would, however, agree in rejecting Hegel's strikingly antiliberal view that there can be no fixed limits on the scope of police surveillance and regulation (PR, §234, Z; VPRHO, 693).

ing. Hegel *is* much closer in spirit to welfare liberalism than to libertarianism, as is generally recognized. But what is less commonly appreciated is that he breaks with both libertarians and welfare liberals on the very point about which they agree: the distinction between civil society and the state.

Hegel would allow that the libertarian and welfare liberal understanding of this distinction does contain a kernel of truth: namely, that the administration of justice and the public authority are both external to the *system of needs*. But he would insist that these institutions are not external to civil society considered as a whole, because he maintains that this sphere contains its own public dimension constituted by a set of public institutions concerned with the protection of the rights and welfare of individuals.[35] Hegel takes his discovery of civil society to consist, not in the discovery of a purely private sphere, but rather in the discovery of a private sphere containing its own public dimension, a social formation that is *civil* as well as *bourgeois*.

And so if we ask, *Could* Hegel accept the proposal to clarify the distinction between civil society and the state by taking the administration of justice and the public authority to be part of civil society and not of the state? it is clear that the answer is no. Hegel most emphatically does not share the common identification of civil society with the private sphere and of the political state with the public sphere. The claim that the administration of justice and the public authority belong to civil society, then, is absolutely crucial to his view.

At least two things should be clear at this point. The first is that Hegel's distinction between the civil society and the state is not to be identified with the distinction between the private and public spheres. The second is that Hegel's distinction cannot be understood in terms of complete institutional separation. Hegel clearly does not think that civil society and the state are distinguished by the fact that they share no institutions in common. Indeed, as we shall see, he holds that the institutional overlap exhibited by the administration of justice and the public authority represents one

---

35 In saying that Hegel maintains that civil society contains its own public dimension, I do not, of course, mean to suggest that this dimension is wholly independent of the political state. Although Hegel takes the administration of justice and the public authority to be integral components of civil society, he also thinks that they are part of the political state. And one essential feature of his conception of civil society is that its maintenance and reproduction require the existence of the political state.

of the crucial points of *connection* between the political state and civil society. And so we need to ask: How, then, does Hegel draw the distinction between civil society and the political state?

He does so by contrasting the "determinations" (*Bestimmungen*), or rationales, of the two spheres. Hegel maintains that civil society and the political state are distinguished, first and foremost, by the fact that their respective determinations are distinct.

In Hegel's view, the determination of civil society is to promote the development of "the particular" (the private ends of individuals and groups) "through the exclusive *mediation* of the form of universality" (e.g., the operation of the system of needs and the corporations together with the administration of justice and the public authority) (PR, §182). Civil society is the social sphere that gives particularity "the right to develop and express itself in all directions" (PR, §184).[36] He maintains that this is what marks civil society as one of the "specific shapes" through which the modern social world actualizes "the right of the subject's *particularity* to find satisfaction" (PR, §124R). This is the right which, it will be recalled, Hegel regards as "the pivotal and focal point in the difference between *antiquity* and the *modern* age" (PR, §124R). The main reason why the administration of justice and the public authority count as integral components of civil society is that they are specifically concerned with the particularity of the members of civil society (their particular rights and welfare) and as such share the determination of this sphere.

We can begin by characterizing the determination of the modern political state by saying that it is to promote the common good of the community, what Hegel calls "the universal" (*das Allgemeine*). By 'the common good of the community', Hegel means the common good of the community as such, a good that is distinct from the separate and particular interests of its members. Hegel takes the fact that the modern political state has this universal end to be one of the features that distinguishes it from civil society. Although the institutions of civil society aim at promoting the private ends of individuals and groups, they do not aim at promoting the good of the community as such.

For Hegel, the familiar contractarian view that the end of the

36 The specific form of particularity that civil society promotes consists in the particularity of separate and particular interests and legally specified rights, in contrast to the 'emotional' or 'psychological' particularity that flourishes within the modern family.

political state consists in "the security and protection of property and personal freedom, *the interest of individuals as such*" (PR, §258R) represents a characteristically modern confusion of civil society with the political state. The "interest of individuals as such," Hegel insists, is the concern of civil society, not the state. Grasping the modern political state in its specificity turns on appreciating that it represents the social sphere concerned with the community as a whole.

Hegel maintains that one of the most important ways in which the modern political state promotes the common good is by providing the institutional framework within which the community can determine its common destiny. Civil society makes it possible for people (men, in any case) to make and act upon their own private decisions, which of course have *consequences* for the community, but it does not provide a framework within which the community can *as a whole* determine and pursue its common ends in a self-conscious and rational way. For this, the political structures of the state are required.

Hegel takes political self-determination – the political self-determination of the community – to represent the highest 'moment' of the community's common good. He holds that membership in a self-determining political community constitutes the highest practical good that a human being can enjoy (see PR, §§153R, 258). In this respect, at least, Hegel is a republican. What Hegel most admires about ancient Greek democracies and the Roman Republic is that they realized the good of political self-determination. And in his view, the significance of the *modern* political state consists largely in the fact that its structure makes it possible to realize this republican ideal in a manner compatible with the basic conditions of modernity, which include the indispensability of bureaucracy and the need to devote oneself to one's private concerns.

Hegel recognizes that the very idea that a modern community could have a set of genuinely common ends is highly problematic. Civil society is, in his view, an inherently pluralizing force (PR, §§182Z, 184,Z, 185Z; VPRHO, 567, 570, 574). He thinks that its form of social life gives rise to the diversity of interests and opinions characteristic of modern social life. But he also holds that the modern political state provides an institutional framework within which the different sectors of the modern social world – the substantial estate, the estate of trade and industry, and the universal estate – can come together, and within which the divisions of interest between the different corporations within the estate of trade and industry can be overcome. Indeed, Hegel takes the coordination of these divergent interests to be one of the central tasks of the state.

It should also be pointed out in this connection that Hegel maintains that the common ends of the community are essentially the product of a particular kind of collective deliberative process. What makes them the *common* ends of the *community* is the fact that they are formed through a collective deliberative process in which the community attempts as a community to determine what *its* ends are. Indeed, it is precisely through the process of collective deliberation that the modern political community forms itself as a unified political community, as a political community with a set of common political goals. Hegel contends that the modern political state makes this collective deliberative process possible by providing an institutional structure within which this process can take place.

This characterization of the modern political state as the sphere that promotes the common good of the community is not, however, complete. Hegel contends that the most distinctive features of the modern political state are, first, that it enables its members to pursue their separate and particular interests and, second, that it unifies these separate and particular interests ("the particular") with the common good of the community ("the universal") (PR, §260). The modern political state enables its members to pursue their separate and particular interests by maintaining and supporting a social sphere distinct from itself – civil society – within which they can carry out these pursuits. Hegel holds that the fact that modern political states contain such a sphere is the feature which most centrally distinguishes them from states of classical antiquity. This is what he means when he says that in these states "particularity had not yet been released and set at liberty" (PR, §260Z; VPRHO, 717). They did not contain a sphere within which particularity was given the "right to develop and express itself in all directions" (PR, §184), a sphere of civil society. Nor, in Hegel's view, *could* they have: "the self-sufficient development of particularity . . . is the moment which appears in the states of the ancient world as an influx of ethical corruption and as the ultimate reason for their downfall" (PR, §185R). Seen from this point of view, the first thing that stands out about the modern political state is that it, unlike the states of classical antiquity, does contain a sphere within which particularity has been "released and set at liberty" (PR, §260Z; VPRHO, 717).

But for Hegel the very fact that the modern political state contains such a sphere raises the question whether particularity can be "brought back to universality, i.e. to the universal end of the whole" (PR, §260Z). There are really two worries here. The first worry is whether the modern political state can be understood as "harmoniz[ing]" (PR, §261R) the separate and particular interests of the members of the community with the common good of the community as such. Can it provide mechanisms that will ensure that there are no fundamental conflicts between the common good of the community and the separate and particular interests of its members? And can it provide mechanisms that will ensure that there is some fundamental unity between the separate and particular interests of its members and the common good of its members? The second worry is whether the modern political state can make it possible for its members to promote the common good of the community without abandoning their separate and particular interests. Can people in the modern social world combine the life of the *citoyen* with the life of the *bourgeois*?[37]

In claiming that the modern political state unifies the common good of the community with the separate and particular interests of its members, Hegel is saying that the answer to each of these queries is yes. This is at least part of what he is getting at when he says in that most evocative passage: "The principle of modern states has enormous strength and depth because it allows the principle of subjectivity to attain fulfillment in the *self-sufficient extreme* of personal particularity, while at the same time *bringing it back to substantial unity* and so preserving this unity in the principle of subjectivity itself" (PR, §260).

So far we have been focusing on the distinctive features of Hegel's understanding of the institutional side of the modern political state. It should be pointed out that there is another respect in which Hegel's conception of this configuration is distinctive. Hegel denies that it consists exclusively in a set of institutions. The modern political state contains an essential subjective dimension as well. He maintains that it is also constituted by what he calls the political disposition or attitude (*Gesinnung*), which he identifies with patriotism, properly understood (PR, §268). When ordinary people carry out their ordinary activities in the family and the workplace with a

---

37 This is one of the ways in which Hegel formulates the question concerning the possibility of reconciling the liberties of the ancients with the liberties of the moderns.

certain attitude, they are part of the modern political state. Thus, for Hegel, the state is not only 'out there' (in a constellation of governmental bodies) but also 'in here' (in our habits and outlook). Moreover, in order for the modern political state to attain full actuality (*Wirklichkeit*), a significant number of its members must exhibit the 'political attitude'. This, he contends, is one of the most important ways in which the modern political state exists.

We have already had occasion to consider the content of this political attitude, but it will be instructive to consider it once again in the context of the present discussion. "This disposition is in general one of *trust* (which may pass over into more or less educated insight), or the consciousness that my substantial and particular interest is preserved and contained in the interest and end of an other (in this case the state), and in the latter's relation to me as an individual" (PR, §268). We are now in a position to see what Hegel means here. By my "substantial" interest, Hegel means my interest as a citizen, which is to say my interest in the common good of the political community. By my "particular" interest, Hegel means the range of separate and particular interests I have as a private person. Thus, the trust that constitutes the political attitude is the trust that the true interest of the political state consists precisely in promoting both my substantial and my particular interest. It is the confidence that the political state is organized in such a way as to allow me to live a life in which I can realize myself both as a *bourgeois* and as a *citoyen*.

I conclude this exposition of Hegel's basic conception of the state by observing that, in addition to speaking of "the strictly political state" (*der eigentlich politische Staat*), Hegel also speaks of the state in a broader sense, as the politically organized community.[38] The politically organized community, as Hegel understands it, consists not only of the political state but also of the family and civil society. The strictly political state is thus one component of the commu-

---

38 The phrase 'politically organized community' originates I believe with Taylor (1975, 387). Cf. Pelczynski 1971, 1984b. It might be useful to distinguish between the broader idea of a politically organized community and the narrower idea of a political community. As we have seen, one of the striking features of Hegel's conception of the modern *political* state is that it *is* a conception of a political community, a community that consists not only of governmental officials (the political community, very narrowly understood) but also of ordinary citizens who exhibit what Hegel calls "the political attitude." I propose that we use the phrase 'political community' to refer to *this* (narrower) political community and reserve the phrase 'politically organized community' to refer to the (broader) community formed by the family, civil society, and the political state.

nity as a whole (the apex Hegel thinks) – but only one component. Hegel no more identifies *it* with the community as a whole than he identifies the family or civil society with this larger unit. But Hegel does identify the state understood as the politically organized community with the community as a whole. He thinks that the proper way of understanding the community as a whole is precisely to see it as a *politically organized* community, as a state, in the broad sense of the term. And, finally, it is the state understood in this broader sense that Hegel takes to be the basic ethical and political unit.

2. I will now provide a brief sketch of Hegel's account of the "constitution" (*Verfassung*), or normative structure, of the modern political state. We have seen that Hegel regards constitutional monarchy as the specifically modern form of government and that he holds that a modern constitutional monarchy consists ideally of three branches: the crown, the executive, and the legislature (PR, §273). Let us briefly examine these three branches in turn.

The crown (or "princely power," *die furstliche Gewalt*), as Hegel represents it, consists of a hereditary monarch together with a council of ministers (PR, §§275, 279–80, 283). The monarch, Hegel maintains, is the head of state who formally holds the final power of decision within the government. He is the bearer and personification of the sovereignty, or supreme authority, of the political state (PR, §279), the symbol of the unity and individuality of the political state (PR, §279, R), and the locus of the political state's subjective choice and decision. He is advised by the chief ministers of state – experts responsible for the formulation of policy and the initiation of legislation who serve at his pleasure (PR, §§283–4). Although the *formal* power of decision rests exclusively with the monarch, these ministers, not the monarch, perform the substantive work of the office of the crown. Hegel even goes so far as to say that the monarch's personal character is (or ought to be) irrelevant to the exercise of his office. "In a fully organized state, it is only a question of the highest instance of formal decision, and all that is required in a monarch is someone to say 'yes' and dot the 'i'; for the supreme office should be such that the particular character of the occupant is of no significance" (PR, §280Z; VPRHO, 764; cf. VPRW, 161–3).

The real political significance of the monarch consists in the fact that he is the subject through whom the community makes its decisions. Hegel takes the monarch to be the locus of the community's self-determination, the seat of its ultimate decision. When the monarch says, "I will," he is acting as the representative of the community, lending it the structures of his subjectivity (his ability to say, "I will"), so that, through him, *it* can perform the final, formal act of decision.

Hegel's insistence that the community's final decision must be made by a single human being (rather than a collective body) reflects his commitment to the principle of subjectivity. He argues that "subjectivity attains its truth only as a *subject* and personality only as a *person*" (PR, §279). He contends that "a so-called *moral person* [*moralische Person*], a society, community, or family, however concrete it may be in itself, contains personality only abstractly as one of its moments. In such a person, personality has not yet reached the truth of its existence" (PR, §279R).

Tracing Hegel's views about the monarch to their philosophical source in his commitment to the principle of subjectivity helps us to understand the philosophical motivation for these views. It does not, however, make Hegel's defense of monarchy convincing. But the real oddness of Hegel's insistence that the subjectivity of the political state must be realized by one single human being has to do with the fact that it comes from the very philosopher who perhaps more than any other figure in the history of philosophy has taught us to appreciate the conceivability of forms of subjectivity that are realized not by single human beings but by groups. And here one cannot help but think that democracy – a form of government Hegel explicitly rejects as being unsuitable to the modern social world (PR, §§273R, 279R, 301,R; VPG, 306–8/250–2, 310–13 /254–6) – makes it possible for the moment of subjective free decision to be realized by each individual voter. In a democracy, the locus of individual subjectivity, which Hegel takes to be so crucial, is not a monarch but myself. Why should I look to a monarch to provide the locus for the essential subjectivity of political decision when I can find it in my own vote? In any case, even granting Hegel's claim that the subjectivity of the political state must be located in one single human being, it is by no means obvious that this single human being must be a monarch. Virtually no one today finds Hegel's arguments for this claim to be compelling. However, if one's concern is with the distribution of power in Hegel's political state, as well it might be, the proper source of worry is not the monarchy, whose powers are rather restricted, but rather the bureaucracy, the real seat of power in the modern political state as Hegel represents it.

This leads us naturally to the executive (the executive power, *die Regierungsgewalt*), the bureaucratic center and administrative heart of the modern political state. The executive is the governmental body through which the community *acts* as a whole. As Hegel conceives of it, this branch of government consists of a body of highly trained civil servants and higher advisory officials, who are devoted to the common good of the community. (One of the most striking, and disturbing, features of Hegel's conception of the modern political state is the extraordinary faith he places in the dedication and public-mindedness of the civil servants.) The central task of the executive is to apply the law made by the legislature and to execute the policies determined by the crown (PR, §287). This branch of government is also responsible for the regulation and supervision of the corporations (PR, §§288, 289, R). And, as we have seen, the executive includes the administration of justice and the public authority as subordinate powers (PR, §287). These institutions function both as organs of civil society and as organs of the state. Insofar as they operate within the private sphere and have the protection of individual rights and welfare as their ends, they are organs of civil society. Insofar as they derive their authority from the state and have as their end the maintenance of the general framework that provides the community with a sphere of particularity, they are part of the state. The executive is thus a mediating governmental body that serves to connect the political state to civil society (PR, §302). It has the task of preserving the stable operation of the institutions of civil society quite generally (PR, §287) and, more specifically, the task of ensuring that the corporations, which have their own particular ends (PR, §§251, 256), do not transform civil society into an instrument of their particular interests.

Finally, the legislature ("the lawgiving power," *die gesetzgebende Gewalt*) is the branch of government responsible for the formulation of law. The legislature passes the laws that define and protect the rights of property and contract, thereby giving legal expression to the private sphere and conferring upon it the protection of the state (PR, §§212, 217, 298). This branch of government consists of the crown, the executive, the assembly of estates, and public opinion (PR, §300). That both the executive and the crown are working parts of the legislative machine illustrates Hegel's general rejection of the Montesquieuian understanding of the separation of powers (PR, §§272R, 300Z; VPRG, 704). The motivation for Hegel's division of government into different powers is not to guarantee that each power will check and restrain the other but rather to allow for full development and institutional expression of the central tasks of government (allowing the community as a community to deliberate, decide, and act). The institutional overlap exemplified by the active role the executive and crown play in the legislature reflects the fact that Hegel takes interconnection among the different governmental powers to be essential. Without such interconnection, he contends, the political state would fail to exhibit the sort of unity it must have if it is to be "*a single individual whole*" (PR, §272R).

The assembly of estates, as Hegel conceives of it, is a bicameral representative body (PR, §303). Its upper chamber consists of members of landed aristocracy, entitled to their place in this chamber by birth, who at least ideally represent the point of view of the substantial estate (PR, §§305–7) as a whole. Its lower chamber consists of deputies (*Abgeordneten*) of the estate of trade and industry who are elected from the corporations (PR, §§308–9) and reflect the diversity of opinion and points of view characteristic of civil society.

One of the fundamental sources of Hegel's view that the deputies in the lower house should be elected through the corporations rather than directly is his commitment to the idea that the point of the assembly of estates is to provide a body that represents the community as a community and allows the community to deliberate as a community. Civil society, as Hegel understands it, is not an aggregate of private individuals but instead an articulated body of different corporations, which represent the different branches of civil society (e.g., commerce, manufacturing industries, etc.) (PR, §311, R). Hegel says, "If the deputies are regarded as *representatives*, this term cannot be applied to them in an organized and rational sense unless they are *representatives* not of individuals as a crowd [i.e., as a "formless mass"], but of one of the essential spheres of society, i.e. of its major interests" (PR, §303R). This is what Hegel is getting at when he speaks of these representatives as being "elected by *civil society*" (PR, §311; my emphasis). And this, in turn, is why Hegel says:

> In so far as these deputies are elected by civil society, it is immediately evident that, in electing them, society acts *as what it is*. That is, it is not split up into individual atomic units which are merely assembled for a moment to perform a single temporary act and have no further cohesion; on the contrary, it is articulated into its associations, communities and corporations which, although they are already in being, acquire in this way a political connotation. (PR, §308)

The idea that the assembly of estates is supposed to be a body in which the community deliberates about the common good also motivates Hegel's view that the representatives are not to serve as "commissioned or mandated agents" of the community or corporation that elected them but rather to give their "essential support" to the "universal interest," the good of the community as a whole (PR, §309).

Hegel maintains that the assembly of estates constitutes the central forum for the public discussion of political affairs (PR, §309). It is the body through which public opinion is articulated and clarified, given institutional expression, and communicated to the executive and crown. It is also the body that allows citizens to gain insight into the workings of government and come to view themselves as citizens (PR, §§314–15).

In Hegel's view, one of the characteristic features of modern social life is that ordinary citizens insist upon understanding and participating in the public affairs of state. The assembly of estates, Hegel contends, is the body that makes this possible. Ordinary citizens gain insight into public affairs by following the debates and discussion that take place within this body. Just as jury trials allow citizens to gain insight into the workings of the judicial system, so the assembly of estates allows citizens to gain insight into the workings of government. Ordinary citizens participate in the affairs of state by participating in the larger public discussion of which the exchanges and deliberations within the assembly of estates are a part: the larger public discussion that constitutes public opinion (*öffentliche Meinung*). And it is worth noting that this larger public discussion is itself an essential component of the modern political state (PR, §§316–18). Having sketched Hegel's conception of the constitution of the modern political state, I now turn to a central problem to which this conception gives rise.

3. One of the most striking claims in the *Philosophy of Right* is Hegel's assertion that "the vocation of individuals is to lead a general life" (*ein allgemeines Leben*, PR, §258R). By a "general life," Hegel means a life that transcends the private sphere of family and civil society, a life in which one realizes oneself as a citizen. It is a life devoted to the common good and, more specifically, to the preservation of the politically organized community. Just as striking as Hegel's claim that leading a general life constitutes the vocation of modern individuals is his claim that the modern political state makes it possible for them to do so. Taken together, these two claims might

lead us to expect that Hegel would maintain that the modern political state must be organized in such a way as to maximize the participation of the ordinary citizen in the workings of the state. Certainly Hegel's talk of a "general life" conjures the image of the ordinary citizen as a politically active, fully engaged, decision-making member of the political community. But this is by no means the conception of modern citizenship that Hegel actually holds.

What stands out about his account of the modern political state is precisely the restricted character of the ordinary citizen's participation. Unlike the citizen of ancient Athens or republican Rome, the ordinary citizen in the modern social world does not participate directly in the decisions of the state. Hegel's modern political state is not a democracy but a constitutional monarchy in which the real work of governing is carried out by civil servants. In the state Hegel describes, the political participation of the ordinary citizen (i.e., the ordinary burgher) is limited to voting (through the corporations), paying taxes, engaging in public discussion, and (in times of national emergency) serving in the common defense of the politically organized community – in the military (PR, §§299Z, 311, 316–18; VPRHO, 791). Indeed, Hegel himself says that "in our modern states, the citizens have only a limited share in the universal business of the state" (PR, §255Z; VPRHO, 709).[39]

This basic fact that "citizens have only a limited share in the universal business" of the modern political state raises a fundamental question concerning how the modern political state can possibly be said to afford ordinary citizens the opportunity of leading a general life and what precisely Hegel takes a general life to be. This fact also raises a fundamental question concerning the state's role in the project of reconciliation. Central to the way in which the family and civil society reconcile individuality and social membership in Hegel's view is his claim that each provides a sphere within which ordinary citizens can directly actualize their individuality and social membership. Ordinary citizens can participate fully and directly in the family by marrying and having children. And by getting jobs and becoming members of a corporation, they can participate fully and directly in civil society. But, as we have seen, ordinary citizens cannot participate fully and directly in the business of government. How then can they possibly actualize their individuality and social membership in the political state? How then can the

---

39 Cf. Walzer: "Citizenship, taken by itself, is today mostly a passive role: citizens are spectators who vote" (1991, 299).

political state possibly reconcile individuality and social membership?

We can begin to address these questions by considering why Hegel thinks that the ordinary citizen's participation in the modern state will inevitably be restricted. Hegel contends that the complexity of the modern nation-state precludes extensive citizen involvement. Modern government has become a highly specialized and technical matter, calling for a wide variety of different sorts of administrative expertise (PR, §290,Z; VPRG, 689–90). The ordinary citizen lacks the aptitude, skill, and training that the administration of governmental affairs requires (PR, §301R). In the modern world, the business of government has become the business of experts (PR, §§291, 308R). More precisely, modern government requires a bureaucracy. And, in any case, the modern nation state is simply too large for direct citizen participation (VPG, 311/255).

Another reason why for Hegel the central tasks of government must be assigned to a body of civil servants is that ordinary citizens simply do not want to devote themselves to the political state. The demands of work and the claims of family, friends, and private projects leave ordinary citizens too little time to engage in public affairs. Ordinary citizens simply have too many other things to do to devote their main energies to politics. In the modern social world, private and public affairs have each become full-time occupations. Participation in the corporations represents the limit of the willingness of ordinary citizens to engage directly in public affairs. Thus, Hegel recognizes what Constant regards as the specifically modern need for a private life free of politics.[40] A requirement that all citizens take an active and direct part in the affairs of government (e.g., that they meet in the modern equivalent of the Athenian Assembly) would – practicalities aside – be unacceptably onerous from a modern point of view. More importantly, such a requirement would also constitute a serious restriction on civic freedom: on the freedom of individuals to pursue their own private affairs in their own way, in particular their freedom to choose their own trade or profession and to make it the center of their life (PR, §206). Thus, Hegel would reject Rousseau's contention in the *Social Contract* that "the better a State is constituted, the more do public affairs outweigh privates ones in the minds of the Citizens."[41] Although Hegel deeply admires the devotion to public life displayed by the ancient Greeks

40 Constant 1814, 104.   41 Rousseau 1762, 159.

and Romans, he does not think that the modern social world can or should be structured so as to force the ordinary citizen to live in this way (PR, §§185Z, 206Z, 260, Z; VPRHO, 578, 718). It must be possible, he thinks, for modern individuals to live a life that is bourgeois, which is to say, private and nonpolitical. And the professionalization of government makes this possible.

Of course, the professionals that serve in the government come from someplace. And Hegel maintains that many people within the middle class (*Mittelstand*) do want to dedicate themselves to public affairs (PR, §297, R). These are the people who enter the universal estate and work as professionals within the modern political state. And it must be mentioned that there is an important sense in which direct and active participation *is* open to ordinary citizens. Hegel insists that "it remains open [to the individual] to enter any sphere, including the universal estate for which his aptitude qualifies him" (PR, §308R). No one, or in any case no male adult, is prohibited by birth from entering governmental service (PR, §291). Because government has become professionalized, ordinary citizens must choose to devote their lives to public service if they want to participate personally in governmental affairs. Admittedly, this does involve trading the life of the ordinary citizen for the life of the civil servant: one cannot both participate personally in governmental affairs and lead the life of an ordinary citizen. But this, Hegel would say, *is* a choice that is open to ordinary citizens. The civil service is not a caste.

Hegel's conception of the division between civil servants (members of the universal estate) and ordinary citizens (members of the estate of trade and industry) reflects his acute recognition of the fact that the modern middle class is marked by two different and opposing tendencies: a drive toward private and a drive toward public concerns. Part of the appeal of Hegel's approach is that he attempts to provide room for both tendencies. In his view, civil society provides a sphere for individuals who want to devote themselves to their separate and particular interests, and the political state provides a sphere for those who want to devote themselves to public affairs. If the professionalization of government frees individuals whose basic orientation is private from the burdens of politics, it also provides individuals whose basic orientation is political with a sphere within which they can lead lives devoted to the community.

What these considerations make clear is that Hegel regards the fact that ordinary citizens cannot participate fully and directly in the workings of the political state to be a basic structural feature of modern social life. From his standpoint, the task of modern political philosophy is to show how it is possible for ordinary citizens to lead a general life *given* that the modern political state requires a bureaucracy and *given* that ordinary citizens do not want to lead intensely political lives. It is crucial to remember that, for Hegel, the central question is not how modern citizens can lead the life of the *citoyen rather than* the life of the *bourgeois* but how they can act as *citoyens* while remaining *bourgeois*. Hegel would certainly concede that compared with the political participation offered by the Greek polis, the Roman Republic, or the late medieval city-state, the political participation available to the ordinary citizen in the modern social world *is* restricted, but he would also deny that the sort of political participation modern citizens enjoy is inconsequential. He maintains that what they need is a form of genuinely meaningful political participation compatible with leading their own private lives. And he would argue that, *properly understood*, the forms of political participation the modern political state makes available to the ordinary citizen (voting through the corporations, participating in public discussion, paying taxes, and serving in the military) meet this need. Let us consider why.

Hegel thinks that voting through one's corporation represents a meaningful form of participation because it gives corporation members a genuine voice in the government. The deputies that they elect represent their point of view, the point of view they share as members of their corporation (PR, §§309,Z, 311; VPRG, 718). The presence of these deputies in the assembly of estates guarantees that their basic interests, values, and attitudes will figure in the deliberative process through which laws are enacted and policies are adopted (PR, §309Z; VPRG, 718). Representatives that are elected from geographical districts, by contrast, must represent the varied interests of their constituents: there is no guarantee that the distinctive points of view that people have as members of civil society will be represented. Individual suffrage also has the disadvantage of diminishing the significance of each individual vote (ibid.). Voting through the corporation gives one clout. One final advantage of voting through the corporations is that it connects and integrates the social and political life of corporation members (PR, §303, R). Hegel thinks that individual suffrage also has the highly undesirable effect of sundering one's 'identity' as citizen from one's 'identity' as a member of civil society (ibid.). To vote as an individual is to vote as an "atom" (ibid.). And this, Hegel contends, amounts to "separating civil and political life from each other and leaves political life hanging, so to speak, in the air; for its basis is then merely the abstract individuality of arbitrary will and opinion" (PR, §303R; see §303). When, however, people vote through their corporations, they vote as members of civil society who occupy a determinate and meaningful place in society. In this way a genuine link between civil and political life is forged.

Hegel maintains that, in the modern social world, taking part in the public discussion of political affairs constitutes a significant form of political participation, because the modern political community is itself a discursively formed body. To take part in the discourse through which the political community forms itself as a political community is to take part in the basic political process. This activity is open to ordinary citizens; although they cannot participate directly in the assembly of estates, they can participate directly in the larger public discussion of which the assembly's discussion is a part. Moreover, participating in this larger public discussion is also an activity that is compatible with pursuing one's private life, because it consists of such things as reading the newspaper and engaging in conversations about politics and public affairs with friends, neighbors, colleagues, and co-workers. Clearly, this need not be an all-consuming project. Participating in public discussion is thus a form of political participation that makes it possible to act as a citizen without being fully absorbed in the affairs of state.

Of course, the natural worry about this form of participation is that it will have no real political significance, no impact on the decisions of the institutions of the political state. It is here that Hegel's conception of the assembly of estates comes in. The role of this assembly is not simply to allow citizens to gain insight into the workings of government but also to provide a body through which citizens can clarify their views and make these views an integral part of the discursive process through which legislation takes place (PR, §§314–15). The assembly of estates functions as a mediating body that brings the larger public discussion into the workings of the institutions of the modern political state and invests this larger public discussion with real political significance. It is, in principle, the body that provides ordinary citizens with a real voice in the modern political state, preventing modern citizenship from collapsing into mere spectatorship.

Hegel maintains, rather unromantically, that paying taxes represents a form of citizen participation ideally suited to the circumstances of the ordinary citizen (PR, §299R,Z; VPRHO, 791). This claim might seem remarkable since, at least on the face of things, paying taxes represents a form of political participation that is "abstract, lifeless, and soulless" (see PR, §299Z; VPRHO, 791). To be sure, considered as the act of giving a portion of one's hard-earned income to the state, paying one's taxes is concrete enough. But, considered *as a form of political activity*, and when compared to direct engagement in the process of political decision making, the paying of taxes may well seem abstract. Paying taxes simply does not have the heroic character of participating in the Athenian Assembly. Paying taxes is essentially prosaic. And so it is no surprise that paying taxes may seem to be a form of political participation that is less than satisfying.

Hegel, however, maintains that the very abstractness of tax paying – its lack of extensive personal engagement – is precisely what makes it well suited to the circumstances of ordinary citizens.[42] He contends that the great advantage of paying taxes over other, more direct forms of government service is that it provides a way of supporting the state that leaves ordinary citizens free to lead their own private lives.

Of course, from the standpoint of the *bourgeois*, taxes appear to be nothing but a burden imposed by an external government. The only reason the *bourgeois* pays taxes is to avoid the sanctions attached to not paying them. But, according to Hegel, the standpoint of the *citoyen* (a standpoint made available in modern times by the modern political state, the assembly of estates in particular) provides an entirely different way of understanding things. Seen from this standpoint, the body that imposes taxes is not an external or alien institution but the political organ of the community of which the citizen is a member. The ends supported by the taxes one pays are, at least ideally, ends that one shares as a member of the political community. From the standpoint of the *citoyen*, taxation is not a burden but instead the means through which the national community collects resources from itself to support itself. Taxation makes it possible for the national community to be self-standing and autonomous. As a *citoyen*, Hegel maintains, one does not pay taxes because one is coerced; the reason one pays taxes is that one supports the institution of taxation, the process of public deliberation

42 Cf. ibid.

through which one's taxes are fixed, and the common ends the taxes support. The reason one pays taxes is that one supports the state.

The form of citizen participation represented by military service in times of emergency is certainly concrete. One is asked to leave one's private pursuits, to take up arms, and to place the whole of one's existence at risk for the sake of the politically organized community. Hegel maintains that in normal circumstances the state cannot require ordinary citizens to serve in the military. He holds that the defense of the state is in general the responsibility of a professional armed service (PR, §§325, 326, R, 327, Z, 328, R; VPRG, 736). This division of labor makes it possible for ordinary citizens to pursue their own concerns in normal circumstances without the interruption that military service would bring. But ordinary citizens *can* be called to serve in the army in times of national emergency: "in so far as the state as such and its independence are at risk, duty requires all citizens to rally to its defense" (PR, §326). Hegel thinks that this form of service is meaningful because, in coming to the defense of one's country, one comes to recognize the depth of one's commitment to one's country, a commitment that is normally formed as the result of having lived one's life within this community and having adopted its form of life. In risking one's life for the sake of the politically organized community, one comes to recognize in an especially vivid and acute way that one conceives of oneself as a member of this community and that one values its existence and independence more than one's own life.

Let us return now to the question of how, according to Hegel, the modern political state makes it possible for ordinary citizens to lead a general life. It will come as no surprise to say that one of the ways in which it does so is by providing the modes of citizen participation we have just considered. Hegel thinks that participating in the military when the independence of the state is in danger represents a special component of the sort of general life available to ordinary citizens. He thinks that paying taxes and participating in the public discussion represent normal components of the sort of general life available to them. But the crucial thing to appreciate about Hegel's conception of a general life is that leading such a life is much less a matter of performing a particular set of specifically political acts than it is a matter of (i) identifying with the common ends of the politically organized community and (ii) coming to view one's activities within civil society as ways of supporting the politically organized community. And so, the question concerning how the modern political state makes it possible for ordinary citizens to lead a general life comes down to the question of how the modern political state enables ordinary citizens to (i) identify with the common ends of the politically organized community and (ii) view their private pursuits as ways of supporting this community.

We have, in effect, already considered Hegel's answer to this question. In response to the first part of the question, he would say that the modern political state makes it possible for ordinary citizens to identify with the common ends of the politically organized community by providing a set of institutional structures – the assembly of estates in particular – that enables them to understand and identify with these common ends and to view themselves as citizens. He would also add that the modern political state is the institution that provides the set of structures – those of the legislature – through which these common ends can be formed. In response to the second part of the question, Hegel would say that the modern political state makes it possible for ordinary citizens to view their private pursuits as ways of supporting the politically organized community by providing a set of institutional structures – those of the executive – that guarantee that private activities carried out within the family and civil society will support the ends and existence of this larger community. And he would add that one of the functions of the assembly of estates is precisely to give ordinary citizens access to this aspect of the operation of the executive power.

Part of what Hegel has in mind by leading a general life, then, is doing such things as participating in the public discussion of political affairs, paying taxes, and serving in the military in times of national emergency. And part of what he has in mind by leading a general life is identifying with the common ends of the politically organized community. But the most distinctive thing he has in mind by "leading a general life" is carrying out one's everyday activities within the family and civil society with a certain frame of mind. One views these activities not only as one's private pursuits but also as ways in which the politically organized community of which one is a member actualizes *its* shared form of life. And one engages in these activities not merely for one's own sake or the sake of one's family but also for the sake of the politically organized community itself. One "wills the universal" (*das Allgemeine*) in one's private life (see PR, §260).

Hegel's conception of a general life is thus one in which it is possible to lead a life that is general (*allgemein*) while also leading a life that is otherwise bourgeois and to lead a life that, although otherwise bourgeois, is also general. Hegel contends that the final way in which the modern political state reconciles individuality and social membership is by making it possible to lead a life that is both general and bourgeois. In leading a life that is general, one actualizes oneself as a member of the state, as a citizen. In leading a life that is bourgeois, one actualizes oneself as an individual, as someone who pursues his own separate and particular interests. In leading a life that is both general and bourgeois, one leads a life in which individuality and social membership are reconciled.

7

DIVORCE, WAR, AND POVERTY

In this chapter, I discuss those features of the modern social world that, from a Hegelian perspective, are especially problematic: divorce, war, and poverty. My aim is to consider why, in his view, these problems do not undermine the modern social world's claim to be a home. I address these problems in what, from the standpoint of reconciliation, might be considered the order of increasing seriousness. Thus, I begin with divorce, turn to war, and finally consider poverty.

I. Divorce

Marriage is haunted by the possibility of divorce. The disappointment associated with the fact that marriages can and do collapse may cast doubt upon the institution itself. How could we accept an institution so fraught with risk? How could we accept an arrangement that is so fragile? Nor are the hopes and expectations that are frustrated by divorce merely subjective (merely private, personal, or psychological). They are generated by the nature of the institution. Marriage itself offers the promise of permanence. That is what Hegel means when he says that marriage "*ought* to be indissoluble" (PR, §176Z; VPRHO, 555) and maintains that it "should be regarded as indissoluble *in itself*" (PR, §163Z; VPRHO, 519). Why then doesn't the possibility of divorce violate the institution's own promise of permanence? Why doesn't it show that the institution is deeply defective?

Hegel responds to this concern by looking into the nature of the institution. Marriage, he says, is essentially (although not exclusively) an affective unity (PR, §176,Z; VPRHO, 554). The most fundamental bond connecting husband and wife is the bond of love (PR, §158). But feelings, Hegel suggests, are by their nature contingent (PR, §§163Z, 176; VPRHO, 434). The love connecting husband and wife may die, and the two may become totally estranged (*total entfremdet*) (PR, §176). This is not to say that married people cannot take steps to preserve their love, that they are simply at the mercy of fate. Couples can try to avoid circumstances that might threaten their marriage and try to work through the obstacles they cannot avoid. And in good marriages couples do. But whether any given couple will take these steps is a contingent matter. And whether they will succeed is a contingent matter too. Even good marriages can fail. Thus, "since marriage contains the moment of feeling within it, it is not absolute but unstable, and it has within it the possibility of dissolution" (PR, §163Z; VPRG, 434).

Should it come to pass that a married couple becomes totally estranged, then the essential inner bond of their marriage has broken, and their marriage, considered as a spiritual and affective union, has already collapsed. Under such circumstances divorce must be granted (PR, §163Z; VPRG, 434). This is why Hegel says "marriage certainly *ought* to be indissoluble, but this indissolubility remains no more than an *obligation*" (PR, §176Z; VPRHO, 555). The granting of divorce simply represents the official public recognition of the fact that the differences between the married partners are irreconcilable and that the marriage has collapsed.

Now whether a given couple has reached this point is, according to Hegel, something that must be determined by an impartial, institutionally authorized third party (e.g., the church or the court; PR, §176Z). He rejects the view that people should be allowed to divorce simply because they no longer feel like remaining married. And he further contends that merely transitory conflicts and divisions, however painful, do not constitute grounds for divorce. The couple's estrangement must *in fact* be total – deep, comprehensive, and unresolvable – if they are to be granted a divorce. No possibility of reconciliation can remain. Hegel's view of divorce is by no means latitudinarian, but *if* this (subjective) condition (objectively) obtains, then, Hegel maintains, the couple must be granted a divorce. "Just as there can be no compulsion to marry," Hegel writes, "so also can there be no merely legal or positive bond which could keep the partners together once their dispositions and actions have become antagonistic and hostile" (PR, §176).

Hegel thinks we can become reconciled to the possibility of divorce by grasping the intimacy of the connection between the feature that makes marriage attractive and the feature that makes it fragile. What makes marriage attractive is, inter alia, the fact that it is an affective union, but it is precisely because it is an affective union that it is so fragile. The contingency of marriage flows out of the contingency of feeling (PR, §163Z; VPRG, 434). Because marriage is an affective union, the permanence of marriage cannot be guaranteed. Hegel says "since marriage is based only on subjective and contingent feeling, it may be dissolved" (PR, §176Z; VPRHO, 554). Divorce could, of course, be forbidden as a matter of law, but even that would not guarantee the permanence of marriage considered as an affective unity. Given that marriage is an affective unity, it can at best be quasi indissoluble. And, in any case, the real tragedy of divorce consists not in the legal act of total separation but in the interpersonal estrangement that precedes it.

Thus, in Hegel's view, coming to a full understanding of the nature of marriage involves understanding both that the institution aspires to permanence and that the fulfillment of this aspiration cannot be guaranteed. And, he contends, once we understand why the fulfillment of the aspiration cannot be guaranteed, the fact it cannot be guaranteed will cease to be so troubling. The sadness that results from particular cases of divorce or from the general fact that marriages sometimes fail will remain, but the disappointment that results will no longer lead us to doubt the institution of marriage. Our understanding of the institution of marriage will instead provide a point of view from which we can come to terms with this disappointment. Because we understand that the possibility of total estrangement is built into the nature of marriage, we will be less troubled when such ruptures occur.

II. War

Surely one of the most disturbing features of the political life of states is the phenomenon of war. Its horrors are too well known to need recounting. The fact of war – the fact that wars occur – obviously poses a problem for the project of reconciliation. How can we be reconciled to a social world in which wars occur? This problem arises in an especially acute way for Hegel since he regards war, not as a deviation from the norm of peace and harmony, but rather as a normal feature of the political life of states. This is not to say that Hegel denies the horrors of war or that he celebrates armed conflicts between states.[1] It is certainly not to say that he endorses a general posture of militarism, let alone that he thinks that states ought actively to seek out wars. He does not. The point is rather that Hegel maintains that war is no less a normal feature of the political life of states than peace. He, like Plato, regards war as a permanent feature of human existence. The fact that war plays a central role in the actual life of states is, in his view, a fact with which political philosophy must come to terms. He contends, quite plausibly, that *if* we are to become reconciled to the modern social world *as it actually is*, we must become reconciled to it as a place in which wars occur.

Reversing the order of Hegel's presentation, we can think of Hegel's account of war as proceeding in two stages, the first relating to external relations between states and the second relating to the internal life of the state. The first line of argument starts from the fact of the plurality of sovereign states. Hegel maintains that the requirement of *sovereignty* precludes the possibility of the establishment of an international organization (by which he has in mind the "league of peace" proposed by Kant in his *Perpetual Peace*) that could guarantee that states settle their disputes peacefully (PR, §§324R, 333, R). He contends that the requirement of *plurality* precludes the possibility of different states forming one common and sovereign world state that could prevent the outbreak of war.

Hegel's commitment to the principle of sovereignty flows out of his commitment to the ideal of political self-determination. To say that a state is 'sovereign' is to say, inter alia, that it is independent and that there is no higher body with the authority and power to police its actions; each sovereign state is, in effect, a law unto itself (PR, §333).[2] Hegel maintains that states must be sovereign if they

---

1 Cf. Popper 1966, 2:68–9.
2 Hegel recognizes the existence of international law (and, indeed, regards it as one of the essential features of the modern social world), but he holds that "since no power is present to decide what is right in itself in relation to the state and to actualize such decisions, this relation [the legal relation between states] must always remain one of obligation [*Sollen*]" (PR, §330Z; VPRHO, 832–3). This point is addressed more fully farther on.

are to actualize the good of political self-determination (and freedom). Were a state to be subject to the authority of a higher power,
it could not determine its own fate, and its citizens would fail to
enjoy the good of being a member of a self-determining political
community. For a state to surrender its sovereignty would be for it
to relinquish the highest good it can offer its members, the highest
practical good they can enjoy. Because of this, Hegel concludes that
sovereignty is something that states must preserve.

Hegel adduces two reasons for rejecting the possibility of a world
state. The first is that there is a plurality of national peoples (*Völker*),
each of which needs its own state in order to realize its own distinctive "anthropological principle" – that is, a principle expressing its
distinctive form of life (VG, 59/51-2). The existence of a single all-
encompassing world state would be unacceptable because it would
preclude national peoples from expressing their own distinctive
anthropological principles. The second reason starts from Hegel's
assumption that states are, by their nature, individuals (PR, §§321-
4, 324R, Z; VPRG, 735). In speaking of states as "individuals"
(*Individuen*), Hegel presumably does not mean that they are individuals in precisely the same sense in which single human beings
are. He does not, for example, regard states as subjects of conscience; still less does he think they are the subject of phenomenal
mental properties (pains, colors, etc.). His claim that states are individuals involves the idea that politically organized communities are
unified collectivities with their own ends, which are distinct from
the separate and particular aims of their members, and which, when
considered in relation to the ends of other states, can themselves
be regarded as separate and particular. The claim that states are
individuals also involves the idea that states conceive of themselves
as individuals, in that they conceive of themselves as single, independent, and sovereign bodies (see PR, §324).[3]

In any case, Hegel maintains that *because* states are individuals,
they need other individuals (i.e., other states) from which they can
(i) distinguish themselves and (ii) attain recognition (see PhG, 145-
55/111-19). Hegel is committed to the general philosophical thesis
that individuals (single human beings or states) can fully actualize
themselves as individuals only if they are recognized as individuals
by other individuals from whom they have distinguished them-

---

3 The idea that groups can be the subjects of self-conceptions is discussed in Chapter 2.

selves.[4] Part of what it is to *be* an individual, for Hegel, is to be recognized as an individual by other individuals and to recognize that one is recognized as an individual by other individuals. The establishment of a world state would therefore eliminate a condition – the existence of other states – that must obtain in order for that world state fully to actualize itself as an individual state. And so a world state, in addition to being undesirable, is not a real possibility.

Thus, in Hegel's view, the basic circumstance of international relations is this: states face each other as sovereign powers with no higher power between them capable of enforcing the peaceful settlement of disputes. Sovereign states can and do enter into treaties to prevent the violent resolution of disputes, but because there is and can be no international body with the authority and power to enforce these treaties, the bindingness of these treaties ultimately remains contingent upon the will of particular states (PR, §333). Hegel concludes that when states face grievous disputes unresolvable through peaceful means, they have no recourse other than war (PR, §334). The possibility of war, Hegel maintains, arises from the basic circumstance of international relations.

Hegel also claims that the basic character of international relations makes it necessary not only that war be possible but also that war be actual, that wars take place. It is crucial here to appreciate the level of generality of Hegel's claim. In his view, the fact that *any particular* war occurs is a contingent matter. This is to say both that (1) any given war might not have occurred and (2) the principal immediate cause of any given war will lie in something other than the basic structural relations of states. What is not a contingent matter is rather the *general* fact that wars occur. The fact that wars occur is, Hegel maintains, a necessary feature of human social life, whose necessity is explained by the basic character of relations between states and the fact that each state has its own separate and particular interests, which are liable to come into conflict with the particular interests and concerns of other states. Things being as they are, contingencies will arise that do in fact lead to war (PR, §334).

Hegel's second line of argument for the necessity of war starts from what he regards as the deleterious effects of extended peace (PR, §324, R, Z; VPRG, 733–4). He maintains that relations between

4 See Siep 1979.

individuals and states deteriorate when states go through long periods of uninterrupted peace. Individuals become increasingly absorbed in the private pursuits of civil society and begin to view themselves exclusively as private persons and burghers. They lose sight of the value of the political community and begin to forget the essentially finite and contingent character of property and life, assigning more value to their own lives and property than these goods actually have. As a result, Hegel contends, *individuals* come to be worse off because *they* then cease to actualize themselves fully as citizens, and the *politically organized community* comes to be worse off because *it* ceases to enjoy its characteristic form of life. And finally, the distinction between the state and civil society becomes blurred, and the state is at risk of being absorbed into civil society.

War, Hegel maintains, is the corrective. When individuals see enemy troops entering their homeland, the finite and contingent character of life and property ceases to be an abstraction (PR, §324, R, Z; VPRG, 733–4). When threats to the state threaten their private pursuits, individuals grasp that the existence of the state makes these pursuits possible. And when the independence and sovereignty of the state are thrown into question, individuals recognize that it is *their* shared form of life that is at risk and consequently grasp the interest they have as citizens. At such times individuals learn to appreciate the value of their state. They grasp both that its existence is a necessary precondition of the attainment of their private ends and welfare and that its shared form of life is something that they value in itself – indeed, something that they value more than the attainment of their own private ends and welfare. When *this* happens, Hegel contends, the ethical health of the politically organized community is restored.

Hegel also holds that in times of war the state most clearly establishes itself as separate from, and superior to, civil society. The central thing at stake in war is not life and property (the central concern of civil society), but rather the existence of the political institutions of the state and the common life lived in and through them (PR, §324R, Z).[5] Even if a perpetual peace were possible,

5 One of Hegel's arguments for the reality of the distinction between civil society and the political state is that this distinction must be made in order to make sense of the possibility of war in the modern social world. If the modern political state were nothing other than a set of arrangements instituted for the security of life and property (if the modem political state were nothing other than civil society), then the fact that citizens are prepared to fight in times of war would be inexplicable. Why should citizens risk their lives and property to protect an arrangement

it would not, in Hegel's view, be desirable, because war is required for the maintenance of the internal life of the state. We need to be careful here. Hegel's account of war is not intended to show that war is good. What he says is that "war should not be regarded as an absolute evil" (*absolutes Uebel;* PR, §324R). In saying this he is acknowledging that war is an evil but denying that it is an *absolute* or *irredeemable* evil. The two lines of argument we have just considered are both meant to establish that war is an evil we can live with.

The first line of argument seeks to show that war is the price we must pay in order for states to exist. It does not deny that the fact that wars occur is a price – a horrible price – to be paid. It proceeds instead from the conviction that the goods that are preserved through war, the goods specific to the state (e.g., political self-determination and the possibility of leading a general life), and that, under certain circumstances, can be preserved only through war are superior to the goods of civil society (life and property) that are placed at risk by war. The fact that Hegel regards the goods specific to the state as superior to the goods of society marks one respect in which Hegel sides with the ancients *against* the moderns and makes clear how he would reply to the objection that his argument that war is an unavoidable consequence of the existence of the state provides an argument *against* the state.

Hegel's second line of argument is meant to reconcile us to war by showing that although it is an evil, war actually has a hidden benefit. It is meant not to show that states *should* go to war to maintain their ethical health (PR, ¶13), but instead to provide a way of understanding the general fact that states do go to war. This line of

whose point is to protect their lives and property? Why not rather flee to another state and remain outside the fray? This is what Hegel is getting at when he says: "It is a grave miscalculation if the state, when it requires this sacrifice [i.e., of life and property], is simply equated with civil society, and if its ultimate end is seen merely as the *security of the life and property* of individuals. For this security cannot be achieved by the sacrifice of what is supposed to be *secured* – on the contrary" (PR, §324R). Hegel is arguing, plausibly I think, that the fact that modern citizens are prepared to serve in the army in times of war shows that their commitment to the state is not merely instrumental and that the ultimate end of the modern political state cannot be understood "merely as the security of life and property of individuals." Here it is important to distinguish between (1) the argument that the fact of modern war shows that the modern political state is distinct from civil society and (2) the argument that war is redeeming because it makes citizens conscious of the importance of the state. One can regard the first of these arguments as plausible without accepting the second. My treatment of this point is influenced by Avineri (1972, 194–7).

argument seeks to establish that war makes something possible that is really valuable: the fully realized life of the citizen and the ethical health of the state. It proceeds from the assumption that there is no other way in which these benefits can be secured. It also seeks to show that war makes it possible for people to comprehend something essential: that they are members of a particular politically organized community and that the survival of their political community is ultimately more important than the preservation of their property or their own individual existences. We are to become reconciled to war by grasping its redeeming affirmative side.

III. Poverty

Perhaps the most serious problem posed by civil society is the problem of poverty. In Hegel's view, poverty is a terrible evil, generated by the basic structure of civil society itself, and is a problem for which there is no apparent solution. As such, poverty clearly poses an obstacle for the project of reconciliation, one that, at least in some respects, is significantly worse than the obstacles posed by war and divorce. How, then, according to Hegel, can we become reconciled to a social world that gives rise to poverty?

Let us begin by considering what Hegel takes poverty to be and why he thinks it is an evil. The most obvious aspect of poverty is, of course, material deprivation. Poverty is a condition of destitution, want, and need. And these are surely evils. But for Hegel, important as it is, material deprivation is by no means the most important feature of poverty. Poverty, as Hegel understands it, consists most fundamentally in the circumstance in which people lack the means – the resources and skills – required to participate meaningfully in the civil and political life of their society (PR, §241; VPRHN, 194–5).

Hegel believes that the poverty level is in effect determined by the level of income required to participate in a particular society and thus may vary across different historical periods and societies (PR, §244; VPRG, 608). One *can* be poor even if one possesses the basic means of physical subsistence. One *is* poor unless one possesses the resources that are necessary for meaningful social participation. The poor "are left with the needs of civil society," by which he means not only the needs for material things but also the need for recognition as full-fledged members of society (see PR, §§189, 253, R), "and yet . . . are more or less deprived of all the advantages of society, such as the ability to acquire skills and education in general, as well as of the administration of justice, health care, and often even of the consolation of religion" (PR, §241). Hegel thinks that poverty can be *aggravated* by gross discrepancies in wealth. Thus, he maintains that one truly horrendous feature of civil society is that some people live in luxury while others live in squalor (PR, §243; VPRG, 608). And he speaks scathingly of civil society as affording "a spectacle of extravagance and misery" (PR, §185). Hegel does not, however, think that poverty is *defined* in terms of such discrepancies. Nor, indeed, is he troubled by social inequality as such. On the contrary, Hegel thinks that the provision of an arena for the expression of *in*equalities of talent, skill, and effort is one of the proper functions of civil society. He regards the expression of these inequalities as a basic way in which human particularity asserts itself (PR, §§200, R; see also PR, §49R, Z; VPRHO, 218). Accordingly, he rejects the view that society should guarantee social equality just as he rejects the idea that social equality is an ideal worth striving toward. He does, however, maintain that society must guarantee the equal rights of its members (this is the task of the administration of justice and the public authority) and he is profoundly aware of the tension that arises between this ideal and the actual position occupied by the poor. In any case, Hegel does not claim that the poor are poor simply because they have less than others, nor does he think that they are poor because they have *dramatically* less than others: what makes the poor poor for Hegel is, again, that they lack the minimum level of income, skills, and resources required for a normal social life.

What Hegel finds *most* disturbing about the modern phenomenon of poverty is that it leads to the creation of a group that we today might call the underclass, the group that Marx derisively calls the *Lumpenproletariat* and the group that Hegel, no less pejoratively, calls the rabble (*der Pöbel*).[6] A subgroup of the poor, the rabble consti-

---

6 It is interesting to note that the second entry under 'lumpenproletariat' in the third edition of the *American Heritage Dictionary* is "the underclass of a human population." According to the *Wahrig Deutsches Wörterbuch*, the German word *Lumpenproletariat* (which Marx uses to refer to the lowest section of the proletariat who lack [proletarian] class consciousness) derives from *Lumpen*, meaning 'rags', and the French *prolétariat*. *Wahrig* also tells us that the German word *Pöbel*, the term Hegel uses, derives from the East Old French *pobel* (by way of the Middle High German *bovel* and *povel*), a formation influenced by the New French *peuple*, meaning 'people'. For discussions of the notion of the underclass see Auletta 1982 and Wilson 1987.

tute the lowest stratum of society, a group whose members, concentrated in cities, are permanently cut off from participation in the mainstream of social and political life. The rabble are wholly immersed in what might now be called the culture of poverty[7] and characteristically exhibit an attitude of inner indignation and rage (*innere Empörung*) directed against the rich, the government, and society in general (PR, §244Z; VPRG, 609). Hegel even goes so far as to suggest that this outlook, which he calls the "rabble mentality" (*Pöbelhaftigkeit*), represents *the* defining feature of the rabble. He maintains that people fall into the rabble when, in addition to being poor, they come to share this hostile outlook (ibid.).[8]

Strikingly, Hegel maintains that this attitude reflects a correct understanding of the rabble's objective circumstances. More specifically, he claims that the rabble mentality results from the rabble's grasp of two facts: (i) that they have a right to the means required for meaningful participation in civil society,[9] and (ii) that their lack of these means results not from a natural process of some kind but rather from the way in which civil society is organized (VPRHN, 195). This is what Hegel is getting at when he says that

> in civil society it is not a purely natural distress against which the poor man has to struggle. The nature which opposes the poor man is not

7 For a discussion of the idea of the 'culture of poverty' see Lewis 1969, 187–200.
8 Although Hegel generally uses the word *Pöbel* to refer to people who are (i) poor and (ii) possess the rabble mentality (*Pöbelhaftigkeit*), there is at least one passage in which he maintains that the rabble need not be poor: "The member of the rabble [*der Pöbel*] is distinct from the person who is poor [*Armuth*]; normally the member of the rabble is also poor, but there are also rich rabble" (VPRG, 608). I take it, however, that in this passage Hegel is using the word *Pöbel* in a nonstandard, sarcastic way to refer to anyone who displays the rabble mentality. Hegel holds that, in the modern social world, one finds the rabble mentality (understood as the nonrecognition of right) not only among the poor but also among the rich. He says: "Although on the one hand, poverty is the ground of the rabble mentality, the non-recognition of right, the rabble mentality also appears, on the other hand, among the rich. The rich man believes that he can buy everything because he knows himself as the power of the particularity of self-consciousness. Wealth can lead to the same mockery and shamelessness that the poor rabble displays" (VPRHN, 196). In saying that there are members of the rabble who are rich, Hegel is not making the absurd suggestion that some members of the *underclass* are rich but rather that some rich people exhibit the same mentality and the same sort of moral degeneration as the lowest segment of the poor. It is this degeneration that Hegel has in mind when he speaks of the "ethical corruption common to both" poverty and wealth (PR, §185).
9 Hegel contrasts the rabble mentality with that of what he calls naive poverty (*unbefangene Armut*), the form of consciousness exhibited by people who are poor but have not "progressed to the self-consciousness of their rights" (VPRHN, 195).

a pure being, but rather my will. The poor man experiences himself as relating to an arbitrary will, to human contingency; and this in the final analysis is the source of his indignation: that he is placed in this state of division through an arbitrary will. (VPRHN, 195)

What fuels the rabble's indignation, according to Hegel, is that they grasp that their circumstances are ultimately the result of society's will: its willingness to accept a form of social organization that excludes them from participating in society.

Hegel's recognition of the fact that the rabble's outlook has an objective ground does not, however, prevent him from criticizing this outlook. Indeed, he maintains quite generally that members of the rabble suffer from a kind of moral degradation (*moralische Degradation*; VPRHN, 194). He thinks that the members of the rabble think that society simply owes them a living. They lack the will to work and the self-respect that comes from supporting oneself through one's own labor, in other words, the work ethic. Moreover, they are frivolous and lazy (*leichtsinnig und arbeitsscheu*; PR, §244Z; VPRG, 609). And this laziness, coupled with their sense of being the victims of injustice, destroys their integrity and sense of right and wrong (*Rechtlichkeit*; PR, §244), making them wicked (*bösartig*; VPRW, 138). This helps explain why Hegel uses the already pejorative word *Pöbel* in an especially disparaging way.

It is crucial to stress that Hegel's views concerning the wickedness of the rabble do not extend to the poor as a whole. It should also be pointed out that he regards the wickedness of the rabble as the inevitable result of the objective circumstances in which they live, and ultimately of the way in which society is organized.[10] Thus, in Hegel's view, modern society is not only organized in such a way as to deprive the rabble of the material necessities of life and exclude them from meaningful social participation, it is also organized

10 It should be clear from this that Hegel's views concerning the rabble cannot be neatly classified as either conservative or liberal. On the one hand, like many contemporary conservatives, Hegel maintains that there *is* an underclass, focuses on the cultural aspect of their situation, and holds that members of the underclass are not only profoundly disadvantaged but also morally degraded. On the other hand, like many contemporary liberals (and leftists), Hegel takes the outlook and behavior of members of the underclass to be a symptom of their class position and a product of the organization of society. It goes without saying that the most obvious difference between Hegel's discussion of the underclass and contemporary American discussions of the same topic is that the dimension of race is entirely missing from Hegel's discussion.

in such a way as to *make them* ethically depraved. If the rabble are wicked, it is society's fault, not theirs.[11]

One reason why Hegel holds that the modern problem of poverty, including the creation of the rabble, poses a serious obstacle for the project of reconciliation is that he maintains that poverty and the creation of the rabble are *structural features* of civil society. These ills are not the result of personal failings or individual vice. Nor are they the outcome of the purely contingent imperfections of this sphere. They are, he maintains, the result of the normal operation of a number of central features of the economic structures of civil society (see VPRW, 138). These features include the fact that civil society has the character of a zero-sum game, so that the rich become rich only at the expense of the poor (PR, §195). They also include the fact that the development of the modern economy standardly leads to increased specialization, which, in turn, leads to a growing class of workers being thrown into stifling, low-paying, unrewarding jobs (PR, §243). Many of these people are unable to maintain a minimal standard of living or are unable to find work at all, and so an increasingly large number of people fall into the rabble (PR, §244). Moreover, the modern economy, as Hegel represents it, is also characterized by recurrent crises of overproduction: periods in which more commodities are produced than the market can support and in which the firms that produce these commodities contract or collapse, throwing people out of work and into poverty (PR, §245). Furthermore, far from representing an *obstacle* to the operation of the economy, the existence of poverty and the formation of a rabble are, Hegel contends, perfectly compatible with its unimpeded (*ungehinderte*) activity (PR, §243). Indeed, it is precisely civil society's simultaneous production of a class of people who are very rich and a class of people who are very poor that accounts for the spectacle of "extravagance of wealth and misery" that Hegel so deplores (PR, §185).

We can begin to get a grip on why poverty poses a far more serious obstacle to the problem of reconciliation than that posed by divorce or war by recalling that Hegel argues that war contains a moment of redemption. We may, of course, doubt this. We may question whether war actually serves the higher pedagogical func-

---

11 Given that Hegel's attitude toward the rabble is profoundly condemnatory despite the fact that he clearly recognizes this point, it is difficult not to draw the conclusion that he is guilty of the offense that it has become fashionable to call 'blaming the victim'.

tion Hegel ascribes to it. Even if we grant that war *can* serve this function, we may question whether this is a function it *normally* serves. And even if we grant that war normally serves this function, we may not share Hegel's view concerning the value of the things he thinks it makes it possible to know. Indeed, we may doubt whether the things Hegel claims war makes it possible to know *can* be known: we may doubt that they are true. Perhaps the survival of the political community is *not* more important than the preservation of the lives of its citizens. Perhaps the good of political community is swamped by the sheer level of suffering war inevitably brings. We may also have similar doubts concerning the therapeutic properties Hegel ascribes to war. Does war really restore the ethical health of the nation? Even supposing that it does, does that really constitute an adequate defense of war? And we may question other aspects of Hegel's account of war as well.

But *if*, for the sake of understanding, we are willing to grant Hegel's basic assumptions concerning the benefits of war, we can understand why he takes war to contain a redeeming moment. It is striking, then, that Hegel makes no attempt to tell a story that shows that poverty has a redemptive moment. And the simple reason for this is that there is no such story to tell. There is nothing redeeming about poverty. Not the least reason why poverty poses a problem for the project of reconciliation that is significantly more serious than the problem posed by war is that poverty represents a serious and unredeemed social evil.

The fact that Hegel refuses to ascribe a redemptive moment to poverty does not, however, distinguish it from divorce. Why, then, is the obstacle poverty poses to the project of reconciliation more serious than the obstacle posed by divorce?

One basic reason is that divorce, unlike poverty, exhibits a special kind of necessity that can be characterized as *reconciling*. Hegel maintains that the necessity of divorce has this property because it flows out of the character of marriage as an affective unity in an especially direct and immediate way. The institution of marriage, properly understood, would be inconceivable without divorce. There could, of course, be marriage-like arrangements – arrangements that one might call marriages – in which divorce was not a possibility. There could also be primitive forms of marriage proper in which divorce was not a possibility. But such arrangements would not respect human subjectivity and, hence, not count as proper forms of the *modern* institution of marriage (see PR, §124R). To accept marriage as what it is, as a unity of feeling, *is* to accept it as a unity that can dissolve. Hegel's suggestion is that *if* we come to appreciate just how intimately the feature of marriage we initially regarded as troubling (the possibility of divorce) is connected to the feature we find attractive (its character as an affective unity), we will come to regard the initially troubling feature as *fully* acceptable and thus attain reconciliation.

Now there is of course *a* sense in which Hegel might be said to regard the problem of poverty and the creation of the rabble as 'necessary': namely, that he regards them as counting among civil society's structural features. But Hegel never suggests that their necessity has the reconciling character exhibited by the necessity of divorce: he never suggests that to grasp the necessity of these features is to be *reconciled* to them. Nor should he. If anything, the thought that poverty and the creation of a rabble represent necessary features of civil society would seem to provide reasons for regarding this social formation as fundamentally flawed.

Moreover, it is clear that Hegel's attitude toward poverty is quite different from his view of either divorce or war. Although he regards divorce and war as highly problematic, he maintains that both ultimately turn out to be fully acceptable features of the modern social world. He believes that it would be fundamentally wrong-headed to attempt to eliminate either divorce or war.[12] Poverty does not have this status. It is instead a problem to be solved. That Hegel views poverty in this way is shown by the fact that he seriously considers a number of candidate solutions for the problem of poverty, which he did not do in connection with divorce or war.

Before considering the possible solutions Hegel examines, we should note that there are three conditions he thinks that proposed solutions to the problem of poverty must meet in order to be acceptable. The candidate solutions must (1) be effective, (2) respect the basic principles of civil society (PR, §245), and (3) be brought about through public agencies (PR, §242R).

The motivation for the effectiveness condition is plain enough, although what precisely will count as an effective solution will be an important point of interpretation. It is also plausible to say that

---

12 Hegel does, it is true, maintain that legislation should make it "as difficult as possible" to get a divorce, so as to "uphold the right of ethics against caprice" (PR,
§163Z; VPRG, 434), but it is clear that he does not think that such legislation
should prohibit divorce altogether. Hegel thinks that it is terribly important that
divorce remain a real possibility.

a proposed solution to the problem of poverty must not violate any of civil society's basic principles. The public agency condition, however, requires clarification. In maintaining that the solution must be brought about through public agencies, Hegel means that it must be brought about through the activity of public institutions. Hegel's main reason for advancing this condition arises from a point we considered in Chapter 6, namely, that people in civil society have a positive right against civil society that *it* provide them with the means required for meaningful participation in its structures (PR, §246Z). As far as the problem of poverty is concerned, Hegel's general view is that "public conditions should be regarded as all the more perfect the less there is left for the individual to do by himself in the light of his own particular opinion (as compared with what is arranged in a universal manner)" (PR, §242Z).

Turning now to the possible solutions Hegel surveys, it should come as no surprise that he rejects the view that private charity can provide an acceptable solution to the problem of poverty. Private charity is, after all, *private* and as such violates the condition of public agency.[13] Hegel also holds that private charity violates the effectiveness condition. Being dependent upon the private decisions of particular individuals, charity is contingent, and hence unreliable. This is not to say that Hegel disapproves of private charity. He thinks that individuals who are in a position to contribute to charity ought to do so. His point is that important and valuable though they are, almsgiving and charitable donations cannot provide a solution to the problem of poverty.

Unfortunately, the two candidate solutions that Hegel examines that do satisfy the public instrumentality condition either contradict a basic principle of civil society or violate the effectiveness condition. Hegel first considers the possibility of providing direct financial aid to the poor that would be funded through taxes imposed upon the wealthier classes or from monies drawn from other public sources such as wealthy hospitals, monasteries, or foundations. But he rejects this proposal since it would contradict the basic principle of civil society according to which people are to support themselves through their own labor. The second possible solution that Hegel examines would be for the state to provide the poor with productive work through the public institutions of civil society. This proposal, however, runs afoul of the effectiveness condition as it

13 Cf. for similarities Nagel 1991, 95–6.

would only reproduce the problem of overproduction, one of the basic underlying causes of poverty (PR, §245).[14]

The upshot of all this is that Hegel can see no way of solving the problem of poverty. Poverty remains for him a problem to be solved that has no apparent solution. He concludes his survey of possible solutions by saying: "This shows that, despite an *excess of wealth*, civil society is *not wealthy enough* – i.e., its own distinct resources are not sufficient – to prevent an excess of poverty and the formation of a rabble" (PR, §245). And in the 1824–5 version of his lectures on the philosophy of right, Hegel expands on this point, saying: "The question how to remedy poverty is very difficult to answer; it is precisely through the excess of wealth that civil society becomes too poor to remedy the excess of the rabble" (VPRG, 611).[15] It is precisely this pessimism that leads him to suggest despairingly that "the best means [of dealing with poverty] is to leave the poor to their fate and direct them to beg" (VPRG, 612; see PR, §245R).

Pessimistic as Hegel's tone in these passages is, it would be a mistake to conclude that Hegel holds that no solution to the problem of poverty *can* be found. In suggesting that poverty and the formation of the rabble are structural features of civil society, he does not mean that they are ineliminable but rather that they are (i) generated by the normal operations of civil society and (ii) com-

---

14 It has become a commonplace to suggest that although Hegel did not consider the Keynesian approach of employing workers in the production of public works, this approach represents a solution that is in principle open to the Hegelian. The advantage of this solution is that it avoids the problem of overproduction. It is far from certain, however, that this solution would work in the long run. It is not as if we today have solved the problem of poverty. One possible solution that Hegel himself did not consider but clearly could have is colonization. Hegel discusses the role that colonization plays in the life of civil society immediately after his discussion of poverty. The idea would be that civil society could solve the problem of poverty by sending surplus workers off to form colonies. Colonization did not, however, solve the problem of poverty in England – arguably the 'best case' of the measure. And even if colonization did succeed in solving the problem of poverty in the home country, once the new colonies established their own civil societies, the same problems that led to the need to form them would reappear. Moreover, after a period of time these problems would presumably reappear in the home country. So, quite apart from what we might regard as its other unattractive features, colonization does not represent an acceptable solution to the problem of poverty by Hegel's own lights.

15 There is nothing anomalous about Hegel's open acknowledgment of the unsolved character of the problem of poverty (cf. Avineri 1972, 154). As was discussed in Chapter 3, it is part of his conception of the project of reconciliation that its task is to reconcile people to the modern social world as a world that contains problems.

patible with its unimpeded economic activity. Although Hegel does think that the formation of the rabble facilitates the creation of wealth (PR, §243), he is not committed to the thesis that the creation of wealth absolutely requires the existence of a rabble. And although he holds that the basic principles of civil society would rule out a number of candidate solutions to the problem of poverty, he never says that its principles are such that they would block every conceivable candidate solution. Hegel does remark in one passage that "the emergence of poverty is in general a consequence of civil society from which on the whole it necessarily results" (VPRHN, 193). But I take it that his point in this passage is to suggest that civil society exhibits a *systematic tendency* to give rise to poverty, *not* that poverty is ineliminable. It is by no means uncommon for Hegel to use the word 'necessarily' (*notwendig*) in similarly flexible ways.

None of this, however, is meant to suggest that Hegel's considered view is actually optimistic. There is, for example, no reason to suppose that Hegel shares the optimism of his student and colleague Eduard Gans, who wrote that because the existence of an impoverished class "is only a fact, not something right, it must be possible to get to the basis of this fact and abolish it."[16] The point I am urging is rather that, for all of Hegel's very real and deeply felt pessimism, the question of whether an acceptable solution to the problem of poverty can be found remains for him an open one.

I close this discussion of poverty and this chapter by considering the implications of the problem of poverty for Hegel's project. The specific question we need to consider is this: Does the fact that the problem of poverty remains unresolved mean that the social world is not a home? Does the project of reconciliation shipwreck on the fact of poverty?

This question becomes all the more pressing if we consider the situation of the poor (including the rabble) more closely. Recall that Hegel defines poverty as the circumstance in which one lacks the skills and resources required for meaningful participation in social and political life. This means that the poor are cut off – objectively cut off – from participation in the modern social world. And what this means is that they cannot actualize themselves as individuals and social members. And this in turn means that they are alienated. Moreover, they are not just *subjectively* alienated – like the reflective members of the bourgeoisie who constitute Hegel's primary

16 Gans 1832–3, 92; cited in Wood 1990, 248.

audience – but are *objectively* alienated as well. The real evil of poverty, as Hegel represents it, is that being poor means being alienated. Poverty is a circumstance of alienation. The poor *cannot* be at home in the social world. They cannot attain reconciliation.

The question arises whether Hegel clearly grasped this point. One reason for thinking that he did not is that to my knowledge he never clearly *states* that poverty is a circumstance of alienation. Now, taken by itself this consideration is not terribly compelling, but when considered in the light of the way in which Hegel has framed the project of reconciliation, the point gains force. As we saw in Chapter 4, Hegel clearly seems to have thought that the specifically *modern* problem of alienation is subjective, not objective, alienation. And as we saw there, he also seems to have thought the people who need reconciliation are reflective members of the bourgeoisie rather than the poor. Had Hegel clearly recognized the problem of poverty *as* a problem of alienation, then, the problem of poverty would, presumably, occupy a far more central place in the project than it actually does. If anything about Hegel's project is clear it is that subjective alienation – not poverty – constitutes the main problem it addresses. This, together with the fact that Hegel never explicitly speaks of the problem of poverty as a problem of alienation, provides a very strong reason for thinking that he did not clearly recognize the problem of poverty as a problem of alienation.

The suggestion that Hegel failed to grasp poverty as a problem of alienation may seem startling. After all, it has become something of a commonplace to say that Hegel recognized this point well before Marx.[17] And, it must be said, there are some good reasons for thinking that Hegel did grasp this point before Marx. The conclusion that poverty is a form of alienation follows straightforwardly from his general conception of alienation and his specification of the nature of poverty. Moreover, the features that most troubled Hegel about poverty are the very features in virtue of which it counts as a form of alienation. It is possible, however, that Hegel failed to grasp or fully appreciate the implications of his own view. We should be reluctant to infer that because it is obvious to us that poverty is a form of alienation, it was obvious to Hegel. It may be that he was deeply troubled by the fact that poverty is a form of alienation without having clearly and explicitly grasped that *this* was what bothered him.

17 Avineri 1972, 87–98.

It would not be all that surprising if the first person clearly to grasp that poverty was a form of alienation was not Hegel but Marx. Marx's central problematic is after all the objective alienation of the proletariat rather than the subjective alienation of the bourgeoisie. The transition from the problematic of the subjective alienation of the bourgeoisie to the objective alienation of the proletariat *is*, in effect, the transition from Hegel to Marx.

It is quite possible that Marx's discovery that the real significance of poverty consists in the fact that it is a form of alienation (supposing for the moment that it was Marx's discovery) has so transformed the way in which subsequent thinkers have understood the problem of poverty that it has become almost impossible to imagine not seeing things in this way.[18] Perhaps, having read Marx, it is difficult not to read Hegel's account of poverty *as* an account of alienation. If the fact that the real problem of poverty is the problem of alienation is clearer to us than it was to Hegel, it is not because we are wiser than Hegel but because we have the benefit of having read Marx.

My own view is that whether Hegel did or did not clearly grasp the problem of poverty as a problem of alienation is simply unclear. Nonetheless, I would like to suggest that the best way of *interpreting* him is to read him as responding to the problem of poverty as a problem of alienation. This approach leads us more deeply into his social philosophy and makes his view more interesting. Moreover, it is plain that the problem of poverty *as he represents it* does constitute a form of alienation. And it is quite clear that, whether or not Hegel recognized or appreciated this fact, the features that most troubled him about poverty are precisely the features in virtue of which it constitutes a form of alienation. Furthermore, Hegel does have available to him theoretical resources that would enable him to address the problem of poverty as a problem of alienation.

So our question then becomes: *Given* that the problem of poverty is one of alienation and *given* this problem remains unresolved, how can Hegel still maintain that the modern social world is in fact a home? Why doesn't the fact that the poor are alienated shipwreck the project of reconciliation?

One might think that the fact of poverty makes it evident that the social world Hegel describes is not a home. If the poor cannot be at home in the modern social world, the question arises whether

18 Marx 1844, 1978b.

anyone can be. Once one recognizes the problem of poverty as a problem of alienation – so the objection continues – it becomes clear that the modern social world, as Hegel represents it, is not a home. And so the project of reconciliation fails.

Hegel is not, however, committed to the doctrine that it must be possible for *everyone* to come to be at home in order for anyone to be. As we know from Chapters 2 and 3, his view is rather that if the modern social world is to be a home, it must be possible *in general* for people to come to be at home in it. And he maintains that the account of the modern social world he provides in the *Philosophy of Right* does show that this condition obtains. We might well think that this condition is too weak, but it is crucial to see that this is the position Hegel holds. Doing so makes it possible for us to see that, at least within his own framework, Hegel could acknowledge that the poor are not and cannot be at home in the modern social world without abandoning his thesis that the modern social world *is* a home.

Nevertheless, the problem of poverty understood as a problem of alienation places enormous pressure on Hegel's view. The case of poverty is not that of a collection of random individuals who, as it happens, cannot come to be at home in the modern social world. The case poverty presents is instead one of *a whole class* whose objective (and subjective) position is one of alienation generated by the normal workings of civil society.

This in turn raises still another point, one that returns us to an issue we considered at the beginning of our investigation of Hegel's project (in Chapter 1). If, as clearly seems to be the case, Hegel holds that the social world's being a home is compatible with the fact that its normal operation generates a whole class of people who are alienated, why doesn't the reconciliation his project offers collapse into resignation? How could acceptance of such a deep and serious flaw amount to anything other than resignation?

First of all, we should recall that Hegel is not committed to the view that the problem of poverty is insoluble. Nor does he think that there is anything inherently wrongheaded with trying to eliminate poverty. Thus, for Hegel, being reconciled to the modern social world *is* compatible with working to find ways to solve this problem. Becoming reconciled to the modern social world as a place that gives rise to poverty does not mean that one has to sit back and do nothing.

Still, the world to which one is to become reconciled *is* a world that contains poverty. Hegel is not arguing that the modern social world *would* be a home *were* the problem of poverty overcome. He is committed to the much more radical, even shocking view that the modern social world is a home despite the fact that it gives rise to poverty. This reflects his general view, discussed in Chapters 1 and 3, that the aim of the project of reconciliation is to reconcile people to the modern social world as it is here and now.[19] And so we have to ask again: How could reconciliation to such a world amount to anything other than resignation?

Hegel's basic reply to this question would be that although poverty does represent an extremely serious flaw, the *basic* features of the modern social world (i.e., the central social institutions) are nonetheless good. He would suggest that, imperfect though these structures are, they do make it possible for most people – men and women, landowners and peasants, workers and employers, not to mention the members of the universal estate – to be at home in the modern social world. It is important to remember that the sort of society Hegel has in mind is not one in which most people live in poverty. It is rather one in which most people are reasonably well-off and poverty is the condition of the few. Although Hegel takes the problem of poverty to be *very* serious, he does not think that it is *so* serious as to undermine the modern social world's claim to be a home.

Hegel would also suggest that to allow the fact that the modern social world gives rise to alienation to lead one to fall into resignation would amount to the error of placing too much emphasis upon the shortcomings of the world. Hegel maintains:

> To see only the bad side in everything and to overlook all the positive and valuable qualities is a sign of extreme superficiality. Age, in general, takes a milder view, whereas youth is always dissatisfied; this is because age brings with it maturity of judgment, which does not simply tolerate the bad along with the rest out of sheer lack of interest, but has learnt from the seriousness of life to look for the substance and enduring value of things. (VG, 77/66)

Here it must be stressed that Hegel is not saying that one should look at the bright side and ignore the defects of the modern social world. He is not denying the real evil of poverty or alienation. Nor is he advocating complacency. His view is rather that even if one

---

19 See Chapter 1, sections I and IV.1.i–ii, and Chapter 3, section II.

clearly recognizes the very real defects of the modern social world, it is still possible to accept and affirm it. And, indeed, as we saw in Chapter 3, the sort of affirmation Hegel has in mind *requires* full appreciation of these defects. Hegel insists that to be genuinely reconciled is to be reconciled to the modern social world *as it is* (PR, ¶14).

There is one aspect of Hegel's treatment of the problem of poverty, however, that does resemble resignation. In responding to the question concerning how we are to come to terms with the fact that the modern social world gives rise to a problem as serious as that of poverty, Hegel would appeal to the inevitability of flaws and defects in the finite world. He would argue that although poverty is a structural feature of civil society, it nonetheless represents a *contingent* failure of this sphere to "protect its members and defend their rights" (PR, §238Z; VPRHO, 700). This failure is contingent in the sense that, although no adequate solution to this problem has yet been found, it is not impossible that an adequate solution can be found.[20] And contingencies of this kind, Hegel would argue, are unavoidable. It would be unreasonable to expect that we should have a solution for every problem. It is in the nature of things that some problems of this sort will, at least provisionally, remain unsolved. "[W]here there is finitude," he maintains, "opposition and contradiction always break out again afresh" (VA, 1:136/1:99).[21]

Thus, in Hegel's view, we are to accept the existence of poverty as a part of accepting the general fact that defects and imperfections are an ineliminable feature of the social world. This acceptance, Hegel contends, will inevitably contain a moment of melancholy. As well it should, for it is precisely this moment of melancholy that makes it possible, in his view, to combine full acceptance of the modern social world with clear-eyed recognition of its defects.

20 It should be stressed that this argument does not turn on taking poverty to be a *purely* contingent feature of civil society – as not being rooted in any of its structural features. The argument is compatible with recognizing that poverty is generated by the normal operation of the economy and that any number of possible solutions to poverty would be blocked by civil society's basic principles. Cf. Wood 1990, 249.

21 Hegel could appeal to the inevitability of the flaws and defects of the finite sphere even if he regarded poverty as ineliminable, for then the argument would be that the fact that poverty constitutes an ineliminable structural feature of civil society is to be explained by the inherent limitation of all finite arrangements.

CONCLUSION

We have, at last, reached the end of our investigation. At this point it is natural to want a comprehensive assessment of Hegel's project of reconciliation. We may want to ask, Does the project succeed? Can we become reconciled to our social world? To ask whether we can become reconciled to our social world is to ask whether the modern social world is a home. One of the things we have learned from Hegel is just how large this last question is. It is much too large to answer fully here. Still, it might be thought that the question concerning the success of Hegel's project is more manageable. Perhaps it is. But to ask whether the project of reconciliation succeeds is to ask whether Hegel's social philosophy as a whole succeeds, and that is a very large question indeed. My aim in this book has been not to provide a comprehensive account of Hegel's social philosophy but, rather, to show that it can be understood as a project of reconciliation. A final assessment of Hegel's social philosophy would be out of place here. Nonetheless, we need to find a way of considering what we have accomplished and where we stand. We need to say something about how we are to view the project of reconciliation.

We would do well to begin by recalling the force and power of the project's guiding question: Can I – or can *we* – become reconciled to the social world? To ask this question is to entertain the possibility that the social world may not be a home. It is to recognize the possibility of being 'split' from the social world, the possibility of alienation. The question also brings to consciousness the fact that our relation to the social world includes a significant element of subjective assessment and choice. It raises the general issue (personal, ethical, political) of how we are to *relate* to the social world, the question of what attitude we are to take toward the social roles and institutions our social world provides. I have tried to indicate in this book just how important these issues are. The significance of Hegel's social philosophy consists largely in the fact that it provides a general framework within which these issues can be addressed.

As we have seen, the project's guiding question arises naturally from the felt experience of alienation – a feeling that is widespread in our culture. Alienation is what one feels when one regards one's social arrangements as foreign, bifurcating, and indifferent or hostile to one's needs. The feeling can be characterized as one of being split from the world, of not fitting in there. It is the feeling of not being at home in the social world. Contained within this feeling is a wish: the wish to *be at home* in the social world. And contained in this wish is another wish: the wish that the social world would be a home. The ideal of reconciliation (of being at home in the social world) and the ideal of having a social world that is a home are both born of the felt experience of alienation. One virtue of Hegel's account is that it makes it possible to grasp these connections.

The idea of the social world's being a home may of course appear to be hopelessly metaphorical. But one of the strengths of Hegel's account is precisely that it gives real content to this idea. For Hegel, the social world is a home if and only if it makes it possible for its members to actualize themselves both as individuals and as members of society. He also offers a conception of what it is to actualize oneself as an individual and as a social member that is rich, interesting, and attractive.

Hegel maintains, quite plausibly, that actualizing oneself *as an individual* is inter alia a matter of pursuing separate and particular interests, exercising individual rights, and acting on the basis of private conscience. He contends, interestingly, that actualizing oneself as an individual in the strong sense requires participation in civil society and, still more interestingly, that actualizing oneself as an individual in the complete sense also involves participation in the family and the state. In his view, being a member of a particular family and a citizen of a particular state is no less a part of one's individuality (individuality in the complete sense) than one's separate and particular interests or individual rights. This too seems quite plausible.

Hegel contends that actualizing oneself *as a member of society* is largely a matter of participating in the family, civil society, and the state. The form of social membership the family ideally provides is one within which people develop and satisfy their need for intimacy and emotional recognition. At least ideally, civil society provides a form of social membership within which people can pursue their separate and particular interests and come together in voluntary associations. The form of social membership provided by the modern political state is ideally one in which people can pursue the common good of their political community without prejudice to their private pursuits in the family and civil society. Moreover, fully actualizing oneself as a member of society also involves absorbing into one's subjectivity the roles of family member, member of civil society, and citizen. The appeal of this conception of social membership is, I think, clear.

Now, it might seem odd that Hegel should appeal to the structures of the family, civil society, and the state to explicate the idea of social membership. His project is, after all, addressed to a group of people who regard these institutions as alienating. But here it will be recalled that Hegel maintains that the reason his (reflective) contemporaries are alienated is that they fail to understand their social world – and this failure consists more precisely in their failure to understand that the central social institutions enable them to actualize themselves as both individuals and members of society. The aim of Hegel's account of the modern social world – the account he provides in his *Philosophy of Right* – is precisely to enable his reflective contemporaries to grasp this fact. In grasping it, they would grasp that their social world is a home. And in grasping this, they would come to be at home in its arrangements, thereby attaining reconciliation.

It is worth pointing out that, when presented in broad outline, Hegel's account of the modern social world provides a conception of what it is for the social world to be a home *we* can take seriously. According to his account, a modern social world that is a home will consist of three central institutional spheres:

(i) A domestic sphere of affective personal relations within which people can express their psychological particularity and provide one another with emotional recognition

(ii) A private sphere of contractual and civil relations within which people can pursue their private and associational ends and provide one another with objective recognition of their individual talents, skills, and achievements, their determinate position in society, and their general status as members of society

(iii) A political sphere of republican relations within which citizens can collectively determine and pursue their common good and recognize one another as members of a politically organized community

I refer to this account as the *broadly Hegelian conception* of a modern social world. A social world that corresponded to this conception might well be a place in which people like ourselves could be at home. The conception represents one of the most important things we can take away from Hegel's social philosophy, for it gives us a sense of what a world that we would regard as being worthy of reconciliation might be like.

Obviously this conception is very abstract. Too abstract, it might be said, to be genuinely illuminating. But here we should recall that the conception has been abstracted from the account of the modern social world Hegel provides in his *Philosophy of Right*, and that account is surely rich and detailed enough to give us an imaginative grip on the conception. Having gone through Hegel's account of the family, civil society, and the state in some detail, we now are in a position to appreciate the appeal of the broader conception.

The central motivation for abstracting from the details of Hegel's own account is to make it possible to appropriate the features of his account of the modern social world that are attractive while avoiding those that are unattractive. One unattractive feature is Hegel's traditional understanding of the division of gender. Hegel maintains that the family is the special province of women and that civil society and the state are the exclusive domain of men. For those who reject the traditional understanding of the natures of men and women that underlies this view, the world described in the *Philosophy of Right* will present itself as a world of alienation. They will insist that it is a condition of the social world's being a home that the structure of the family be egalitarian rather than patriarchal and that civil society and the state be open to women as well as men. Hence, to form a conception of a world that we can regard as worthy of reconciliation, we must abstract from Hegel's conception of gender.

Many will also take exception to Hegel's hierarchical conception of politics. One thing that stands out about his conception of the modern political state is just how little power it assigns to ordinary citizens. The modern political state, as Hegel represents it, is not designed to enable ordinary citizens to govern themselves. Although it is true that it enables them to vote through their corporations for deputies who at least ideally will represent their point of view in the lower chamber of the assembly of estates, governing is basically the function of the executive and the crown rather than the assembly of estates. The real power in the Hegelian state lies in the hands of a professional class of civil servants. This – and not the fact that it is a monarchy – is the profoundly antirepublican and disturbing aspect of Hegel's account of the modern state.

I do not, however, mean to suggest that Hegel's political state is simply authoritarian. He maintains that both the executive and the crown must work in consultation with the assembly of estates, that is, the political state's representative bodies. He also maintains that the deputies in the lower chambers must consult with the members of the corporations and townships from which they are elected. Hegel's political state is a consultation hierarchy.[1] And as we have seen, Hegel insists that it is essential that ordinary citizens be able to participate in public discussion of political affairs and gain insight into the workings of the government. Thus, the sort of hierarchy Hegel endorses is essentially public. Nonetheless, Hegel's conception of political life is fundamentally hierarchical, and many readers will find this feature objectionable.

Hegel is certainly right in claiming that ordinary citizens must be able to participate meaningfully in the workings of the state if the modern social world is to be a home. But he is wrong in thinking that the world he presents in the *Philosophy of Right* satisfies this condition. In order to be genuinely meaningful, political participation must involve the exercise of political power. Without power, political participation becomes a mere show. Therefore, to form a conception of a social world we can regard as a home, we must also abstract from Hegel's commitment to hierarchy.

1 The phrase 'consultation hierarchy' belongs to Rawls 1993.

The broadly Hegelian conception of modern social life abstracts from Hegel's hierarchical conception of politics, from his patriarchical conception of gender, and from other unattractive features as well. It enables us to see, for example, that we can accept the basic Hegelian conception of the family as a domestic sphere of intimate personal relations without accepting the patriarchal features of the traditional family and that we can accept the basic Hegelian conception of civil society as the sphere of individual and associational pursuits and the state as the sphere dedicated to the pursuit of a common good without accepting the view that these spheres ought to be the exclusive domain of men.

None of this is to suggest, however, that the broadly Hegelian conception provides a complete account of a social world that we would regard as a home. It is one thing to suggest that we want to preserve the attractive features of Hegel's conception of the modern social world while rejecting the features we find unattractive and quite another to explain how in detail this can be done. Obviously, the broadly Hegelian conception does not provide an explanation of this sort. To attempt to provide such an account here would amount to adapting Hegel's project of reconciliation to our ends, aspirations, and self-understandings – and that is certainly more than can be attempted here. My concern in this book has been to enable us to understand Hegel's project and to see its interest and appeal. If we now find ourselves asking whether our social world is a home and looking to Hegel's social theory for help in addressing the question, if we now find ourselves asking which features of Hegel's account we find attractive, which features we find objectionable, and how the attractive features can be preserved while the objectionable ones are rejected, this book has accomplished one of its primary aims.

One of the most important ways in which Hegel can help us in thinking about our social world is by making it possible for us to get a deeper sense of the problems it poses. Indeed, if we look more closely at Hegel's conception of the modern social world, something rather interesting emerges. Although it is possible to imagine a Hegelian world in which women can participate fully in civil society, Hegel's basic conception of the modern social world requires that one marital partner – male or female – devote himself or herself more or less exclusively to the life of the family and that the other partner – male or female – devote himself or herself more or less exclusively to his or her occupation. The basic division between the family and civil society (i.e., the basic division between the domestic sphere and the world of work), as Hegel conceives of it, depends crucially on a strict division of labor between the roles of homemaker and wage earner.

If, however, the idea of a genuinely egalitarian society is not simply one in which individuals face the exclusive choice of being *either* homemakers *or* wage earners, if it is rather the idea of a society in which individuals can participate fully in *both* the family and civil society, then each of these spheres must be reconceived and restructured in fundamental ways. How they are to be reconceived and restructured is obviously a difficult question. But the point to emphasize here is that this is not just a problem within Hegel's account of the modern social world: It is a problem posed by the modern social world, a problem that becomes especially clear when one considers it from the standpoint of Hegel's basic conception.

Hegel can also help us better understand a basic problem of modern political life, for he provides an especially clear articulation of a basic aspiration of modern citizens: the wish to have a form of political participation that is both genuinely meaningful and compatible with the pursuit of one's private life. I have already indicated why I think Hegel's solution to this problem is not satisfactory. The point I want to urge here is that the question of how meaningful political participation can be combined with the possibility of leading a private life is a real question of modern political life. Hegel can help us see why we could not be satisfied in a social world in which we had to devote all our energies to the tasks of citizenship or one in which there was no possibility of meaningful political participation. Moreover, Hegel's account of the modern political state as a large and complex administrative unit helps explain why it will be difficult to arrive at a satisfactory solution; it helps explain why modern citizenship tends to be a largely passive affair.

It is not, however, the case that *all* we are left with is a clearer sense of the problems that face us in relating to our social world. As I have suggested, one of Hegel's most important contributions is his specification of the basic ideal of a social world that is a home. Even if we do not have a complete account of how the social world would have to be organized in order for it to be such that we could regard it as a home, we do have the basic idea of the social world as a home. Moreover, we can, in fact, say rather a lot about how a social world would have to be organized in order to be a home. Although abstract, the broadly Hegelian conception is far from empty. We can use it to articulate the general features a social world must have if it is to be a home. And we can further specify the features a social world must have if it is to be a home by looking at the features of Hegel's account we find objectionable. Ultimately, it is no less instructive to be clear about those aspects of Hegel's conception of the modern social world that we reject than those aspects of his conception we accept. In both cases, clarifying our relation to Hegel provides a way of clarifying our relation to the social world.

Before ending, I need to say something about Hegel's view of poverty. It must be emphasized that Hegel recognizes that poverty constitutes a flaw in the modern social world. Whereas we may disagree with Hegel about the desirability of the traditional division of genders or of a hierarchical political state, there will be no disagreement between us concerning the desirability of poverty. Hegel would agree that poverty is a bad thing – that it is an evil.

The difficulty arises because Hegel is willing to say that the modern social world is a home despite the fact that it contains poverty, despite the fact that it gives rise to a whole class of people who are objectively alienated from its arrangements. One thing this indicates is that Hegel is committed to the principle that a social world that exhibited these features *could* be a home. I assume that this is a principle few readers would be willing to accept and, indeed, that it is a principle most readers would find repugnant.

This, in turn, allows us to articulate further our understanding of the conditions the social world must meet if it is to be a home. It seems natural to suggest that if the social world is to be a home, there must be no class of people who are excluded from participating in its central arrangements. We might try to convey this point by suggesting that, in assessing our relation to the social world, the guiding question should not be, Can *I* be reconciled to the social world? but rather, Can *we* be reconciled to the social world? And so I close by commending the ideal of a social world in which it is possible for all of us to be at home.

SELECTED BIBLIOGRAPHY

Aristotle. *Nicomachean Ethics* (EN).

   Politics (Pol.).

Auletta, Ken. 1982. *The Underclass*. New York: Random House.

Avineri, Shlomo. 1972. *Hegel's Theory of the Modern State*. Cambridge: Cambridge University Press.

Beauvoir, Simone de. 1949. *Le deuxième sexe II: L'Expérience Vécue*. Paris: Editions Gallimard.

   1989. *The Second Sex*. Translated and edited by H. M. Parshley. New York: Vintage Books.

Bellah, Robert N., Richard Madsen, William M. Sullivan, Ann Swidler, and Steven M. Tipton. 1985. *Habits of the Heart: Individualism and Commitment in American Life*. New York: Harper & Row.

   1992. *The Good Society*. New York: Vintage Books.

Berlin, Isaiah. 1969. *Four Essays on Liberty*. Oxford: Oxford University Press.

Camus, Albert. (1942) 1955. *The Myth of Sisyphus and Other Essays*. Translated by Justin O'Brien. New York: Vintage Books.

Carnap, Rudolf. 1932. "Ueberwindung der Metaphysic durch logische Analyse der Sprache." *Erkenntnis* 2: 218–41.

   1959. "The Elimination of Metaphysics through Logical Analysis of Language." Translated by Arthur Pap. In *Logical Positivism*, edited by A. J. Ayer. Glencoe: Free Press.

Cohen, G. A. 1978. *Karl Marx's Theory of History: A Defense*. Princeton: Princeton University Press.

Cohen, Jean L., and Andrew Arato. 1992. *Civil Society and Political Theory.* Cambridge, Mass.: MIT Press.

Cohen, Joshua. 1988. "Lectures on Hegel." Unpublished lecture notes. Massachusetts Institute of Technology.

Cohen, Joshua, and Joel Rogers. 1992. "Secondary Associations and Democratic Governance." *Politics and Society* 20, no. 4: 393–472.

Constant, Benjamin. (1814) 1989. *Political Writings.* Translated and edited by Biancamaria Fontana. Cambridge: Cambridge University Press.

Crites, Stephen D. 1967. "Hegelianism." In *The Encyclopedia of Philosophy*, edited by Paul Edwards. New York: Macmillan.

Elster, Jon. 1983. *Sour Grapes: Studies in the Subversion of Rationality.* Cambridge: Cambridge University Press.

Fackenheim, Emil L. 1969–70. "On the Actuality of the Rational and the Rationality of the Actual." *Review of Metaphysics* 23, no. 4: 690–8.

Frankfurt, Harry G. 1988. "The Importance of What We Care About." In *The Importance of What We Care About: Philosophical Essays.* Cambridge: Cambridge University Press.

Freud, Sigmund. 1930. *Civilization and Its Discontents.* London: Hogarth Press.

Fulda, Hans Friedrich. 1981. "Georg Wilhelm Friedrich Hegel." In *Klassiker der Philosophie II: Von Immanuel Kant bis Jean-Paul Sartre.* Edited by Otfried Höffe. Munich: C. H. Beck.

Gans, Eduard. (1832–3) 1981. *Naturrecht und Universalrechtsgeschichte.* Edited by Manfred Riedel. Stuttgart: Klett-Cotta.

Geuss, Raymond. 1981. *The Idea of a Critical Theory: Habermas and the Frankfurt School.* New York: Cambridge University Press.

Habermas, Jürgen. 1971. *Theorie und Praxis: Sozialphilosophische Studien.* Rev. ed. Frankfurt: Suhrkamp Verlag.

1973a. *Legitimationsprobleme im Spätkapitalismus.* Frankfurt: Suhrkamp Verlag.

1973b. *Theory and Practice.* Translated by John Viertel. Boston: Beacon Press.

1975. *Legitimation Crisis.* Translated by Thomas McCarthy. Boston: Beacon Press.

Haym, Rudolf. 1857. *Hegel und seine Zeit.* Berlin: Rudolf Gaertner.

Heidegger, Martin. (1927) 1962. *Being and Time.* Translated by J. Macquarrie and E. Robinson. New York: Harper & Row.

(1947) 1977. "Letter on Humanism." In *Basic Writings*, edited by D. F. Krell. New York: Harper & Row.

Heiman, G. 1971. "The Sources and Significance of Hegel's Corporate Doctrine." In *Hegel's Political Philosophy: Problems and Perspectives*, edited by Z. A. Pelczynksi. Cambridge: Cambridge University Press.

Henrich, Dieter. 1983. "Einleitung des Herausgebers: Vernunft in Verwirklichung." In *Hegel: Philosophie des Rechts: Die Vorlesung von 1819–*

20 in einer Nachschrift, edited by Dieter Henrich. Frankfurt: Suhrkamp Verlag.

Hösle, Vittori. 1986. "Eine unsittliche Sittlichkeit: Hegels Kritik an der indischen Kultur." In *Moralität und Sittlichkeit: Das Problem Hegels und die Diskursethik*, edited by Wolfgang Kuhlmann. Frankfurt: Suhrkamp Verlag.

Humboldt, Alexander von. (1862) 1969. *The Limits of State Action*. Edited by J. W. Burrow. Cambridge: Cambridge University Press.

Ilting, Karl-Heinz. 1973. "Einleitung: Die Rechtsphilosophie von 1820 und Hegels Vorlesungen über Rechtsphilosophie." In *Vorlesungen über Rechtsphilosophie, 1818–1831*, vol. 1, edited by K.-H. Ilting. Stuttgart: Klett-Cotta Verlag.

Inwood, Michael J. 1983. *Hegel*. London: Routledge & Kegan Paul.

——— 1984. "Hegel, Plato and Greek 'Sittlichkeit'." In *The State and Civil Society: Studies in Hegel's Political Philosophy*, edited by Z. A. Pelczynski. Cambridge: Cambridge University Press.

Kant, Immanuel. (1786) 1968. "Was heißt: Sich im Denken orientieren?" In *Schriften zur Metaphysik und Logik 1, Immanuel Kant Werkausgabe*, vol. 5, edited by Wilhelem Weischedel. Frankfurt: Suhrkamp Verlag.

——— 1949. "What Is Orientation in Thinking?" In *The Critique of Practical Reason and Other Writings in Moral Philosophy*, translated and edited by Lewis White Beck. Chicago: University of Chicago Press.

Knox, T. M. 1952. "Translator's Notes." In *Hegel's Philosophy of Right*, translated with notes by T. M. Knox. New York: Oxford University Press.

Kraut, Richard. 1979. "Two Conceptions of Happiness." *Philosophical Review* 88: 167–97.

Lacey, W. K. 1968. *The Family in Classical Greece: Aspects of Greek and Roman Life*. Ithaca, N.Y.: Cornell University Press.

Lasch, Christopher. 1977. *Haven in a Heartless World: The Family Besieged*. New York: Basic Books.

Lear, Jonathan. 1990. *Love and Its Place in Nature: A Philosophical Interpretation of Freudian Psychoanalysis*. New York: Farrar, Straus, Giroux.

Lewis, Oscar. 1969. "The Culture of Poverty." In *On Understanding Poverty: Perspectives from the Social Sciences*, edited by Daniel P. Moynihan with the assistance of Corinne Saposs Schelling. New York: Basic Books.

Löwith, Karl. 1941. Rev. ed. 1978. *Von Hegel Zu Nietzsche: Der Revolution im Denken des 19. Jahrhunderte*. Hamburg: Felix Meiner Verlag.

——— 1964. *From Hegel to Nietzsche: The Revolution in Nineteenth Century Thought*. Translated by David E. Green. Garden City, N.Y.: Anchor Books, Doubleday.

MacIntyre, Alasdair. 1981. *After Virtue: A Study in Moral Theory*. Notre Dame: University of Notre Dame Press.

Marx, Karl. (1843–4) 1956. "Zur Kritik der Hegelschen Rechtsphilosophie: Einleitung." In *Marx Engels Werke*, vol. 1. Berlin: Dietz Verlag.

(1844) 1956. *Oekonomisch-philosophische Manuscripte aus dem Jahrn 1844.* In *Marx Engels Werke,* Ergänzungsband: Schriften bis, 1844 Erster Teil. Berlin: Dietz Verlag.

(1845) 1956. "Thesen über Feuerbach." In *Marx Engels Werke,* vol. 1. Berlin: Dietz Verlag.

1978a. "Contribution to the Critique of Hegel's Philosophy of Right: Introduction." In *The Marx–Engels Reader,* 2d ed., edited by Robert C. Tucker. New York: W. W. Norton.

1978b. "Economic and Philosophical Manuscripts of 1844." In *The Marx–Engels Reader,* 2d ed., edited by Robert C. Tucker. New York: W. W. Norton.

1978c. "Theses on Feuerbach." In *The Marx–Engels Reader,* 2d. ed., edited by Robert C. Tucker. New York: W. W. Norton.

Mill, John Stuart. (1859) 1978. *On Liberty.* Edited by Elizabeth Rapaport. Indianapolis: Hackett.

Nagel, Thomas. 1979. *Mortal Questions.* Cambridge: Cambridge University Press.

1991. *Equality and Partiality.* New York: Oxford University Press.

Neuhouser, Frederick. 1993. "Fichte and the Relationship between Right and Morality." In *Fichte: Historical Context and Contemporary Controversies,* edited by David Breazeale and Tom Rockmore. Atlantic Highlands, N.J.: Humanities Press.

Nietzsche, Friedrich. (1883–5) 1980. *Also Sprach Zarathustra: Ein Buch für Alle und Keinen.* Vol. 4 of *Friedrich Nietzsche: Sämtliche Werke, Kritische Studienausgabe,* edited by Giorgio Colli and Mazzino Montinari. Berlin: Deutscher Taschenbuch Verlag.

(1886) 1980. *Jenseits von Gut und Böse: Vorspiel einer Philosophie der Zukunft.* Vol. 5 of *Friedrich Nietzsche: Sämtliche Werke, Kritische Studienausgabe,* edited by Giorgio Colli and Mazzino Montinari. Berlin: Deutscher Taschenbuch Verlag.

1966a. *Thus Spoke Zarathustra: A Book for All and None.* Translated by Walter Kaufmann. New York: Viking Press.

1966b. *Beyond Good and Evil: Prelude to a Philosophy of the Future.* Translated by Walter Kaufmann. New York: Vintage Books.

Nussbaum, Martha C. 1986. *The Fragility of Goodness.* Cambridge: Cambridge University Press.

Okin, Susan Moller. 1989. *Justice, Gender, and the Family.* New York: Basic Books.

Pelczynski, Z. A. 1971. "The Hegelian Conception of the State." In *Hegel's Political Philosophy: Problems and Perspectives,* edited by Z. A. Pelczynski. Cambridge: Cambridge University Press.

1984a. "Introduction." In *The State and Civil Society: Studies in Hegel's Political Philosophy,* edited by Z. A. Pelczynski. Cambridge: Cambridge University Press.

1984b. "Nation, Civil Society, State: Hegelian Sources of the Marxian Non-theory of Nationality." In *The State and Civil Society: Studies in Hegel's Political Philosophy*, edited by Z. A. Pelczynski. Cambridge: Cambridge University Press.

1984c. "Political Community and Individual Freedom." In *The State and Civil Society: Studies in Hegel's Political Philosophy*, edited by Z. A. Pelczynski. Cambridge: Cambridge University Press.

Peperzack, Adriaan T. 1987. *Philosophy and Politics: A Commentary on the Preface to Hegel's Philosophy of Right*. Dordrecht: Martinus Nijhoff Publishers.

Pippin, Robert. 1981. "Hegel's Political Argument and the Problem of Verwirklichung." *Political Theory* 9, no. 4, November, pp. 509–32.

Plamenatz, John Petrov. 1963. *Man and Society: A Critical Examination of Some Important Social and Political Theories from Machiavelli to Marx*, vol. 2. London: Longman.

Plant, Raymond. 1973. *Hegel*. Bloomington: Indiana University Press.

Popper, Karl R. 1966. *The Open Society and Its Enemies*, vol. 2. Rev. ed. Princeton: Princeton University Press.

Rawls, John. 1971. *A Theory of Justice*. Cambridge, Mass.: Harvard University Press, Belknap Press.

1985. "Justice as Fairness: Political Not Metaphysical." *Philosophy and Public Affairs* 14, no. 3: 223–51.

1987. "Lecture Notes for Philosophy 171." Unpublished lecture notes. Harvard University.

1989. "The Domain of the Political and Overlapping Consensus." *New York University Law Review* 64: 233–55.

1993. "The Law of Peoples." In *On Human Rights: Oxford Amnesty Lectures 1993*, edited by Stephen Shote and Susan Hurley. New York: Basic Books.

Riedel, Manfred. 1974. "Hegels Begriff der bürgerlichen Gesellschaft und das Problem seines geschictlichen Ursprungs." In *Materialien zu Hegels Rechtsphilosophie*, edited by Manfred Riedel. Frankfurt: Suhrkamp Verlag.

1984. "'State' and 'Civil Society': Linguistic Context and Historical Origin." In *Between Tradition and Revolution: The Hegelian Transformation of Political Philosophy*, translated by Walter Wright. Cambridge: Cambridge University Press.

Ritter, Joachim. 1965. *Hegel und die französische Revolution*. Frankfurt: Suhrkamp Verlag.

1982. *Hegel and the French Revolution*. Cambridge, Mass.: MIT Press.

Rosenzweig, Franz. (1920) 1982. *Hegel und der Staat*. Reprint (2 vols. in 1). Aalen: Scientia Verlag.

Rousseau, Jean-Jacques. (1762) 1974. *The Social Contract, or Principles of Political Right*. Translated and edited by Charles M. Sherover. New York: Meridian Books.

Sandel, M. J. 1982. *Liberalism and the Limits of Justice*. Cambridge: Cambridge University Press.

Sartre, Jean Paul. (1943) 1966. *Being and Nothingness*. Translated by Hazel E. Barnes. New York: Washington Square Press.

Schacht, Richard. 1971. *Alienation*. Garden City, N.Y.: Anchor Books.

Schiller, Friedrich. (1801) 1967. *On the Aesthetic Education of Man*. Translated and edited by Elizabeth M. Wilkinson and L. A. Willoughby. New York: Oxford University Press.

Shklar, Judith M. 1971. "Hegel's Phenomenology: An Elegy for Hellas." In *Hegel's Political Philosophy: Problems and Perspectives*, edited by Z. A. Pelczynski. Cambridge: Cambridge University Press.

Siep, Ludwig. 1979. *Anerkennung als Prinzip der praktische Philosophie: Zu Hegel's Jenaer Philosophie des Geistes*. Munich: Alber.

Stone, Lawrence. 1979. *The Family, Sex, and Marriage in England, 1500–1800*. New York: Harper & Row.

Strawson, Peter. (1959) 1964. *Individuals, an Essay in Descriptive Metaphysics*. Reprint. London: University Paperbacks, Methuen.

Taylor, Charles. 1975. *Hegel*. Cambridge: Cambridge University Press.

———. 1985a. "Atomism." In *Philosophy and the Human Sciences: Philosophical Papers*, vol. 2. Cambridge: Cambridge University Press.

———. 1985b. "Self-interpreting Animals." In *Human Language and Agency: Philosophical Papers*, vol. 1. Cambridge: Cambridge University Press.

———. 1989. *Sources of the Self: The Making of Modern Identity*. Cambridge, Mass.: Harvard University Press.

Theunissen, Michael. 1970. "Die Verwirklichung der Vernunft: Zur Theorie–Praxis–Diskussion in Anschluß an Hegel." *Philosophische Rundschau*, Beiheft 6.

Thomson, Judith Jarvis. 1990. *The Realm of Rights*. Cambridge, Mass.: Harvard University Press.

Toews, J. E. 1980. *Hegelianism: The Path Toward Dialectical Humanism, 1805–1841*. Cambridge: Cambridge University Press.

Trilling, Lionel. 1972. *Sincerity and Authenticity*. Cambridge, Mass.: Harvard University Press.

Walsh, W. H. 1969. *Hegelian Ethics*. London: Macmillan.

Walzer, Michael. 1991. "The Idea of Civil Society: A Path to Social Reconstruction." *Dissent*, Spring, pp. 293–304.

Weil, Eric. 1950. *Hegel et l'état*. Paris: College Philosophique.

Westphal, Merold. 1984. "Hegel's Radical Idealism: Family and State as Ethical Communities." In *The State and Civil Society: Studies in Hegel's Political Philosophy*, edited by Z. A. Pelczynski. Cambridge: Cambridge University Press.

White, Stephen K. 1991. *Political Theory and Postmodernism*. Cambridge: Cambridge University Press.

Williams, Bernard. 1981. "Conflicts of Values." In *Moral Luck*. Cambridge: Cambridge University Press.

———. 1985. *Ethics and the Limits of Philosophy*. Cambridge, Mass.: Harvard University Press.

Wilson, William Julius. 1987. *The Truly Disadvantaged: The Inner City, the Underclass, and Public Policy*. Chicago: University of Chicago Press.

Wood, Allen W. 1990. *Hegel's Ethical Thought*. Cambridge: Cambridge University Press.

INDEX

272 INDEX

Hegel, Georg Wilhelm Friedrich (*cont.*)
Phenomenology of Spirit, 1n, 33–4, 46;
Philosophy of Mind, 194n; *Philosophy
of Right*, 10, 24–5, 27–30, 67–71, 74,
79, 80, 122, 123, 129, 131, 137–8,
158, 162, 165n, 185, 248, 253, 254,
255; *Positivity of the Christian
Religion*, 32–3; *Science of Logic*, 4, 63;
"The Wurtemberg Estates," 123
Hegelianism, left and right, 4, 27
Heidegger, Martin, 120n
Heiman, G., 197n
Henrich, Dieter, 52n, 65n
Historicism, 49, 73
Hobbes, Thomas, 128, 141
Holism, 98
Home, social world's being: defined,
95–6; and being world that makes it
possible for people to actualize
themselves as individuals and social
members, 102–7; and being world
that is not other than its members,
109; and being good, 109–10; and
being world of freedom, 116; and
happiness, 117–19; and being split,
118; institutional articulation of
gender as condition of, 186;
communitarian aspects of, 187–9.
See also Being at home in social world
Homo oeconomicus, 191n. *See also*
Burgher; Person, private
Hösle, Vittori, 28n
Human beings: as *Geist*, 47–52, 158–9;
as vehicles of *Geist*, 47–52; as
spiritual beings, 47; as social and
cultural beings, 47–8; as vehicles of
national communities of which they
are part, 50; as political animals,
119, 153. *See also* Individuals
Human spirit, self-understanding of:
highest level of, available in given
historical period, 66; correct, 66, 73,
75, 80, 132, 159; and world history,
66
Humboldt, Wilhelm von, 188
Hume, David, 7
Husband who treats wife as property,
177

Idea (*Idee*), 57, 58
Ideal (*Ideal*): of reconciliation, 2, 252;
true (*wahrhaftes Ideal*), 58, 69; of
Plato, 69; gap between, and existing
social arrangements, 71; of making

it possible for people to actualize
themselves as individuals and social
members, 111; republican, 210; of
genuinely egalitarian society, 257
Idealism of Hegel's conception of
reality, 58
Ideals: vocabulary of social, 2; of
wholeness, unity, and harmony, 39–
41; of imagination (*Ideale der
Phantasie*) defined, 59–60, 73, 80,
118; of reason (*Ideale der Vernunft*)
defined, 59–60, 73, 80, 118
Idee. See Idea
Identification, immediate and
reflective, 166–7
Ideologiekritik, 120n. *See also* Ideology
Ideology, 31–2, 120. *See also*
Frankfurt school; Geuss, Raymond;
Marx, Karl
Illusion (*Schein*), 53
Ilting, Karl-Heinz, 29n
India, 130
Individual social membership, 173
Individual suffrage, 222–3. *See also*
Voting
Individualität. See Individuality
Individuality (*Individualität, Einzelheit*):
atomic, defined, 145; and
eccentricity and idiosyncrasy, 145,
151; and nonconformity, 145; full-
fledged, 145; in minimal sense, 146–
8; in strong sense, 148–53, 165, 168,
172, 186–9, 204; and conceiving of
oneself as self, 148–50, 165–7; and
conceiving of oneself as bearer of
separate and particular interests,
149; and conceiving of oneself as
possessor of individual rights, 149;
and conceiving of oneself as subject
of conscience, 149–50; and social
membership, 165, 167–9; and
reflective identification, 166–7;
social dimension of, 169–72; in
complete sense, 169; as unity of
particular and universal, 171; and
Begriff, 172; and individual social
membership, 173; and recognition,
235
Individuals: reconciled, 26; reflective,
129–31, 134, 137–8, 145, 246;
philosophically reflective, 130–1,
135–6, 141–2; reflective, as locus of
modern culture's subjectivity, 135;
atomic, 140–1; in minimal sense,